# Atlantic
# Salmon Flies and
# Fishing

## Also by Joseph D. Bates, Jr.

Spinning for American Game Fish

Trout Waters and How to Fish Them

Streamer Fly Fishing
in Fresh and Salt Water

Spinning for Fresh Water Game Fish

Spinning for Salt Water Game Fish

The Outdoor Cook's Bible

Streamer Fly Tying and Fishing
*(With a Subscribed Limited Edition
of 600 Copies)*

Elementary Fishing

Atlantic Salmon Flies and Fishing
*(With a Subscribed Limited Edition
of 600 Copies)*

# Atlantic Salmon Flies and Fishing

by Joseph D. Bates, Jr.

Line Drawings by Milton C. Weiler

STACKPOLE BOOKS

Harrisburg, Pennsylvania

Designer: Ernst Reichl
Color plates by Walter Whittum, Inc.

ISBN 0–8117–0180–8
*Library of Congress Catalog Card Number 76-123401*
Printed in U.S.A.

To

The Reverend

**ELMER JAMES SMITH**

a Friend of Man, and of

the Salmon

The Author Expresses His Appreciation
to the Anglers and Fly Dressers
Who Have Added Their Skill and Knowledge
to This Book, including:

Arno Adlivankin, A. I. Alexander, III, Dan Bailey, (Mrs.) Carmelle Bigaouette, (Miss) Megan Boyd, Joe Brooks, Don Brown, (Miss) Bessie Brown, Geoffrey Bucknall, Louis M. Butterfield, Burt D. Carpenter, Robert H. Cavanagh, Jr., Clayton R. Cronkite, Edward A. (Ted) Crosby, Bing Crosby, Harry A. Darbee, Charles De Feo, Wallace W. Doak, Lt. Colonel Esmond Drury, Jean-Paul Dubé, Bob Elliot, Philip L. Foster, W. L. Frith, Keith C. Fulsher, François deB. Gourdeau, Preston D. Griffin, Arthur H. Grove, Edward Gruber, Norman Hathaway, Austin S. Hogan, Herbert L. Howard, Maurice Ingalls, Robert V. Jacklin, Dick Jennings, Yngvar Kaldal, William J. Keane, C. Otto v.Kienbusch, Bernard ("Lefty") Kreh, Paul Kukonen, David E. Lawrence, Sr., B. Martinez, Leon Martuch, Werner Meinel, Bert Miner, Arthur Oglesby, Olaf Olsen, Bill Rosgen, Wilson Russell, Erling Sand, Ben Schley, Charles Shoppe, Johann Sigurdsson, Alex and Colin Simpson, The Reverend Elmer J. Smith, John Veniard, Harry Willcox, Ted Williams, Ian Wood, Lee Wulff and Jimmy Younger.

# Contents

# Contents

## PART TWO  Atlantic Salmon Flies

# List of Illustrations

## COLOR PLATES

# Preface

About 1925 the renowned American angler and salmon fly originator, John C. Cosseboom, sent a Christmas card to his friends.
The folder contained a photograph of himself dressing flies aboard
the steamer *Fleurus* en route to Anticosti Island; one of his poems;
and the printed comment, "I have written this little verse in honor
of those old school salmon fishermen whom I admire and respect
but whose thinning ranks fill me with sadness."

Since the traditions, equipment and techniques we enjoy while
salmon fishing are largely dependent upon the "old school salmon
fishermen," in honor of them it seems appropriate to include here
John Cosseboom's verses. He called the poem "Old Time Salmon
Fishing":

> Did you ever cast for salmon in the Spring,
> For the big bright shining fish fresh from the sea,
> With the leaping strength and vigor that they bring
> To the swollen flood-fed river running free?
>
> Did you ever feel the fever in your blood
> When a dirty cold Nor'easter threatened rain,
> And you smelled the river clearing after flood,
> And you sensed the salmon in the pools again?
>
> Did you ever wield a rod of eighteen feet—
> A Leonard, old, with handles wound with cane—
> The "Church of England" rods we used to meet,
> Swung by anglers of the old school without strain?
>
> Did you ever use a cast of Hebra size?
> Did you ever cast a sixty-thousandths line?
> Did you ever tie on *Durham Ranger* flies—
> Big 5–0 flies, and cast them in the wind?
>
> Did you ever see a wave behind your fly
> And know it for a fish of monstrous size,
> And when that wave exploded two feet high,
> Feel your great rod bend near double to the rise?

Did you ever have a guide yell in your face,
When your salmon surged across the heavy pool
And dragged your rod down level with your waist,
"Keep your tip up, or you'll lose him, you dumb fool!"?

Did you ever race along the slippery shore
With your rod held high and bended to the fray,
While down across the rushing pool he tore
And jumped two hundred feet and more away?

Did you ever feel your rod and line go slack,
And cry, "He's gone!", in disappointed pain,
And when you found he'd only started back,
Did you madly reel the strain on him again?

Did you ever think you had him tired out,
When his tail began to show above the stream?
Did you ever think him yours without a doubt
Till he rushed and made your old reel fairly scream?

Did you ever back up slowly on the beach
And draw him gently toward the waiting guide,
Then have him stop and stay just out of reach,
And chug those scary chugs from side to side?

Do you recall that long last surging plunge
That took him up and out across the tide,
And how you swung him back down to the lunge
That sank the gaff into his silver side?

Do you recall your fervent thankful prayer,
As his forty pounds lay shining at your feet,
To the Red Gods who had smiled on you so fair,
To the Red Gods who had made your joy complete?

That's the fishing that they called a "sport of kings"—
When they fished in swollen rivers' springtime flow
For the big bright shining fish of other Springs,
With that heavy rugged gear of long ago!

J.C.C.

# Introduction

Few experienced anglers will dispute the paramount opinion that, pound for pound, the Atlantic salmon is the world's most exciting and challenging fish that can be taken with an artificial fly in fresh water. The methods for taking him have been debated and discussed in scores of excellent books and in generations of periodicals and other printed matter. Kings, princes, tycoons and lesser folk have thrilled to his spectacular leaping somersaults; and to his surging runs and his rather human idiosyncrasies ever since the development of practical fly-fishing tackle two or three hundred years ago.

So, what more is to be said, in a book like this? There is now a great deal more to be said, because the old order in Atlantic salmon fishing has changed, and changed very considerably.

We, here in northeastern North America, inherited our salmon fishing tackle and techniques from our fellow anglers across the sea. While their methods have changed from year to year, ours have developed much more widely, and what we have discovered and developed should be of particular interest to them. During the last quarter-century or so we have originated tackle and techniques of our own—very different ones, easier ones, and ones which are at least as successful.

Split-bamboo double-handed rods a dozen feet long or more have given way to the single-handed, nine-footer. Even these are no longer very popular except for big fish in wide, fast rivers. Trout-type

rods from seven to eight and a half feet long, equipped with efficient
reels containing room for 150 yards or more of backing, are much
more popular under average conditions. This trend, here and there,
has been carried farther by trying to take big fish on the very lightest
tackle—a practice considered rather ostentatious by some and a very
sensible way to enjoy fishing fun by others.

The "greased line" no longer is greased because modern plastic
surfacing fortunately makes this rather messy practice unnecessary.
Leaders, formerly of silkworm gut, now are tied from strands clipped
from spools of a range of sizes of cheaper and more reliable synthetic
monofilament. Many of us tie our own leaders, as we dress our own
flies, partly because by doing so we can make leaders to the specifications we want without having to depend on whatever can be found in
stores. Because of technical improvements hooks other than traditional black enamel types are becoming more popular and are considered
by many to be more efficient. While those who can afford them justi-
fiably cherish rare and valuable split-bamboo rods hand-crafted so
painstakingly by revered experts such as Edwards, Hardy, Leonard,
Orvis, Payne and Thomas, excellent counterparts which are factory-
made to precise specifications from glass-fiber cloth may be bought
for a fraction of the price.

Styles in flies have changed even more, and part of the restyling
is rather a pity. The historic British Classics such as the *Jock Scott*,
*Durham Ranger*, *Silver Doctor* and *Wilkinson* are rarely seen on North
American salmon rivers except on the leaders of fine old gentlemen
who still fish them more because of tradition than necessity. These
gorgeous confections, each dressed with parts of the plumage of a
dozen or more exotic birds, have been replaced by simple hair-wing
patterns which any novice fly-tyer can put together well enough to
fool fussy salmon. Fluorescent yarns and floss, strands of mylar, and
other modern ingredients contribute to their effectiveness. The new
hair-wings are only part of the story. Fish that formerly refused to rise
to a fly or take it after rising can often now be coaxed to do so by the
employment of absurdly simple artificial nymphs, by streamer flies
and bucktails formerly used only for black salmon, or by unusual
floating monstrosities only remotely resembling any bug that ever
flew.

If you want to go fishing for Atlantic salmon and don't think you have correct tackle, just bring along your trouting gear—with plenty of backing on the reel. Trout patterns such as the *Dark Cahill, Black Gnat, Royal Coachman* or *Muddler Minnow* work very well at times, if one knows how to present them to the fish! Conversely, much that we are learning about the tackle and tactics for salmon can be used very effectively when we go fishing for trout.

Of course it's nice to know a wealthy person who owns or leases a good piece of water and is kind enough to invite us up for a week or so. Lacking that, we can rent a pool or two in some places and stay at a hotel nearby. We can invest quite a lot of money and join a club, if the members will let us in. But if that sort of thing doesn't fit the family budget, let's not give up! The government tourist bureau in the area we want to visit can provide a list of fishing camps which take in paying guests. Or we can ask the bureau where there are public waters near which we can park the trailer, pitch a tent, or put up at a boarding house. Since many other people will have the same idea, plans should be made well in advance. But please don't write the author about it. He isn't a tourist bureau!

If this book should tread lightly (but, I hope politely) on the toes of such notable angling authors as Kelson, Hill and La Branche, it may be a sort of boon to the rest of us to realize that fishing for Atlantic salmon can be much less difficult than the old-timers made it out to be. The methods are very simple and can be simply stated. With the many modern changes in salmon tackle and tactics, this seems to be the time to try to reduce the techniques to elementals which can be better understood. So, with proper reverence to the hallowed past of Atlantic salmon angling, let's try to make it easier so we can enjoy it more!

Atlantic salmon use a few rivers in northern Maine (where conservation efforts are improving the fishery) and many rivers in the northeastern Canadian provinces. Their range fans out to Greenland, Iceland, the Scandinavian countries, the British Isles and to many rivers in Europe, as far south as Spain. While styles in flies vary widely in various regions and from time to time, the North American equipment and methods described in this book should apply to about eighty-five per cent of Atlantic salmon rivers generally. The exceptions, chiefly, pertain to big, swift rivers harboring very large fish, where sturdier tackle may be more appropriate.

To make this book as complete as possible, notes on the flies, tackle and tactics popular in countries outside North America are included to the extent that the book's size permits. Although sport-fishing with lures other than flies is permitted in some of these areas, this book is concerned only with fly-fishing with artificial flies.

Most experienced salmon anglers agree that the presentation and movement of the fly are several times as important as the choice of pattern. Methods of presentation and of manipulation of the fly have changed perhaps even more than has the modernization of tackle.

These things, and the detailed dressing instructions for about two hundred of the most popular fly patterns, are what this book is about. Whether you still look forward to catching your first salmon, or whether you have landed hundreds, we hope the information offered here will make your days astream much more successful and a lot more fun!

When it was first suggested that I should write this book, I declined because there are many men who have fished for Atlantic salmon many more years and in many more places than I have. In recent years I have been fortunate to have fished with several of them, some of whom have devoted entire seasons for a decade or more to learning the fine points of the game. In acceding to a bit of pressure I accepted their promises of cooperation because I have always thought that any definitive book on angling should never expound the opinions of only one man.

So this book is a cumulative effort in which I have tried to present information based on many lifetimes of salmon fishing. I am grateful to the many people in many countries who have contributed flies and facts, and I have tried to express my appreciation herein. But there is one gentleman who must be thanked more specifically, because, during the many weeks of our fishing together, he has acted as my Father Confessor on the entire project. He is well qualified, because he has devoted entire seasons to almost constant Atlantic salmon fishing for over twenty years. Therefore, it my privilege to dedicate this effort to him.

I am also grateful to a sympathetic publisher who, among other things, agreed that a book of this sort merited publication in a specially designed limited edition, and that all editions should contain outstanding color plates so readers can see (and perhaps copy more accurately) the beauty of some of the salmon flies discussed herein.

Finally, I am grateful to my lifelong friend, the celebrated angling artist, Milton C. Weiler, for the book's jacket and drawings, and especially for the beautiful painting of a salmon pool on the Matapedia which graces the limited edition. Both of us caught a "big one" there.

The Atlantic salmon is a revered fish which, in its development, has survived so many perils that relatively few return to their rivers. To enjoy salmon fishing to the fullest, we should learn to respect the salmon and, especially, to understand him.

So before becoming involved with the new tackle and tactics of the sport, let's learn something about the varying characteristics of typical salmon rivers, and then let's become better acquainted with the very beautiful, unusual, smart and sturdy fish we hope so often to catch—Salmo Salar, whose name means "the leaper"—the noble Atlantic salmon.

JOSEPH D. BATES, JR.

*Longmeadow, Massachusetts, U.S.A.*

# PART ONE
# Atlantic Salmon Fishing

# I

# The Lure of the Rivers

Salmon rivers are ever-changing, to the fascination, elation and frustration of the addicted anglers who fish them. In spate in the spring they may run deep, dark and turbulent, often overflowing their banks to necessitate farms and fishing camps being built on high ground. In summer and fall they may sleep, warm and shallow, with barely a trickle shimmering over the riffles, thus imprisoning the salmon in the pools until the rains come.

Between these extremes come the rains, the rising water which brings shoals of salmon up from the estuaries and which frees the fish in the pools so all may surge forward, joyfully leaping and sturdily swimming upward and onward to their spawning grounds.

When the rains afford moderate flow the rivers are "right" because the salmon can rest or can move on, as they choose. These are the days of elation for the angler: the hours of the smashing strike, the spectacular leap, the powerful run, and the victory when the prize can be led to gaff, to net, or up onto the gravel of the beach.

The days of easy fishing are when the rivers are "right" and the salmon are on the move. The challenge comes at other times, when the fish are land-locked, lethargic and moodily suspicious of even the most artfully crafted and carefully presented confection of fur and feathers. The challenge then is how to select and how to present the fly in a manner that will tempt the fish to take it. Because the water is low and clear, the salmon often can be seen, and a big one can be selected to fish over. This is the time for knowledge, for skill and for patience. Cast after cast may bring not a flicker of a fin. Then, suddenly, an unusual presentation or the offering of a different pattern may result in reaction—perhaps so little as a suddenly enhanced quivering of fins and tail, or perhaps a majestic rise to inspect the new temptation more closely.

When a fish can be made to show such interest, there are many who say the angler can catch him, although I have not always found this to be so. But when, perhaps after many casts and changes of flies, interest can be aroused, a smaller fly or a different fly, thoughtfully presented, may tempt the salmon to take it.

If this implies that there are "tricks of the trade," old hands on the rivers will agree that there are many of them. Some are ancient tricks, while others are very new. They will be discussed as we go on. A true story about one of them may serve to illustrate the point.

On a late July day under such conditions a neophyte angler arrived at Wendell Allen's camp, where the Cains River pours into the Miramichi near Blackville, in New Brunswick. He stowed his equipment, dressed in new fishing clothes, and sauntered into the dining-room for early dinner. His new vest was crammed with fly boxes, little bottles filled with one preparation or another, and whatever else he thought he needed. Dangling from his vest were clippers, scissors and so forth. His hat was festooned with flies. Quite obviously he was well prepared for any eventuality.

Four older anglers relaxed at their table, finishing their evening meal. They had fished the river for many years, usually during the middle of July and again in the last week of September. They were in no hurry because the fishing was poor. Only a grilse had been taken during the past three days.

The neophyte greeted them cheerily as he sat down at his table and examined the salad.

"Hi, fellers! How's the fishin'?"

The old-timers eyed him morosely. He seemed the type who would ask too many questions, offer too many answers, and probably barge uninvited onto their porch during the "happy hour."

"The fishing is lousy," one of the old gentlemen said, "but there are a few fish in the lower part of the pool. One big one, maybe twenty pounds. He lies to the left of the rock that breaks water. We've fished over him all day. Why don't you go down and give him a try?"

The younger man wolfed his dinner, and all went out together. He picked up his fly-rod and proudly offered it for inspection.

"Brand-new," was his unnecessary comment. "Weight-forward floater with sinking tip. Nine-foot leader to eight pounds. *Gray Ghost* streamer fly that Mrs. Stevens tied herself. Quite deadly for land-locked salmon on Lake Sebago, you know!"

One of the older men suggested that he might do better with a *Red-Butt* or a small *Gray Wulff*.

"Nope," the neophyte said. "This one always works for me. You guys coming down?"

"We've fished quite a bit today," one of the old-timers said. "You can have the pool all to yourself. We're going to play bridge."

Half an hour later, comfortably settled at a card table on the porch with drinks beside them, the foursome was playing a hand of five spades which had been doubled and redoubled. The gentleman whose chair faced downstream looked there.

"Great gawdamitey," he ejaculated as he dropped the last trump card on a hand already won by his partner. "That barsted is into a fish!"

All four leaped up, ignoring the shaken table that had tipped a tumbler of bourbon and water onto the floor. One reached for binoculars.

The neophyte was waist-deep in the pool. The salmon had made a long run, and leaped as they watched.

"I think it's the big one," the man with the binoculars said.

They watched the young angler as he battled the salmon for twenty minutes. They saw the fish brought to net. They saw the guide dispatch him and hold him up for the sport to admire.

The neophyte, carrying his fly-rod and followed by the guide with the fish, walked up the path to the porch where the old-timers stood.

"Congratulations!" the four men exclaimed, and they truly meant it.

"Uh, thanks," the young man said, "but I damn near bitched it up. The wind took the fly and, in trying to pick it up for a better cast, it skittered right over where the salmon was. He came up and took it!"

The young man didn't realize it but, under the circumstances, the things he had done were right. The salmon for days had seen conventional flies fished over him in the orthodox manner, and he wanted no part of them. But suddenly there appeared an unusual streamer pattern, skittering over him in a way that was entirely new. He couldn't resist it!

In a future chapter it may be interesting to discuss the fairly recent discoveries of the advantages of streamer flies and bucktails in fishing for bright salmon in the rivers of Maine and Canada. They, and unusual ways of handling other types of flies, both wet and dry, are among the techniques that contribute to making salmon fishing somewhat different from what it used to be.

I have fished the Miramichi many times when it was "right" and many times when it wasn't.   Sometimes we have fished hard and long, all week, and have rarely taken a fish. Sometimes it is a bonanza. But the lure of the river and the challenge of the fishing can get into one's blood and call one back, year after year. It is the challenge of the fishing more than it is the catching of many fish.

Two years before I wrote this I didn't go to the Miramichi when I should have gone there. We had reservations for the last week of September at Wendell Allen's camp. Just before we planned to go, Wendell phoned to say the river was low and the fishing was very poor. This news, combined with business matters, influenced canceling the trip.

A couple from Worcester went up anyway. He had fished the river many times, and his wife had finally determined to go on the next trip. So he bought her all the proper clothes  and all the proper tackle. He made her read books on salmon fishing, and he devoted many hours to teaching her the various techniques of casting, knot-tying, fly-selection, fly-presentation, and so forth. He periodically quizzed her on what she had learned. He instilled in her the belief that she must do her homework assiduously because, if she didn't, she would never catch a salmon. After all, salmon fishing is a man's game (he said) and one has to know all the intricacies of the sport to be successful at it.

When they returned they invited us to a dinner which featured broiled fresh salmon. As soon as we had settled down with cocktails I asked how the fishing had been.

"I'll answer that," she exclaimed, suddenly boiling with indignation. "That damn husband of mine! He wasted days and days of my time because he had the nerve to tell me that salmon fishing is difficult."

She glanced at him fondly.

"Do you know what happened? It rained all the way up, all six hundred miles. We arrived late at the camp after being stuck in the mud on the way in. The river was high, so we couldn't fish much on Sunday and Monday. Two whole days gone! Well, on Tuesday morning the river had gone down, and salmon were jumping all over the place. The guide set us ashore on the far bank and I waded out a bit and made a cast with a number six *Green Butt*. I flubbed the cast and everything landed in coils. But the current took the line and straightened it out. The minute it straightened out there was an awful strike, and a salmon was on. He raced and jumped all over the place, and I slipped and fell in. But I got up and held on, and you're having the salmon for dinner!

"Jim had a salmon on, too. When he got it in he came over and sat me on the ground and lifted up my feet and all the water in my waders poured down my back, but I didn't really care because I had caught my first salmon!

"Well, to make a long story short, both of us took our limit of four fish in less than two hours each morning, and we did it every day!

"Now, where does he get all this stuff about salmon being so hard to catch? He made me work all summer to learn how, and he makes out that he is a great expert or something and the fact is that all this stuff about selection and presentation is a lot of bunk. He fooled me about how hard it was and he cheated me out of days and nights when

I wanted to do something else besides reading all those books about salmon. The fact is that anybody can catch them."

Then she looked at me, accusingly. "And furthermore," she said, "you are no better than he is. You make out that all this salmon fishing is an occult science and you talk Jim into buying scores of flies and lots of rods and reels and all kinds of stuff that he doesn't need. You two boys have been found out. You positively glow with perfidiousness. All one has to have to catch salmon is one set of tackle and my little number six *Green Butt,* and all one needs is to throw it in. The current and the salmon will do the rest!"

Jim gave me a small shrug and a "What's the use?" expression and poured the second cocktail.

I asked her, "Just how many hours have you spent actually fishing for salmon?"

She counted quickly on her fingers. "Maybe twenty."

"When you have spent fifty," I said, "please tell Jim and me all that again!"

Last year they went back in July and again in September. Last year was a very poor one on the Miramichi because of lack of rain. Jim totaled only one small salmon and a very few grilse, and his wife didn't take a fish. She gave him a box of new flies for Christmas, and he gave her an Orvis eight-and-a-half-foot rod fitted with reel and line. Last time we saw them the table in the den held several books about salmon fishing, beside which was a pile of magazines such as *The Atlantic Salmon Journal* and the British *Trout and Salmon.*

"Looks like you're reading up on it," I said to Jim.

"Well, some," he replied, "but Jane borrowed all these. Now she reads everything on salmon she can get hold of."

Many years ago, when I knew much less about the sport than I do now, we fished the famous Wasson Bar Pool, in Blissfield, New Brunswick. The river was moderately high and the salmon seemed to be running up without stopping in the pool. Under such conditions, anglers wade the bar down the pool with slack and usually fishless water on the left and deeper, fishable water on the right. One constantly casts quartering downstream to let the fly swing on a tight line. After fishing out the cast he moves forward a few feet, thus covering all the good water and hoping his fly will swing near fish

*(B. Schley)*

Fig. I-1

A HIGH JUMPER ON THE MIRAMICHI

9

swimming up. If an angler hooks one downstream everyone in the procession of five or six rods fishes with extra care on the presumption that a run of salmon is at hand.

Since the water was rather deep and the current fairly strong I used a sinking line with a fourteen-foot leader—one that I since have found to be much longer than necessary. Although fish were taken by everyone else that morning, I didn't have even a strike.

That afternoon I changed tackle, selecting an eight-and-a-half-foot fiberglas rod which was rigged with a white floating line with ten feet of sinking green-colored tip. Wading to the upper end of the bar I took a place behind the other anglers who were working downstream. On the first cast I hooked a grilse, beached him, and took the end spot again. This trip proved unsuccessful. As I waded out for another try I checked the leader and noted a wind-knot near the tip. Carelessly assuming the leader would be strong enough I worked down the bar again.

Suddenly there was a strong strike and a fairly large salmon jumped. Lowering the rod during the jump I tightened on him again, but he was off. He jumped once more, with my fly in his mouth. The leader had broken at the wind-knot.

On several more excursions down the bar I hooked and beached a fish on nearly every trip, releasing all but two and finally ending as the high-scoring rod of the afternoon by a very comfortable margin.

This taught me two things, among many others that I learned as the years went by. One should frequently check the leader for wind-knots if there is even a suspicion that one might be there. If it is, it should be mended immediately, because carelessness frequently costs one the best salmon of the day.

Also, under average wet-fly conditions, I have become very partial to a floating line with a sinking tip. A leader only the length of the rod is as long as necessary, and it can be as strong in the tippet as the size of fly permits, because salmon are not very leader-shy.

With this equipment one always knows where his fly is. The end of the white line is very visible, and the fly is about twenty feet in a straight line beyond that. In addition, the line can be picked up very easily because most of it is floating. The sinking tip and the leader combine to sink the fly only a foot or so, which seems to be the depth where the fish seem to want it in most rivers under average conditions.

On this occasion, the longer leader and the sinking line evidently didn't allow the fly to fish properly. As I envisioned it later, the too deeply sunken fly was disturbed by rocks and currents down in the pool. It didn't swing and present itself as it should. Salmon rarely will take a fly that is being fished improperly.

Salmon rivers are ever-changing also because of the difference of each one from all the others. In this chapter we have dwelt on the famous Miramichi, which is a giant river system very handy to anglers living in the northeastern United States. Parts of it flow through towns and farmlands where its banks are sprinkled with small homes and fishing camps. Other parts flow through wilderness areas where moose and deer and other animals distract anglers from their fishing. Boats are often used for transportation, but most of the fishing (except for black salmon) is done by wading, with waders usually preferred to hip-boots so that deep spots can be negotiated.

The beauty of the rivers, and the differences between them, compete with the interest in the fishing and combine to make every excursion to a new river a different and very rewarding experience.

The Province of Quebec enjoys amazing variety in its rivers, and most of them harbor much bigger salmon than the average found in the Miramichi. It is a pity that no one ever can fish them all.

The first visit to a river is like an orientation process, because one learns what could be expected on the next trip. One remembers the "hot spots" where a good fish was taken, and looks forward to returning to try the spot again. Among the difficult decisions an angler has to make is whether to return to familiar places or whether it would be more interesting to try new ones. The lure of the rivers, whether they be familiar or unvisited, is that, in their ever-changing moods, they always seem new.

The Grand Cascapedia, which partially splits the Gaspé Peninsula, is big and sophisticated. It flows majestically through mountainous country in a constant succession of bends and deep, rock-bound pools. Long rods usually are needed in this heavy water to cast large flies for very large salmon often weighing thirty pounds or more. Since all, or nearly all, of the river is privately owned or leased, it is not available to anglers lacking an invitation.

On the contrary, the welcome signs are out on the nearby Matane, which flows into the St. Lawrence. This is a smaller, more placid stream whose many well-marked pools are available to licensed anglers for a small daily fee. Since it is public water accessible by a good road bordering most of it, one may find too many anglers there when the fishing is good. But .one man's chances are as good as another's and camping spots on the upper stretches make the river popular for those with moderate budgets. If camping isn't your cup of tea, one can live luxuriously at the Belle Plage Hotel and Motor Inn in the nearby city of Matane and can travel by car to the pools.

Farther up the Gaspé Peninsula beckons the St. Anne, whose headwaters are in the beautiful Gaspé Park wilderness. Although on the lower stretches beats are available by arrangement, the highlight of a visit here is the day-long boat trip on which two guides pole one or two anglers down very fast water from pool to pool, stopping at each one for the fishing. This is a wilderness excursion which must be arranged long in advance, because only one or two boats are allowed on the river at a time. The wild and beautiful trip is exciting, regardless of how many salmon are in the river, or how few.

No North American angler should claim to be a salmon fisherman until he has caught at least a twenty-pounder with a trout rod on the Gaspé's famous Restigouche or Matapedia, which meet near the small city of Matapedia and flow into the Bay of Chaleur. During the season, anglers are accommodated at the comfortable Restigouche Hotel and its luxurious motel across from the railroad station. The hotel is very convenient to the liquor store and to Carmelle Bigaouette's fly shop, where excellently dressed salmon flies can be purchased from her abundant supply, or she will dress them overnight on special order.

Fishing on the Government stretches of the Matapedia is by arrangement with the Provincial Park Service in New Carlisle, and by paying a daily rod fee. Arrangements should be made months in advance. Each of the many pools is assigned to one angler (sometimes two) with a guide and a boat. He fishes each pool in rotation for half a day, so, for example, an angler who stays for four days would fish eight pools. After taking a bright twenty-three-pounder I asked

( W. Meinel)

FIG. I-2

READY FOR THE BEACH

the guide what average could be expected. He said that, under usual conditions, a competent angler should expect to take one and a half fish per day, or three salmon in two days. To many of us, only one salmon of twenty pounds or so, caught on a relatively light fly-rod, would be an amply rewarding memento of such a trip! Unlike the Miramichi and many other rivers, there are few, if any, grilse in the Matapedia early in the season. One does, however, occasionally catch a sea-run Brook Trout. Trout weighing a pound or more, which would be considered quite satisfactory on our trout streams at home, are treated as nuisances on salmon rivers and usually are referred to as "those damn things" by the guides.

Each of these typical salmon rivers is different from the others, and each differs in its own characteristics from day to day during each season. The fishing may be a feast or a famine, but usually it is somewhere in between. A map of the Atlantic salmon rivers of Canada* shows hundreds in that country alone. There are a few in Maine, and almost countless others in Iceland, the Scandinavian countries, the British Isles, and in France and Spain. Each has its own type of beauty, its own characteristics, and its own methods of fishing. No man can live long enough even to sample quickly more than a small fraction of them all, but the varied beauties and challenges of the great salmon rivers get into one's blood, as do the varied characteristics and challenges of the salmon themselves.

The battle to save the salmon rivers from the greed and abuses of man is never-ending. In the days of our forefathers, Atlantic salmon were so abundant in New England's rivers that often they were considered a nuisance. Then man built dams for his factories, thus barring the salmon from their spawning grounds upstream. Illegal poaching, excessive netting and the scourge of pollution did the rest, eventually driving all the salmon from nearly all the rivers in the United States. To further compound the felony, people from European countries discovered where the salmon migrate while they grow and fatten in the sea. There (in areas south of Greenland) they are being drift-netted and caught with long-lines in quantities which dangerously deplete the stock before they can return to their rivers

* Obtainable (for $5 as this is written) from The Atlantic Salmon Association, 1225 University Street, Montreal 2, Canada.

and attempt to run the gauntlet of nets, dams, poaching and pollution at home.

While all this sounds very discouraging to anglers who want their sons and grandsons to be able to enjoy the thrills of salmon fishing when they grow up, it may not be quite as bad as it seems. During the past few years the State of Maine has been showing that salmon rivers can be rehabilitated and that salmon caught by fly-fishermen are worth many times more to the economy than are salmon caught by netters to be sold commercially. Associations have been formed to protect the salmon for sport-fishing, at the same time acknowledging that commercial interests deserve their fair share, but not such an excessive amount as could endanger future stocks for all concerned. International councils have been formed to insure that adequate quantities of salmon can return to the rivers of their birth.

Most of the nations which have an investment in the salmon fishery increasingly realize that the salmon must be protected from avaricious interests in the sea, in the estuaries and all the way up the rivers to their spawning grounds. To this end, netting rights gradually are being purchased; dams are being destroyed; or adequate fish-ladders are being provided for them; and the battle of river pollution is being fought.

Both the lure of the rivers and the lore of the salmon combine to make Atlantic salmon fishing with the fly-rod and the fly the transcendent angling sport that it has been for so many generations. Let us all join together, sportsmen and commercial fishermen alike, to insure that this priceless heritage can be preserved so that our descendants as well as ourselves can always enjoy the incomparable thrill of hooking the Atlantic salmon with a fly!

# I I
# The Lore
# of the Salmon

Far up a small tributary of a salmon river, deep down in its gravel, the warmth of early spring was causing an annual occurrence as old as the ages. Late the previous fall a salmon had laid her eggs there. She had dug the bed more than six inches deep because instinct born of heredity had warned her that shallower planting would expose the nest of eggs to the depredations of insect larvae and the questing of hungry fish and birds. Instinct also had told her not to deposit all her eggs in one place, so she had laid them in several such nests, covering each one carefully as she prepared the next, until her supply was exhausted. Then, also exhausted, she had slowly returned to the rehabilitating vigor of the sea.

Now, as warming pure water trickled deep through chinks in the gravel, the eggs were quivering with life. Soft, orange-pink, and little larger than buckshot, fish-like heads and tails emerged from them, but the rest of the egg remained suspended from each newly born fish until the yolk-sack had completed its mission of nourishment and

16

had become absorbed. The baby salmon, called "alevins," were no more than half an inch long.

This stage of development required several weeks but, when it was completed, the eggs had been transformed into inch-long tiny fish. One by one they slithered up through the gravel and hid in schools of hundreds on the stream-bottom under whatever protection each could find. There, as the weeks passed, those that survived the raids of birds and of larger fish grew steadily as they sucked in the minute micro-organisms of the river.

Salmon, in their several stages of development, are given various names by scientists. When the alevin has absorbed its yolk-sack, it is called a "fry." On reaching the length of longer than an inch, but still below finger-size, it becomes a "fingerling." Exceeding finger length it develops a dark back and lighter belly, with vertical bars (called "parr-marks") along its sides. In this stage it is termed a "parr" and closely resembles a small Brook Trout, except primarily for its deeply-forked tail.

The life of the parr in the river is a dangerous one. As they subsist and grow by devouring nymphs, insects and later-born alevins, their numbers are constantly depleted by larger fish and by diving birds. The little parr remain for a year or more in the river (the length of time depending on environmental factors) and, as they grow, gradually drift downriver to the sea.

The avidity of the parr for insects is well known to anglers who go fly-fishing for salmon. Very often there is a slight tap on the fly, which can't be recovered properly because a hungry parr has caught his little mouth around the hook. Then the angler (if he deserves that term) carefully draws in the baby fish, lifts him by the hook, turns its barb over, and lets him wriggle off—usually with an invitation for him to return when he grows up!

As the parr reach the river's estuary they gradually take on a silvery color which hides the parr marks. In this stage, the brightly shining fish is called a "smolt," his color transformation indicating that he is almost ready to go to sea. His age at this point is two or three years, occasionally more or less, depending again on environmental conditions. His life is never free of dangers: the man-made dangers of power-dams and factory pollution, and the dangers of

Nature in the form of diving cormorants and gulls. But the smolts that survive school together, often in tremendous numbers, awaiting by instinct the tide that is to take them to sea.

Where the salmon go while they grow to adulthood in the sea remained an enigma until 1965, when two fishing boats in the Davis Strait between Greenland and Canada drift-netted over ten thousand adult salmon, a quantity that each year since has doubled or much more than doubled, creating a drain on the salmon supply of extremely dangerous proportions. This is of very special concern to North Americans because research indicates that "the majority of salmon (taken) in the West Greenland fishery originate in Canada*." It is also having an effect upon the excellent work the State of Maine is doing in reclaiming its salmon rivers: "The effects of the Greenland fishery on salmon rehabilitation in Maine is cause of great concern."*

Evidently this vast area in or near the Davis Strait is a major international feeding ground for Atlantic salmon because other nations (the United Kingdom, especially) have noticed dangerous depletions in the numbers of salmon which return to their rivers. We have noted that an international Conference on Conservation of Atlantic Salmon has been deliberating on the problem. A ten-year moratorium on the netting of Atlantic salmon has been suggested. The matter needs more than deliberation while this destructive netting still goes on. Immediate and definite action must be taken if our remaining salmon stocks are to survive.

After one or more years of growth in the sea, the surviving salmon return to their rivers. That they almost all return to the rivers of their birth (as learned from the tagging of smolts and from other research), and even to the very tributary wherein they were born, is a constant source of wonder and astonishment to man. Since no man ever has been a salmon, the solution to the enigma is a matter of conjecture. Of course it must be a God-given instinct similar to the unerring migrations of birds, wherein one or a pair may winter thousands of miles away and return in the spring to a familiar acre of ground, there perhaps to remodel or to build a nest in the same tree they formerly occupied.

* Sport Fishing Institute *Bulletin*, May, 1969.

Scientists seem to conclude that when this instinct brings the salmon to the region of their river, a remembrance of the characteristics of the river itself guides them into it. The presumption is that every river has an individual identifying combination of chemical composition, odor, water-pressure, taste and, perhaps, of temperature and that salmon remember these characteristics and can follow them home. Considerable experimentation has been done to substantiate this conclusion, but perhaps we needn't bother to consider it here.

When the salmon return to the region of their rivers and travel up or down the coast to identify their own, they must survive a new set of dangers. At this time they are in their prime, having become big, strong and fat by feasting on the bounty of the sea. Their flesh is firm and is red or pink, depending on the quantities of shrimps and other crustaceans they have eaten, because these types of foods color it so. Their strength and swiftness may enable them to avoid predators such as seals, porpoises and lampreys, but they are no match for the maze of nets in the estuaries or the nets and weirs in the tidal waters. Here the majority of the survivors are taken by commercial fishermen. Governments controlling most rivers dictate that the nets must be raised or removed at certain times to allow a reasonable proportion of the salmon to get through. This is not always done. Having passed the hazards of the estuarial and tidewater nets, there are dams the salmon must leap, fish-ways and counting stations to be negotiated and, too often, the nets of poachers.

In some of the rivers with which I am familiar, illegal netting is much too prevalent. Because of the complexity of the river systems, policing in most areas cannot be efficient. Fines for poaching are usually so small that only one of many nights of thievery will pay for all of them on the rare occasion when a poacher is caught and convicted. Towns along the rivers are usually small. People overlook offenses of their friends, if they consider them to be offenses at all. The poacher may be married to the judge's daughter! The sad fact remains that the relatively few salmon which survive from egg to their return to the river are spawning stock, minus the small proportion taken by anglers. These survivors are very valuable fish. Poachers can net scores of them from a single pool and, when conditions are right, they can do it time and time again. Anglers invest valuable days and considerable money on fishing trips to Canada, perhaps to find some of the trips unsatisfactory because too few fish are in the river. Authorities would greatly help the economies of their areas if they would radically increase the penalties for illegal netting, spearing and other forms of poaching.

Salmon may enter their rivers at any time of the year, although there are peak periods. Their runs upriver in spring, summer and fall vary from river to river and depend on the conditions of the rivers themselves. Thus, by their peak periods, rivers may be known as spring rivers, summer rivers or autumn rivers. By knowing when the runs of fish should occur, anglers can visit one river after another and can expect good fishing throughout the season.

The strength and determination of salmon running upriver is a sight to behold when quantities of them are negotiating an obstacle such as a waterfall or a dam. In his book *The Salmon*, Dr. J. W. Jones describes a measured leap of eleven feet, four inches by a salmon going over a perpendicular waterfall. This required a vertical speed of twenty miles per hour as the fish left the water. Since they have never done this before, their instinct for negotiating falls and fast water is amazing. Failing to make the leap, they will try and try again, until it is accomplished. In one place, where the current of a small stream swept downward over a rocky chute caused by an inclined ledge, the salmon were smart enough not to try to swim the chute. Instead, they selected the thin, slower water at the edge of the ledge, and slithered upward over it easily in water insufficient to float them! For one reason or another, they move mostly during the night, or during the hours approaching night or daylight. During the day, or when the flow is insufficient for travel, they rest in the pools. A pool devoid of salmon one day or even one hour may be full of them the next!

Salmon may spend one, two, three or even four years in the sea, growing bigger year by year. A salmon returning after his first year in the sea is called a "grilse," and normally weighs between two and eight pounds, usually at least five or six. When a salmon is termed a grilse and when he becomes a full-fledged salmon sometimes goes by local rules. On the Miramichi, for example, a fish of five pounds or more is called a "salmon," so it is possible for a fish, having spent

FIG. II-1

THEIR INSTINCT FOR NEGOTIATING FALLS
AND FAST WATER IS AMAZING

21

only one year in the sea but having returned as a five-pounder, to be dignified by the term of salmon.* In the Miramichi the proportion of grilse to salmon is very large, sometimes as large as ten grilse to one salmon. This may be due to the gill-netting in the estuary, which takes the larger fish but which lets the smaller ones get through. Or it may be because grilse will take a fly quicker than the salmon will. I have been told by people who have observed a few salmon and many more grilse in a pool that the grilse nearly always will go for the fly first. In other rivers the grilse habitually run at different times. If one fishes the Matapedia in early July, for example, one will almost always take salmon. But if he goes there later in the season, he will take a larger proportion of grilse.

Often the size of the salmon is proportionate to the size of the river, but not always. Thirty-pounders occasionally are caught on the Miramichi, and they are fairly common on the Matapedia, a river of about the same size. Forty-pounders, or even larger, are taken on bigger rivers such as the Restigouche and the Grand Cascapedia. In his excellent book *The Atlantic Salmon*, Anthony Netboy says, "No generalizations are possible about the size of adult salmon, although some countries like Norway and Scotland seem to breed heavier fish than others. Salmon weighing up to 70 pounds and more have been taken in these lands and the world's record, as far as I can ascertain, is a 103-pounder landed in the River Devon in Scotland."

Mr. Netboy might have added that the 103-pounder was caught in 1901 or 1902 in a net by poachers. Records kept by *Field and Stream* indicate that the rod and reel world's record is a 79-pound, 2-ounce fish taken in 1928 on the Tana River, which separates Norway and Finland. The data does not say whether or not it was caught on a fly. The Canadian record is a 55-pounder taken on June 27, 1939 on Quebec's Grand Cascapedia River by Esmond B. Martin, who

---

* The five-pound classification comes from the law that says that any fish under five pounds cannot be taken commercially or offered for sale in New Brunswick. Consequently all salmon under five pounds must be released by nettors. So even a mature salmon could be classified as a grilse, and a grilse over five pounds could be, and is, classified as a salmon albeit the first could have spent two or possibly three years at sea while a six-pound fish could still be a one-year-at-sea fish. The size and weight of salmon are governed by many factors, including heredity, genes, their start in life as parr and smolt and the length of time they spend in the river before going to sea.

used a Leonard rod, vom Hofe reel and a *Lady Amherst* fly. In the United States the record breaker is a 26-pound, 8-ounce salmon taken on July 16, 1959, on Maine's Narraguagus River by Harry E. Smith, who used a Phillipson rod, Pflueger reel and a special dry fly tied by himself. Presumably the day is not far off when this record will be broken.

When the salmon first arrive in the river they are in their prime—bright, fat and strong, a joy to catch and trophies to be proud of. But, as they do not feed to any appreciable extent after entering the river, their beauty and strength gradually decline. As their appearance wanes, their sexual organs develop, nearly filling the body cavities of the males with milt, and of the females with roe. Their minds are no longer on feeding although, very fortunately for anglers, they will by instinct take insects occasionally, and sometimes other things. They are totally occupied with sex, and are determined to reach their nuptial gravel beds as quickly as possible to get started with it!

Salmon do not necessarily enter the rivers with their supply of milt or of roe in an advanced stage of development. In the fall of 1969 the author took a gorgeous female salmon on a Quebec river. Bright, fat and lusty, she was over three feet long and weighed better than twenty pounds. On preparing her for the freezer I found that her eggs were very small, occupying an area hardly bigger than a golf ball, and weighing less than three ounces. Fresh from the sea, her sexual development had hardly begun.

The trip up the river to the nesting areas in the tributary streams may take several weeks, delayed perhaps by low water or possibly because the fish do not want to reach their destinations until they are almost ready to spawn.

Although the spawning of salmon has been discussed in angling classics as far back as Walton, evidently earlier writers lacked the facilities to observe it with complete accuracy. The best description this author has found is in Dr. J. W. Jones' excellent and authoritative book *The Salmon* (1959), published in the United States by Harper & Row, of New York. Dr. Jones obtained an endowment to build an observation tank on the River Alwen, a tributary of the Welsh Dee. After considerable experimentation he accurately observed more than ninety spawnings in the tank over a period of more than three thousand hours. Essentially, his observations are these:

The males and females spend a considerable time resting in the pools at either end of the spawning bed, though the dominant male will frequently prod a female with his snout, push against her, or bully any other male. Dominance may be an indication of imminent readiness for spawning: it is certainly not primarily dependent on size. The next stage is the movement of a female out of the pool and over the gravel. After exploratory wanderings the female starts cutting a bed (making a depression in the gravel). As this continues the dominant male quivers with increasing frequency and intensity alongside her. As the cutting continues the tenant female tests the result of her activities with her ventral fins, particularly the anal; and when she has made a saucer-like depression about six inches deep, her efforts appear to be directed principally to perfecting the shape of the bed. The end result is a hole at the bottom of which the current is much reduced. At the bottom of the hole are two or three large stones between which she can thrust her anal fin as she presses her body into the shape of the bed.

When, after hours or even days of fidgety cutting and feeling, the bed is suitable, she assumes the "crouch" position, opens her mouth, and is joined by the male. He also opens his mouth and quivers violently; and the eggs and sperm are extruded almost simultaneously. Immediately after the orgasm the male moves away, generally into the pool below, while the female moves a foot or so upstream from the bed and by vigorous cutting sends down gravel to fill the depression and cover the eggs. In most spawnings nearly all the eggs are ejected into the crack between the stones at the bottom of the bed, where they are difficult to see and reasonably well sheltered from the shower of gravel which the female afterwards sends down. The "covering up" is usually continued as the beginning of the next spawning sequence. As many as eight such sequences, each farther upstream than the previous one, may be carried out before the female has deposited all her eggs.

Other observations indicate that the ovaries of hen fish are so full of soft and not very round eggs that they fill most of the body cavity. Once extruded, however, the coating of mucous on the eggs causes them to adhere to whatever they touch on the stream bottom, where their shells gradually harden and become more spherical. Depending on their size, adult females usually will deposit between 5,000 and 10,000 eggs in a succession of beds (the whole area of which is called a "redd"). Usually, over 95 per cent of the eggs which are laid are successfully fertilized.

A male salmon may fertilize the eggs of several females. The reproductory functions of living things are wonderful in many ways. In the case of salmon, for example, nature has insured that, when a ripe female and a spent or nearly spent male are together the female's eggs may be successfully fertilized even if insufficient milt remains in the male. Instances are recorded of male parr (weighing only fractions of an ounce) invading the beds of giant salmon while the male salmon is too occupied to drive them away (or perhaps he doesn't notice that one or two of the neighborhood boys are getting into the act!). The little parr, with their tiny vents close to the big one of the large female, have the instinct to deposit their milt over the eggs at the proper time.

Although this disparity in sizes, somewhat resembling that between a dinghy and an ocean liner, may seem rather ludicrous, scientific experiments in observation tanks have been made wherein, although the big male had been sterilized, the little parr fertilized the eggs as well as the adult might have done it.

After spawning in the late fall or early winter, the salmon, exhausted by their efforts and lack of food, are ugly, emaciated caricatures of the lordly fish they once were. They are called "kelts" ( or "spent fish" or "unclean fish" or "black salmon"). Some die of disease; others (unlike all Pacific salmons) drift downriver to the sea, where they can feed and cleanse themselves and perhaps return, as beautiful as before and larger than ever, to spawn again or perhaps to provide superlative sport to the angler with his fly-rod and his fly.

In some regions the surviving salmon, which do not return in the fall or early winter to the sea, may become icebound, thus being forced to remain in deep pools until spring. In the spring they may be in even worse condition, although anglers (in regions such as New Brunswick, where they are allowed to fish for them) maintain that they do gradually cleanse themselves to an extent and take on a more silvery appearance during the weeks that follow the breaking up of the ice. This "black salmon" fishing has been allowed in New Brunswick mainly because of the tourist traffic it brings in. The short season has been shortened, and the practice may be barred altogether. Fishermen are divided quite radically into two very divergent schools of thought about it.

Proponents of black salmon fishing maintain that it is exciting to fish from boats in the fast spring run-off and to hook perhaps a dozen or more big fish a day with large streamer flies or bucktails even though, at this time, fly pattern and size are unimportant and all one needs to do is to shake some line out into the current to catch fish. They maintain that, after the ice goes out, the salmon do feed, fill out in size, take on more of a silvery color, and furnish good sport. They say the flesh is palatable even though they admit it can't compare with that of fresh-run fish. Finally, they maintain that the practice doesn't harm the fish, because most of them are released.

Opponents of black salmon fishing maintain that it requires no skill, is not sporting, and does great harm to the fishery. They feel that, whether or not the fish do feed, they couldn't do so very much because, if they did, they would consume nearly all the parr, trout, smelt and other small fish in the river. While, soon after ice-out, they may look more silvery and filled-out, this is mostly an illusion because their bodies are highly liquid, causing them to deflate after being killed. They consider the flesh so flavorless and unpalatable that no self-respecting gourmet would touch it.

Perhaps the main point in this difference of opinion is that, after the exhaustion of fighting their way many miles upriver, of spawning, of going for many weeks with little or no food, and after a hard winter in the river, the salmon's chances of survival are poor indeed. When their strength is further exhausted by battling rod and reel, their chances are almost nil. Fishermen usually do not release black salmon, unless perhaps they have taken a plethora of them. Those that are released, in their extremely exhausted condition, have almost no chance of surviving to reach the sea.

Statistics indicate that, of the black salmon which do live to return to the sea, a very significant proportion return to their rivers fully rehabilitated, bigger and lustier than ever before. The percentage varies in various rivers but in the Miramichi it is in the neighborhood of ten or twelve per cent. These are the trophy fish we seek to catch and occasionally hear about. Who can say that, after all a salmon has been through, he should be denied the chance to be one of them?

Readers may wonder why this brief discussion of the life history of the Atlantic salmon should be included in a book on flies and fishing. It is included because an integral part of fishing for salmon is the basic understanding of them. When we realize why they are in rivers at some times and not in others, when we understand the several periods in their development, and when we know something about their habits, we are much better able to fish for them success-fully. Then, when one suddenly boils up to slam at our fly, the thrill of the fishing will be greater than it could have been before!

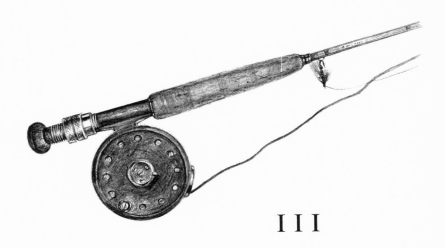

# I I I

# The New Look
# in Salmon Tackle

As late as 1950 heavy two-handed rods, of greenheart or split-bamboo, from 12 to 14 feet long and weighing between 12 and 26 ounces, were favored for salmon on both sides of the Atlantic. Their modern uses are confined to a relatively few very large rivers. There they are needed to cast the tremendous flies, of size 5/0 or so, which are selected because, due to their heavy irons, they will sink quickly and, due to their size, be more visible deep in immense pools or in swift, murky currents. They also are needed to handle super-size salmon in these wide, torrential streams. Otherwise, during recent decades, salmon rods have been getting lighter and shorter until the great majority of them have become fairly well standardized in 8- to 9½-foot lengths.

## RODS

Diminution in size is part of the "new look" in rods. The other major part is the change from split-bamboo to tubular rods fabricated from fiberglas cloth. The former has been influenced by the latter because the very dependable power and strength of properly made glass rods have made the long, heavy sticks much less necessary.

Discriminating anglers in large numbers still seek and cherish hand-crafted rods of split-bamboo. If these anglers understand the revolutionary improvements which have been made in glass rod construction, they will have to admit that their preference for split-bamboo is due to pride of possession rather than to superior efficiency. In a way, I side with them, because rods made by famous craftsmen such as Orvis and Payne are a joy to use and to own. But, in fairness to progress, let's look at the other side of the coin.

Last fall I took turns with a highly experienced angler in fishing a famous salmon pool from a boat. He used a 9-foot split-bamboo rod made by a renowned New York State rod builder. He was a bit contemptuous of the two I brought along, both being Wright & McGill "Eagle Claw" glass rods in 8½- and 9-foot lengths. Noticing that he had picked up only one rod, it seemed prudent to take along a spare!

During his turn to fish a drop he hooked a large salmon. He lost it when his rod broke at the ferrule, the tip sliding ignominiously down the line into the water. He accepted my glass 9-footer, and both of us caught salmon in the 25-pound class. We did it in considerably less time than the proverbial average of a minute to the pound. He used my rod in preference to his others for the rest of the week, and shortly thereafter he wrote that he had purchased one of his own.

The improvements made in glass rods in America during recent years have been astounding, and have largely been due to a fascinating chain of breakthroughs in modern manufacturing technology. Glass rods vary widely in quality and in the characteristics built into them by various manufacturers. Quality is not entirely based on price, because there are low-priced and high-priced rods which are excellent —and others which are abominable. The best guarantee to the uninitiated is the integrity of the manufacturer.

In the days of split-bamboo, rods were individually made from cane strips of varying strengths with the result that no two rods were exactly alike. Prospective purchasers tested the actions of one after another until, after many wogglings and wigglings and other displays of profound knowledge, each buyer had selected the one with "perfect action," as far as he was concerned.

Thanks to modern glass rod technology, all rods made by the same manufacturer in the same model number are exactly alike, and their actions are planned to suit the great majority of people who will buy them. But, since there are many ways in which each manufacturer can vary the action of his rods, including specifications of the glass cloth and the design of the template which governs the shape of its cutting, the rods of one manufacturer will vary in action from those of another. Generally, however, all manufacturers plan their rods so they will handle the lines which fit them with maximum efficiency. Usually they are general purpose rods with medium action, which is just what we want for use with most types of salmon flies.

If one is so fussy that he is not content with a general purpose rod he may want to shop around to find one with faster action for dry-fly work, or one with slower action for heavier flies or streamers. In salmon fishing, however, dry flies usually are rather bulky for best flotation, and big streamers also can be handled very well with a medium-action rod, so this type should prove excellent for all purposes. Flies of all types most commonly used on average-sized rivers are in sizes 4, 6 and 8, which can be handled excellently with a System 8 or a System 9 rod size, the former usually being about 8½ feet long and the latter about 9 feet long. Larger flies might cast better with a more powerful rod, and smaller flies might work better with a less powerful one. The power of the rod, however, should be more in keeping with the nature of the water being fished than with the sizes of flies which are used with it. Rods longer than 9 feet are tiresome to cast with one hand. A two-handed rod presents difficulty in handling the line. Rod length primarily is dictated by the distance of cast needed, although we may want a longer one for deep wading and a shorter one for shore and boat fishing. Detachable butts, formerly common on the larger rods, are not as prevalent as they used to be. Many of us consider them an unnecessary nuisance, and we will show later why they should not be needed.

Rods of 8 feet or more nearly always are fitted with locking reel-seats. Be sure the reel can be locked on tightly because any wobble in the connection is dangerous and bothersome. If, when the connection is tightened, the reel does wobble a little, this can be adjusted by building up the reel-seat with adhesive tape.


## LINES

There have been difficulties in selecting proper line sizes which best bring out the actions of rods generally. Manufacturers usually print on the rods, or specify on the tube labels, the line size recommended. A size larger often is better. Since rods of similar lengths may vary widely in power, selecting line sizes by rod lengths is too rough a generality. Matching the line to the rod is of paramount importance because poorly matched tackle simply won't cast properly.

This problem has been solved as well as it can be by Scientific Anglers, Inc., a manufacturer of glass fly rods, fly reels and fly lines located in Midland, Michigan. They classify their tackle, and the rods of all other major manufacturers, by "Systems" or sizes ranging between System 4 and System 11. Atlantic salmon fishermen generally will be concerned only with Systems 8, 9 and 10. System 9, for example, is the designation of a medium-powerful rod suitable for average rivers requiring a size 9 line. The designation goes further to include the type of line, and is indicated by letters such as DT for "double taper," WF for "weight-forward (or torpedo-taper)," S for "sinking," F for "floating," etc. Thus, for example, if a rod requires a System (or "size") 9 line and the owner wants it to be a weight-forward floating line with a sinking tip, the designation would be WF-9-F/S.

This simplification was made necessary when, after World War II, fly lines were no longer made entirely of silk, but also of other materials such as nylon (which is lighter) and dacron (which is heavier). Line size designations by diameter no longer meant anything. Accordingly, the American Fishing Tackle Manufacturers' Association set up this new number system wherein every fly line has a number indicating its weight. Its diameter is ignored, as it always should have been. The weight designation is determined on the basis of the forward 30 feet of line, so all types of lines (double-taper, weight-forward, floating, sinking, etc.) which carry the same number weigh the same. Thus, if a rod handles well on one type of line of a certain size, it will handle equally well when fitted with any other type of the same size.

Scientific Anglers, Inc., have further cooperated with fly-fishermen by publishing an annually revised folder on *Fly Line Recommendations* for every model number of every fly-rod distributed by all major manufacturers. In this folder the owner of a new rod can look under the manufacturer's listing to find the model number of his rod and he will find there the recommended line weight (System number, or size) which should fit it best. This information is provided without charge upon request.

All this is a big help to anglers who own several rods and an assortment of reels filled with various sizes and types of lines. One can mark each rod and rod case with the correct line size for it. One can mark each reel or reel spool acording to line size and type. Then, when selecting a few rods to use on a fishing trip, it is easy also to select the reels and lines which belong with them.

Along with the "new look" of synthetic lines, which don't need to be pampered as much as the old silk lines needed to be, is the floating line which doesn't need to be greased because its buoyancy is derived from millions of tiny air cells sealed in the coating. Anglers have said that some of these lines which are made to float don't always do so. The reason may be because they have become dirty. Rubbing them with a small cloth dipped in mild soap and tepid water should remedy this.

Many of us who used to store fly-lines in large coils during the off-season now leave them on the reel spools throughout the year. If they have set in coils, when they next are used stretching them should make them pliant again.

In salmon fishing one needs all the backing the reel-spool will hold—at least 150 yards, or more. Information which comes with the reel usually specifies the amount of backing which can be accommodated with various sizes of line. If it doesn't a solution is to put the line on first and then to reel on backing until the spool is comfortably (but not overly) full. The backing and line then is reeled off (without twisting); the backing is reeled on tightly; and the reel-end of the fly-line is spliced to it.

One way to join backing and line is to splice a small loop in the

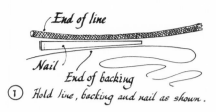

① Hold line, backing and nail as shown.

② Wind backward around line, nail and itself seven times and insert end of backing back through loops.

③ Pull both ends of backing tight. Slip nail out and retighten securely. Clip ends of line and backing.

④ Thread wind and cement to finish.

Fig. III-1

THE "NAIL KNOT"

line and to make a loop in the backing which is large enough to pass over the reel or reel-spool. The backing loop is put through the line loop, then over the spool, and the connection is pulled tight. The backing loop seems neatest when made with a Perfection Loop knot, which is amply strong for this purpose.

A better way, in the author's opinion, is to join backing and line with a Nail Knot, as shown in Figure III-1. This provides a smooth connection which passes freely through the rod's tip-top and which can't slip, cut or pull out when tied properly. Either a tapered nail, a small piece of tubing or something else such as a strong toothpick can be used.

Hold line, backing and tapered nail or tubing together between thumb and forefinger, as shown, with ample backing extending for the windings. Wind the backing end backward over itself and the nail and line (toward fly line end), making seven close coils. Thread the end of the backing back under the coils through the tubing or beside the nail, and pull the connection snug. Then remove nail or tubing and tighten by pulling on the backing and its end, being sure all coils are close

33

together, preferably without overlapping. The connection must be pulled tight enough so the coils of backing bite into the line. Test the knot and then clip the line end and the backing end close to it. Thread-wind and varnish or cement the connection, if desired. This knot also is used to join a leader to a fly line, but a simpler way to do this will be shown in the section of this chapter which discusses leaders.

There are times when we may want to use a favorite reel for salmon fishing, but its arbor is too small to hold the line and enough backing. A remedy for this is to see how far we can cast comfortably with the line, then to pull out about five feet more and to cut the line at this point (which probably will be about 45 or 50 feet, or about half of the line). Backing is put on as previously discussed, and the forward end of the line is joined to the backing. Backing usually is of braided dacron, of about 15 or 20 pounds test. Since this is much finer in diameter than the line, a large amount of backing can be put on a medium-sized fly-reel if the useless part of the line is eliminated.

Normally the tippet strength of the leader will not exceed 15 pounds; it is usually less. So there is no need to use braided backing which is much stronger than the tippet. Since the strength of braided backing may have deteriorated slightly, and since we feel safer with backing we know is strong enough, a strength testing 5 or 10 pounds more than the strongest tippet we will use should be adequate. To avoid error, the backing on all reels should be of the same strength. The author standardizes this at 20 pounds, which should be sufficient for all North American rivers. If one plans to fish in Norway or other regions having extra-large salmon in extra-turbulent rivers, the strength of the tackle should be decided by local custom.

The color of the line (and of the leader) in salmon fishing seems to make no appreciable difference. We will see later that dry-fly fishing for salmon is often a necessary way, and always a pleasant and exciting way, to take them. For this, a double-taper floating line usually is preferred, although some will want a forward taper to cast big floating flies, especially into the wind. A sinking line may be necessary to get flies down deep in big pools but, since it is difficult to present a fly properly in this manner, since it is hard to pick up a sinking line, and since pools and situations which require this are the exception rather than the rule, the selection of a sinking line for salmon fishing is in most cases a last choice. Nevertheless, under some conditions it proves valuable.

For all normal wet-fly fishing, my favorite is the floating line with a sinking tip. The forward ten feet are of a different color (such as a white floating line with a green sinking tip) so, knowing how long the leader is, one always knows where his fly is. The twenty feet or so of sinking leader and tip seem to swim the fly at the ideal depth of a foot or so (depending on current), and seem to help to present it properly to make it of maximum interest to salmon. An alternative is to use a line which floats entirely, and to use a longer leader of eighteen feet or more, if we are in positions which allow us to cast a line long enough to accommodate that length of leader. As mentioned earlier, lines that sink too deeply may swim the fly improperly due to eddies near the bottom of the stream. Also, salmon may not be interested in flies that are fished too deeply. Finally, another argument in favor of the floating line with a sinking tip is that it is very easy to pick up, usually making false casts unnecessary.

Some manufacturers provide tapered lines with an extra length of level line at the tip end so the angler can cut off what he wants to balance his tackle properly. Since this level tip section has no appreciable casting weight, most of it should be clipped off. By doubling the line, we can see where the taper starts, and we should cut off all but a foot of the level section. Failure to do this may mean that the cast will not roll out as it should.

Colors in fly lines vary nearly as much as the opinions of anglers as to what they should be. There are exponents of green lines, brown ones, yellow, white, salmon-pink and probably pistachio. My preference for floating lines is for white because I can see it better, but it never occurred to me that it would be less visible than other colors to fish.

Colonel Esmond Drury, the renowned English angling authority, proved that white lines *are* less visible to fish. During a blitz in Malta in 1941 he shared a trench with a Commando who was a frogman specializing in underwater demolitions. During later conversations the Commando happened to mention that the most difficult target to locate underwater is a ship with a white hull.

Eight years passed before the colonel happened to think that this comment might apply to fly lines. While snorkeling on vacation he observed floating and sinking lines against the sky from underwater and noticed that the traditional brown and green ones looked like black ropes. With some white string and wax he made a makeshift white fly line and noticed that, while it was very obvious when viewed from above, it was much less visible than lines of other colors when viewed from below.

He says, "The initial experiment was done in a deep, calm pool on a very bright day when the cone of vision was quite obvious. That part of the floating line within the cone was comparatively inconspicuous, while the line lying outside the cone of direct vision showed only a long silver indentation in the silvery mirror of the undersurface. I next tried it in fast, streamy water and had difficulty in seeing the line at all, except where it was submerged by the broken water. In later experiments under all conditions the white line proved much less visible from below than the traditional brown or green ones, which invariably looked black.

"On the manufacturing side, Milwards was most helpful and produced the first white fly line to be made. British anglers are conservative people, and the white fly line didn't take on, but the Americans got hold of the idea and today most fly lines are white ones."

If anyone is inclined to debate this point he might consider Darwin's theory of the survival of the fittest. Over the ages, water birds with bellies other than white ceased to exist because they were more conspicuous to predators looking upward from beneath the surface. If any water birds have bellies other than white, I don't know about them; and the same applies to most gamefish, too!

## SHOOTING HEADS

Using only the easily castable weight-forward tapered part of the fly line, connected to monofilament backing instead of to braided line, is an accepted fly-fishing method regardless of reel capacity. This part of the line is called a "shooting head," and shooting heads in all sizes can be bought as such, thus making the cutting of expensive fly lines unnecessary. Shooting heads have long been popular with those who desire to cast to greater distances for competition or to reach distant fish in wide streams, as well as with those who want maximum backing on the reel. Twenty-pound test monofilament is a good compromise between strength and stiffness. The Nail Knot produces less bulk than does joining the ends with interlocking loops, and its smoothness can be further improved with a few coats of good cement such as Pliobond to provide jerkless passage through the line guides of the rod.

Here a word of warning is appropriate. Do not put a large amount of monofilament on a fly reel that is of flimsy construction. If you do the constriction of the coils which builds up under tension can spread the plates of the reel spool, thus causing it to bind against the reel-cage and perhaps cause permanent damage. High quality reels should be strong enough to prevent this.

There are advantages and disadvantages in shooting heads. They allow a maximum amount of monofilament backing on the reel. They make casting possible to longer distances with less false casting and fuss. The narrower diameter of the monofilament gives less water resistance and thus less chance for hook pull-out. If a salmon runs around rocks the monofilament is easier to lift off the water so it can be passed over the obstacle. In the same vein it is argued that a fly can be more readily "let down" the stream to a greater distance without imparting unnatural motion to it.

In spite of these arguments, there are relatively few Atlantic salmon anglers who use a shooting head. Opponents think that unnecessarily long casts are usually more detrimental than helpful. Too many anglers overfish salmon lies even with conventional equipment. Opponents think the shooting head involves too much fuss, particularly in stretching the monofilament to prevent it from coiling and snarling. There is unpleasantness in handling the many coils of flimsy material that must be shot out on the cast if great distance is to be obtained. Even with care and experience, there is more danger of tangling than with conventional lines. Accuracy of fly presentation is reduced.

These seem to be the main arguments, both pro and con. One who does want to use a shooting head should, in fairness to the method, take enough time to learn how to use it efficiently.

## REELS

Fly-fishermen will need few suggestions on reels for salmon fishing because it is obvious that the reel must be large enough to hold the fly-line and between 150 and 200 yards of backing—preferably the latter amount. In addition to adequate reel capacity, quite obviously we need a reel with a smooth drag which can be adjusted to a reasonable extent. Beginners invariably set the drag too tight, thus endangering a snapped leader or a hook that pulls out. Since a salmon will exhaust himself by running and jumping, a fairly light drag is sensible under average conditions. Beginners should test the drag by pulling out line while someone holds the rod up. Invariably they will find that the amount of drag they have adjusted to will be a bit too tight. In dry-fly fishing, where the leader-tippet may be only six pounds or so, a very light drag is most necessary.

Some of the new reels are made to allow anglers to "feather" the spools—that is, to provide extra braking power with the fingertips while the spool is revolving. One of this type is offered by Scientific Anglers, Inc., and is made by the famous firm of Hardy Brothers. Another type, offered by Wright & McGill Company, has a spool handle which remains stationary while a fish takes out line. Its separate line spool revolves under adjustable drag tension until one is ready to retrieve. This is a low-cost reel. Another is the Pflueger Medalist, which comes in several sizes, with extra spools available. One sees it everywhere on North American salmon rivers.

Most fly-reels for salmon are single-action—that is, they retrieve one turn of line with each turn of the handle. There are others of the multiplying type which take in more than one turn, usually 2 or $2\frac{1}{2}$. Although these reels are heavier and bulkier than their single-action counterparts (due to the gearing in them), they do offer an advantage in retrieving line when salmon make long runs. Single-action reels require us to reel furiously when a lot of our backing is off the reel because we must crank in many more turns to regain the same amount of line than we would have to if the spool were nearly full.

When we are taken down into our backing, we must remember that the drag of the reel increases as more line is taken out. Unless the drag has been set fairly lightly, it may be prudent to lighten it a little and then to tighten it when all the backing has been regained. I prefer a lighter drag in the first place because it seems dangerous to fool with it while battling a salmon. This, of course, is a matter of preference.

A third type of fly-reel is the automatic. For many reasons, including the fact that it won't operate properly on long runs of fish, it has no place in Atlantic salmon fishing.

The pitch of the whir of the click on a fly-reel is supposed to tell the angler how fast a fish is taking out line. This seems of minor importance because he should know what is going on anyway!

When buying a reel, it is wise to get one or two extra reel-spools to go with it, and to select one which permits quick and easy changing of spools. Then, for example, if we buy a reel for a size (or System) 8 rod, we can fit the spools with a floating line for dry-fly work, a floating line with a sinking tip for fishing wet flies near the surface, and a sinking line for use when we want to fish deeper. We don't need to buy more than one reel for this size of rod, and the extra spools are easier to carry than extra reels are. Each spool, of course, should be labeled with the previously mentioned symbols for the size and type of line which is on it. It is very easy to forget!

Unlike trout fishing, where the reel's function is primarily to store line, the long runs habitual to salmon make it advisable to own the finest reels one can afford. In selecting them it is fun to see what new models are being offered in the best tackle shops or in mail-order catalogs illustrating high quality equipment.

In fresh-water fishing, reel maintenance is a minor problem. If even a grain or two of sand gets into the reel, of course the spool should be removed immediately so the parts can be washed and wiped dry. Reels should be taken apart for cleaning and light greasing of the moving parts before each trip and every day or two during it. Little things often make a big difference in success with salmon!

## LEADERS

During many years of fishing I long ago concluded that the most neglected part of a fly-fisherman's tackle is the leader. As a result of too great casualness in tying or in buying leaders, they may frustrate the angler by dropping on the water in coils, by having wind-knots cast into them too often, by wrapping themselves around one's neck, or by breaking at the tippet when a big one hits. These frustrated fishermen notice other casters who also lay out a good line, but whose leaders roll over beautifully and without collapsing, thus delivering the fly properly for maximum effectiveness. They wonder how these casters do it. They do it because they understand the simple facts about tying or buying correctly tapered leaders.

Tying one's own leaders is so simple that all fly-fishermen should be encouraged to do it. The alternative is to accept whatever can be found in stores—leaders which invariably are too small in the butt section. When the butt section is too light or too short, the heavy line and the too-light leader act as a hinge instead of as a harmonious continuation of the line. The whole thing collapses!

There is a "Two-thirds Rule" which we shall apply twice in tying correct leaders. We can call it the "Sixty Per Cent Rule," which some experts think is better. If we are somewhere between the two, we can't go wrong.

First, the butt-section of the leader should be about two-thirds (or about sixty per cent) of the diameter of the line. Let us say that the end of a size 8 line micrometers .039. Two-thirds is .026. Sixty per cent is .0234. We put the micrometer on 30-pound monofilament and find it measures .024. (Various brands vary somewhat.) So we decide that the butt section should begin with 30-pound test monofilament.

The second part of the rule is that the heavy section should be two-thirds (or 60 per cent) of the length of the leader. The rest of it consists of a few short graduations down to a longer tippet.

Now, let's decide that we want a 9-foot leader, which is a favorite length in wet-fly salmon fishing, and let's decide that we want to graduate it down to a 10-pound test tippet, which is a favorite strength for flies in the size 4, 6 and 8 category.

We plan the leader on paper so it will graduate down in size according to the rule:

$$
\left.\begin{array}{l}
\text{3 feet of 30-lb. test} \\
\text{2 feet of 25-lb. test} \\
\text{1 foot of 20-lb. test}
\end{array}\right\} \quad 60\%
$$

8 inches of 17-lb. test⎫
8 inches of 15-lb. test⎪   Graduations
8 inches of 12-lb. test⎭
12 inches of 10-lb. test:   Tippet

We could make this leader a little longer and still stay within the rule by adding another six inches or so to the butt section and another six inches or so to the tippet to give us a 10-foot leader and to allow a little extra length in the tippet for changing flies. All that is needed is to plan leaders that come fairly close to the rule. They can be planned to any length and to any tippet size. A friend of mine who is one of our leading fly-rod experts made one forty feet long, as an experiment, and he said it handled just as well as did the tapered line. When properly tapered, the length of the leader has little bearing on performance.

Someone will remind us that there is stiff monofilament and soft monofilament. If both are available, the stiff material can be used for the butt sections and the soft for the final graduations and the tippet. If leaders made according to this formula don't cast well, it would have to be because the monofilament used is exceptionally soft. In that case, we would make each section one size larger and add another graduation to reach the same size of tippet.

This rule is, of necessity, somewhat general because there are variations in diameter per pound test and in the degree of suppleness of various brands of monofilament. In almost all cases it will work very well. If it shouldn't, adjustments can be made as above noted.

It is necessary to learn only two knots to be able to make one's own leaders. An excellent booklet on tying all monofilament knots is *How to Use DuPont "Stren" Monofilament*, obtainable without charge by writing Plastics Dept., DuPont, Wilmington, Delaware 19898.

The Perfection Loop Knot (leader-loop) is used to make the loop at the butt end of the leader and is used when a loop is spliced into the end of the fly-line, the two being joined as will be described. To tie this knot, as illustrated in Figure III-2, hold the piece of monofilament between left thumb and forefinger so that six inches or so of it extend and point upward. Holding the end with right thumb and

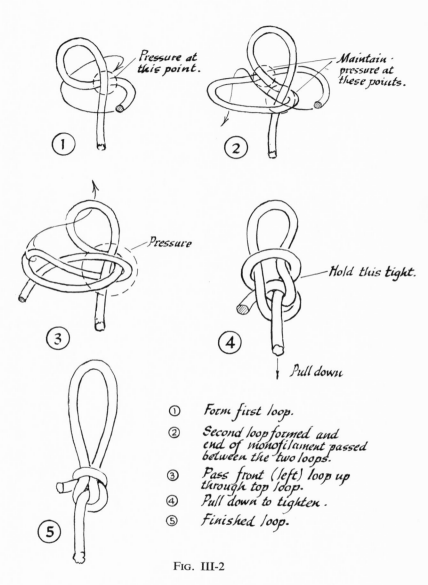

① Form first loop.

② Second loop formed and end of monofilament passed between the two loops.

③ Pass front (left) loop up through top loop.

④ Pull down to tighten.

⑤ Finished loop.

FIG. III-2

THE "PERFECTION LOOP KNOT"

forefinger, throw a small loop to the left so it crosses behind the standing end. Holding this loop, bring the end toward you and pass it around the loop, clockwise, also grasping this between left thumb and forefinger. You now are holding two loops, the second one in front of the first. Now take the short extending end of the monofilament and pass it between the two loops, also holding it between left thumb and forefinger. Now grasp the front loop and work it through the rear loop, at the same time pulling it out a little. Still holding this tightly so the knot won't slip, pull on the lower extension of the monofilament, thus closing the smaller loop. If the remaining loop starts to twist, keep it from twisting and pull downward on the lower extension and upward on the remaining loop until the knot is tight. The knot can now be released from the fingers. Put a pencil or something similar through the loop and pull the loop as tight as possible. The short end of the monofilament will now extend to the left at a right angle from the loop, and it can be clipped off closely. The knot is completed and, by making the loops as small as desired, the Perfection Loop also can be made in any size desired.

The various graduations in the leader are made with Blood Knots, as shown in Figure III-3. Lap the two ends to be joined (held between right thumb and forefinger), with four or five inches of each extending. Twist one end around the other strand five times and place the end between the strands at point "x", holding it there as in sketch #1. Now transfer the knot to the left thumb and forefinger and wind the other end around the other strand five turns *in the opposite direction*. Pass the end through the knot beside the other end, but in the opposite direction from it, as in sketch #2. The knot can be released, and will look as in sketch #3. Now pull on both strands of monofilament, being sure while doing so that the ends don't pull out. The knot will gather as in sketch #4. (If the ends are too long they can be pushed back into the knot, if desired, to conserve monofilament.) Now pull the knot as tight as possible to test it and to make it look like sketch #5. Clip the ends very close to the knot, and it is completed.

One can learn both of these knots in a few minutes, and a bit of practice will make them very simple to tie. Leader material in all necessary sizes is available on small spools at low cost. With this, it is fun to tie our own leaders wherever we may be, and it is a very

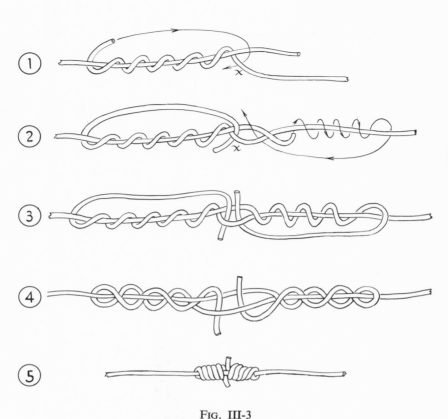

FIG. III-3

THE "BLOOD KNOT"

handy trick-of-the-trade when we want a special leader or when we are far away from stores.

Someone will remind us that there are knotless tapered leaders. There is nothing wrong with them except that we will add knots anyway. Usually we'll have to tie in a heavier butt section because the knotless one is too light. And, if the tippet size was right in the first place, we'll have to tie in a new tippet after changing flies several times.

There are good and bad ways to join the leader to the line. If the line comes with a little metal eyelet stuck into its end, we should cut it off because it probably would pull out when handling salmon. There are other objections, but that one is enough. The Wedge-Knot

44

sometimes used in trout fishing isn't very good either mainly because, if reeled into the tip-top, it won't pass through smoothly.

The author knows of only three really satisfactory ways to join leader and line. One is to splice a small, smooth loop in the end of the line, put it through the leader-loop, string the leader through it by its tip, and pull the connection tight.

Another way is to dispense with the line-loop and the leader-loop and to join line and leader by a Nail Knot. This knot, which has been described in this chapter, can be so simplified, when used to tie a *leader* to a line, that it can be done properly in a matter of seconds. "Lefty" Kreh, one of the foremost fly rod experts of these times, showed the author how to do it. It must be done with a knotless leader but a knotted leader can be tied to the monofilament butt after the knot has been completed.

To tie this Thirty-Second Nail Knot we need a fairly large common pin, a small nail, a needle of moderate size or any thin, stiff piece of metal which is similar. Even a strong toothpick would do because this is only to provide stiffness when tying this knot:

## THE THIRTY-SECOND NAIL KNOT

As indicated in Figure III-4, hold the line end between left thumb and forefinger so it extends about an inch. Also hold the leader butt (leader extending to the right) so about an inch of it is behind thumb and forefinger. Also hold a nail or a pin with its point beside the line end. Take hold of the forward end of the leader and also put it between left thumb and forefinger, holding its tip so that it points to the right and lies beside the line end and the pin. (The rest of the leader hangs in a loop below the fingers. You now have four items grasped between left thumb and forefinger; the line end, the pin, the leader butt and the leader tip.)

Grasp the part of the leader butt extending from thumb and forefinger and wind it clockwise to the left around the above four items, making seven tight, close coils just in front of the thumbnail. Holding these coils in place, between the left thumb and forefinger, take hold of the leader tip with the right thumb and forefinger and pull it to the right so that all of the leader is pulled between the coils

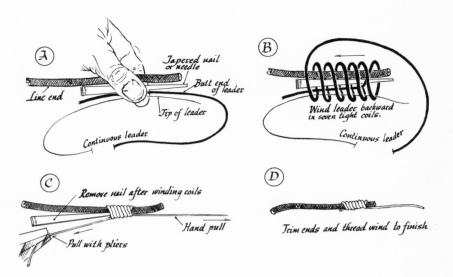

FIG. III-4

## THE "THIRTY SECOND NAIL KNOT"

as far as it will go. (At this point be sure all seven coils lie closely together.) Now you can let go of the knot, pull out the pin, and grasp the rearward-protruding end of the leader butt with a pair of pliers. By also holding the leader which extends from the knot and pulling in both directions the coils will bite into the line to form a rigid connection.

All that remains now is to snip off the excess butt end of the leader and the excess tip end of the line, and to test the connection to be sure it has been pulled tight.

The rest is optional. You can coat the connection with Pliobond cement or varnish to make it smooth. You can leave about a quarter of an inch of leader butt and line end and you can whip them and the knot with thread for added smoothness, also coating the whipped knot with cement or varnish. (This isn't really necessary unless one wants to bother with it.)

This simplified knot is much quicker and easier to tie than to describe. It puts the former method of tying the Nail Knot out of business except for joining line and backing.

46

If one is using a knotted, tapered leader, as most fly-fishermen do, the piece of monofilament we have just tied to the line acts as its butt section, and this butt section should be a little smaller in diameter than the line end and a little larger in diameter than the rest of the leader which will be tied to it. If the leader which is to be tied to it has a loop on the butt end, this loop is snipped off and the leader is tied to the (semi) permanent connection with a Blood Knot.

Perhaps the only objection to rigging line and leader with this knot is that, when storing it on the reel, the leader will be in coils. A piece of inner tube rubber about 3 by $1\frac{1}{2}$ inches in size will remedy this. Double the rubber between thumb and fingers and pull the leader between it. The friction will stroke out the coils. The strength of the leader should be tested frequently by this means or by pulling it to be sure all knots are joined properly and that there are no nicks to cause weakness.

The third way is to join line and leader by what is called a Pin Knot. This is an adaptation of the Nail Knot and the only thing it has going for it is that the leader comes out of the end of the line, an improvement which some readers may deem inconsequential, particularly in view of the fact that the knot requires more time than the former one.

This knot has been described in various publications and, from the descriptions, one wonders if the writers ever tried to tie it because, in some cases, it would be impossible to do so by following the instructions provided. Lefty Kreh showed me a method I won't pass on because it involves tapering the monofilament with a razor blade and threading it through the line end with a needle. While he did it expertly, I invariably ruined the monofilament and finally gave up the project. Following is the author's own variation, which is as quick as any. It also works!

### THE PIN KNOT (or Needle Knot)

Push a moderate-size common pin into the end of the line and out of its side-wall so that one-quarter of an inch of the line is strung on the pin. Pliers are needed for this and for holding the pin during the following operation.

Hold the pinpoint with the pliers and apply heat from a match or cigarette lighter to the pinhead until the part of the line nearest the heat begins to smoke *very slightly*. Push the line towards the pinhead and, holding the pin with pliers at this end, apply heat to the pinpoint until that end of the line which is strung on the pin also begins to smoke very slightly. (Avoid overheating so as not to impair the strength of the line. All that is needed is only enough heat to prevent the hole made by the pin from closing up when the pin is withdrawn.)

Now withdraw the pin and thread the leader material through the hole made by the pin. Thread it all the way through until not over half an inch protrudes from the end of the line. Hold the line between left thumb and forefinger at the part of the side-wall where the leader comes out of it and loop the leader (as was done in tying the Thirty-Second Nail Knot) so that its end also is grasped between thumb and forefinger and there is an inch or so protruding to the left. Also grasp the pin so its point is beside the end of the line.

Grasp the long length of leader which is immediately in front of thumb and forefinger with the right hand and wind it clockwise around the items held between left thumb and forefinger. Starting the winding where the leader comes out of the line, make seven tight close coils, winding them to the left toward thumb and forefinger. Each coil must touch the one before it, and they must not overlap.

Holding these tight coils between left thumb and forefinger, use your right thumb and forefinger to pull the leader material out of the end of the line. Keep pulling it all the way out until no more can be pulled, thus securing the seven coils tightly to the line. Remove the pin. Now grasp the short end of leader material with pliers and pull on the long end until the coils bite into the line and you are sure the connection is strong and tight. Cut off the excess end of the leader material close to the coils and the knot is completed except for varnishing, if desired. For a really smooth job it can be whipped with thread and then varnished.

This knot also is quicker and easier to tie than to describe. Except for threading the pin through the line end, it is almost identical with the Thirty-Second Nail Knot. The only difference between the two is that, in this one, the leader comes out of the end of the line instead of being beside it. Because these two knots are so similar, another descriptive drawing does not seem necessary.

In dry-fly fishing, the tippet can be much longer than in wet-fly fishing, even two or three feet long, to provide a longer float to the fly. Some anglers prefer very long tippets; others don't like the way they cast.

Nearly all salmon flies have eyes which are turned either up or down, usually up. The Clinch Knot, although stronger and quicker to tie, does not give a straight connection, so the Turle Knot is usually preferred. But the Turle Knot has been known to pull out. This can be prevented by tying an ordinary knot in the end of the tippet and cutting off the excess after stringing on the fly. Then tie the Turle Knot and work the ordinary knot up to it before looping it over the eye. This little precaution is a favorite of mine, and I never have known it to fail.

The size of the fly roughly dictates the size or strength of the tippet, which should be light enough to enable the fly to fish normally. Since salmon are not very leader-shy, we can use tippets of between ten and fifteen pounds test with reasonably large flies but, if conditions permit, we should use proportionately lighter tippets with smaller flies, and set the reel-drag lighter to conform to the strength of the tippet. When water is low and clear, tippets in the lighter range are preferable. Strange as it may seem, ten-pound *soft* monofilament will fish a number 8 fly properly. With this as a yardstick the proper size of monofilament for larger or smaller flies can be decided.

Most of the anglers who own efficient tackle and know how to use it prefer tapered leaders and usually are rather fussy about how they are made up. These men may be smirked at by fishermen who favor elementary methods and who therefore think level leaders or more simply tapered ones are just as good. The latter maintain that shorter leaders work as well as longer ones and that the weight of the fly will straighten them out and overcome lack of tapering. Those who follow this line of thought believe that there has been too much application of leader theory (as applied to trout fishing) to salmon angling. Using level or too-simply tapered leaders seems to be a lazy expedient because it is quite obvious that properly tapered ones have greater advantages in fly presentation.

A further note might be added about limp and stiff monofilament. If you find you are casting wind-knots in the end of your leader, try a piece of old-fashioned stiff nylon for a tippet. You will get fewer wind-knots and, if you get one, it can be untied much more easily.

## HOOKS

Fish hooks have been vital food furnishers for centuries. Modern hooks were born in Redditch, England, about 1560, because Redditch was an important needle manufacturing region, and the father of the modern hook was the needle.

Until just before the turn of the nineteenth century, hooks with metal eyes had not been perfected, and the salmon flies of that era were tied with eyes of twisted silkworm gut. Those that remain today fortunately are too weak in the eye to fish with and have become cherished collector's items if they have been preserved. Too often, however, the widows of departed anglers have used them for hat decorations, or have given them to other females in the family for the same purpose.

Hooks of the Limerick shape, which have a half-round parabolic bend and an upturned eye, designed for superior strength, are the traditional salmon hooks. This is true, evidently, more because of appearance than because of superior hooking and holding power. The best ones have a Japanned black finish and are made with a returned eye rather than with the cheaper round eyes. One of the "new looks" in modern salmon fishing is the bronzed Model Perfect trout fly hook which has become equally popular, if not more so, in some regions, such as New Brunswick. This is a hook with a perfectly round bend, which is considered by many to be superior because it helps to prevent enlarging the hole of penetration when the salmon is fighting the fly. These hooks sometimes are "kirbed" or offset in a reverse bend, or double-offset (offset both to the right and to the left), on the proven theory that these offsetting methods tend to pull the hook into a fish's jaw better than non-offset designs do.

In buying hooks for salmon flies, the maker's integrity is the best recommendation of quality. One should obtain highest quality because there are many fine points in hook manufacture, such as modern

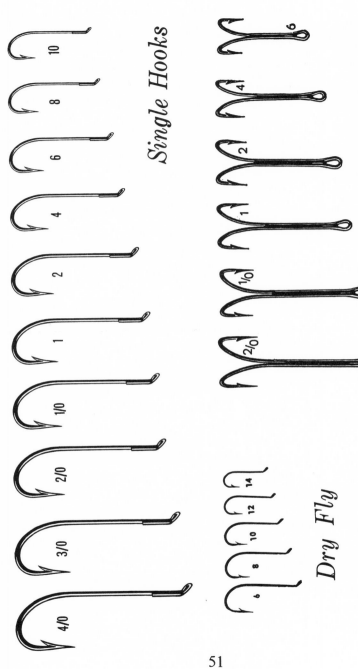

*Single Hooks*

*Double Hooks*

*Dry Fly*

Fɪɢ. III-5

CHART OF SALMON HOOK SIZES

51

heat-treating methods, which are not obvious even to experts. In addition to other indications of lack of quality, improper heat-treating will make hooks too brittle or too soft, thus causing them either to snap or to straighten out. Since Japanned hooks are tumbled after barbs and points have been cut, prudent anglers see that they are touched up to razor edge and sharp needle point with a stone or (in the case of large hooks) with a small jeweler's file.

In addition to various patterns, there are several types of salmon hooks, of which we primarily are concerned with three: the low-water hook, the standard single hook, and the double-hook available both in standard and in low-water weights. Long-shanked hooks also are used for streamers or bucktails and other types of patterns. In general, and within reason, the heavier the hook, the better it is, because heavier hooks are stronger hooks, and they tend to fish deeper. In very big flies with irons two inches long or more, bulk and weight can be reduced by increasing the length of the shank.

Low-water hooks are made with very light wire because the low-water flies dressed on them are very small in proportion to the hook, the dressing usually occupying no more than the forward half of the length of the shank. This provides greater hooking and holding power when very small flies are needed.

In some of the fly patterns discussed here the Wilson dry-fly hook is mentioned. This light-wire hook basically is equivalent to a low-water hook and is very satisfactory for salmon dry flies requiring a longer body, as well as for wet flies requiring hooks of this type. For short-bodied dry flies the typical bronzed hook such as the Allcock Model Perfect is often used. Dry-fly hooks usually are of the round bend variety.

The controversy regarding single hooks versus double-hooks probably never will be settled, the proponents of both types being fairly equally divided.

One experienced angler says, "Double-hooks provide sort of a keel to the fly and thus ride upright in the water and present the fly to the fish as it should be. With single hooks, you never can be sure. I believe there's more holding power, regardless of what some experts say about one of the hooks acting as a lever to work the other one loose. I have seen a lot more fish lost on singles than on doubles, all other things being equal. In several cases I have had one of the hooks tear loose and the fish become hooked with the other before the fly got out of his mouth."

Another says, "It is not valid that the double-hook will carry the fly deeper. Don't try to get the fly down by the weight of the hook. Use a line that will get the fly down, and dress the fly so it will sink most readily. The crucial matter is how the fish takes the fly. Men who have fished double-hooks undoubtedly will continue to do so. The newer anglers will fish them less often."

Thus, this controversy may resolve itself into an individual matter of choice. The author is confident of one thing: double-hooks are superior in rough, swirly water because the two hooks act as rudders to help keep the fly on an even keel. If the fly is not fished upright on an even keel it lacks its best chance to take salmon.

In concluding this chapter it may be appropriate to pass along a useful tip from two old friends, Stu Apte and Lefty Kreh, both of whom are at the very top of the big league in fly-fishing. In rigging a rod, don't start by threading the leader through the guides. This is the hard way and, if you let go, the whole thing will slip back. Instead, double the line near its end and thread the doubled line through the guides, with the leader following along. When a foot or two of the doubled line has been pulled through the tip-top, just shake the rod to pop out the leader! This prevents the line from falling back through the guides, whether there is a leader on it or not.

# IV
# From the Old
# to the New
# in
# Salmon Flies

We who enjoy salmon flies and fishing can learn much about how to select appropriate patterns for various conditions and how to use them properly if we know something of their history, which starts with the simple, expands to the sublime, and then reverts toward the simple again.

Certainly, it all began innocently enough, undoubtedly with the twelve general-purpose patterns attributed to Dame Juliana Berners in 1496. However, little tangible information of value to modern anglers was written until Charles Bowlker (1747) described a few salmon fly patterns in his *The Art of Angling*, wherein he said, "It is needless to treat of any more salmon flies; for salmon flies, in general, are made just as the painter pleases. Salmon, being fond of anything that is gaudy . . . will rise at almost any of the trout flies, where salmon are plenty."

This reminds us that the early salmon flies essentially were trout flies, dressed in larger sizes which supposedly were necessary due to the larger sizes of the fish. We shall see that patterns in salmon flies run full cycle because modern anglers use trout flies and their variations very successfully for salmon, even in sizes as small as 12's.

From the middle of the eighteenth century to the middle of the nineteenth, very little is worthy of note except slow and gradual development. Numerous angling books were written, all contributing bits and pieces of lore available to those who want to search their pages. Salmon flies were relatively drab and simple, especially those made in Wales. But, toward the end of the nineteenth century, fly-dressing came into full flower, so to speak. A plethora of gay and gaudy patterns were developed, each fly-dresser seeming to vie with every other to create more intricate ones. These comprised bits of plumage of many exotic birds such as the several species of Pheasant, Summer Duck, Indian Crow, Bustard, Jungle Cock, Blue Chatterer, Toucan, and Macaw, and of many common dyed and natural feathers from various kinds of ducks, swans, turkeys, geese and other birds. To these were added bright tinsels and an abundant array of colored silks, wools and other materials.

These were the days of Victoria (1819–1901), queen of the United Kingdom, empress of India (from 1876) and ruler of other lands beyond the seas. They were the days when British warships and merchantmen roamed the oceans, and when British regiments guarded the queen's domains in far-flung places.

It is not surprising that British officers, hunting and trading in these exotic regions, sent home the skins of beautiful birds so the ghillies and their families could wile away dreary winter evenings dressing flies for their lords and masters to use when they returned home. It is not surprising that intense competition rapidly spread to see who could conceive the most gorgeous and fruitful patterns.

Many classics of British angling literature picture and describe these colorful and complicated flies. Of these, three books stand out, partly because of their illustrations of flies in excellent color: *The Salmon Fly*, by George M. Kelson (1895), *How to Dress Salmon Flies*, by Dr. T. E. Pryce-Tannatt (1914), and *Fly Tying for Salmon*, by Eric Taverner (1942). Taverner's includes excellent historical information. Although his book and Pryce-Tannatt's postdate the period being discussed, they are very pertinent to it. Kelson gives dressing instructions for 300 patterns, Pryce-Tannatt 100, and Taverner only 27. Although some are duplicated in each book, they comprise over 300 wet-fly feather-wing patterns, and these by no means are all!

In reviewing these classic patterns one only can conclude that they were designed a lot more to please the artistic sensibilities of the angler and a lot less to tempt the voraciousness of the fish. Of course color combination was considered important but, since what suited one fly-dresser might not please another, almost every combination known to man was available. There is a surprising amount of sameness in the character, style, shape and degree of translucence of most of the era's patterns. Perhaps that is because, in those days just before the turn of the century, more salmon were available, and they were less sophisticated. If salmon didn't take in one place, the angler merely moved on to a spot where they would. It seems that persistent efforts in tempting a risen fish to come back to a fly, and to take it, were hardly worth the effort. So variety in type, size and presentation of the fly was a lot less important than it is today.

This makes me think of what goes on in a salmon's head when he, for example, streaks with violent surface wake after a gorgeous number 3/0 *Jock Scott* swinging past him in the current. Does he fail to take at the last second because he suddenly perceives that the Toucan veiling on the fly's body isn't applied exactly as it should have been, or that the Blue Chatterer cheeks are only blue Kingfisher? We cannot help but admire the superb artistry of these exotic flies, but that's not the way we do it today—at least, that's not the way most of us do it!

The change of outlook from the sublime to the sensible is summed up very well in an article by Colonel Esmond Drury published in the *Journal of the Flyfishers Club*, of London, in 1960. In part, he says:

"The outstanding example of extravagance for extravagance' sake is the insistence of many salmon fly-fishermen of 'fully dressed' salmon flies, of orthodox pattern, for spring fishing. One can only surmise that this demand is based on the assumption that the more expensive the ingredients and the more lavish the garnishing, the better the fly.

"It is no accident that the majority of the more ornate flies were devised in the latter quarter of the last century which may be described as the Mrs. Beaton era. The remarkable fact is that these Victorian relics have survived so long. The more particularly is this the case when one considers that they were, in the main, the product of ignorance and lack of scientific knowledge. Kelson, who came to be regarded as the oracle on matters pertaining to salmon flies, and who was responsible to a large extent for the standardizing of dressings, actually believed that, in fresh water, salmon fed on various highly localized species of butterflies and there is no doubt that this belief influenced, to a very considerable extent, Kelson's whole outlook on salmon flies. The extraordinary fact is, not that Kelson held these beliefs, but that succeeding generations of salmon fly-fishermen have apparently accepted the products of ignorance and misconception without question and, in the main, continue to do so today, and that they catch fish on them.

"From his book, one cannot avoid the conclusion that Kelson was a snob. Possibly he was jealous of the reputation and kudos that Halford achieved for himself in chalk stream techniques and, lacking Halford's scientific background and powers of observation, sought to put salmon fishing on the same erudite and elevated plane.

"In his ignorance Kelson became a slave to ornate extravagance. His craftsmanship as a fly-tyer was of a high order, but his artistic sense was of the age in which he lived. That he failed to include aspidistras and antimacassars in his fly-dressing was an oversight, although he nearly achieved the crinoline.

"It is true that standard patterns of fully dressed salmon flies have undergone some modification since Kelson's day. These have related to profile rather than content, and rare and therefore expensive feathers are still regarded as indispensable ingredients in many flies. Nobody can gainsay that these feathers are things of beauty, but the expense of including them in the dressing of a salmon fly cannot possibly be justified on the grounds of enhanced performance— rather the reverse, for their use generally presupposes a fly with an opaque built wing and other excesses which tend to mitigate against performance.

"From conversations that I have had it would seem that most of the experts have long ago discarded the Kelson type flies and that the demand for them comes mainly from the occasional fisher and from those who fish often and who, one suspects, are as fascinated by the appearance of their tackle as by the prospects of catching salmon."

The colonel's alternate recommendations are in keeping with modern concepts, and we will deal with them later. However, one cannot dismiss the "butterfly" patterns of the Victorian era casually. The *Jock Scotts, Silver Doctors, Thunder and Lightnings, Wilkinsons* and other similar confections of the gay 90's still are being used on many Canadian and other British rivers and on many Continental streams all the way from Finland to Spain. However, year by year, their popularity diminishes in favor of the simpler and more effective modern patterns which will be described in this and in future chapters.

Not wishing to give up the classic favorites entirely, and also not wishing to bother with their complicated built wings and mixed wings, many fly-dressers have retained all or nearly all of the classic's components except for the multi-feathered wing, which they have simplified while trying to maintain an effect similar to the original. Examples of these "reduced" classics are the *Black Dose* (reduced) and the *Dusty Miller* (reduced), which are from the bench of the celebrated American angler and fly-dresser, Harry A. Darbee, of Livingston Manor, New York. These are pretty flies, and relatively simple to put together. Of course they are adaptations, without standard pattern, and each dressing depends upon whatever its dresser wants to put into it.

In going from the ornate to the sensible in modern wet salmon fly design the author has tried to find out where and when the popular hair-wing salmon fly patterns originated. Were they of British origin, or of North American origin, or doesn't it matter? Of course there are many theories and suppositions, but whatever authentic documentation there ever may have been has been lost in the past.

One story, which is interesting regardless of its degree of authenticity, tells of immigrants who came from the British Isles to Newfoundland in the eighteenth century, which is very early in the history of fly-fishing. They brought with them cattle, sheep and dogs, plus other essentials of colonial life, including fish-hooks. Although fishing then was mainly done with nets and by other quantity production means, the colonists occasionally fished with long fly-rods for sport.

Since this was in the pre-Kelson era, fancy flies not only were unknown, but their ingredients for the most part were unavailable. People used what they had, and they quite sensibly named each fly from its ingredients, so its name told the neighbors exactly what was used to catch the "big one" of the day.

When it got nosed around, for example, that old Dave Kirke took a whopper on a *Red Cow* fly\*, everybody knew that this came from the Hereford he had brought from England, and that it had a body dubbed from the underfur of the red cow and a wing made of the guard hairs of the same red cow.

Similarly, it was obvious to everybody that a *Ten Bear Fly* had ten Black Bear hairs in its wing—that is, it was a sparsely dressed one. A *Twenty Bear Fly* probably was considered rather overdressed, except for high water, and an *Ordinary Bear Fly* was composed of a bunch of hairs whose number nobody had bothered to estimate, probably because the fishing was rather good at the time.

The fact that the eighteenth century is mentioned in this story doesn't prove that hair-wing flies were used then. It may have happened a great many years later. In my book, *Streamer Fly Tying and Fishing*, it was documented that a bucktail fly for bass was in use in the United States as early as 1886, and that a rancher in Idaho named A. S. Trude tied hair-wing flies for trout in 1901. This date may be open to question because the June, 1948, issue of *Fortune*, quotes an article previously published in the *Bulletin* of the Angler's Club of New York:

"While trout fishing in Idaho back around 1890 the late Colonel Lewis S. Thompson met a fellow fisherman, one A. S. Trude. Trude tied his own flies, and used hair instead of feathers. So far as is known, he was the father of the hair fly, which in the form of the 'bucktail' is known to most anglers. Colonel Thompson saved some of the flies Trude gave him, and later had other flies tied. These were all trout flies. At least he thought so until he tried them (very successfully) on

---

\* Herbert Howard, a renowned angler, fly-dresser and angling historian, states that he has seen a family Bible which belonged to a Newfoundland family named Stirling in which are handwritten entries dating between the years of 1720 and 1896. One of the entries, dated 1795, described a hair-wing fly called the *Red Cow Fly* and says that salmon were caught on it.

salmon, on the Restigouche about twenty years ago (1928, or before)."
(Colonel Thompson developed a method of fishing hair-wing flies for
salmon which he called "The Patent," which will be described in the
next chapter.)

Undoubtedly the colonel didn't mean to imply that he inaugurated
hair-wing fly-fishing for salmon. In Herbert Howard's account of the
development of the *Rat* series of hair-wings, the date of October, 1911,
is given. Since we don't want to steep in historic minutiae, let's let it
go at that. The important thing is not when or where or by whom
hair-wings were first conceived, but rather that they have helped to
revolutionize modern concepts in salmon fishing.

It is one thing to learn that hair-wing flies will take salmon, and
quite another to know what types and sizes will do it best. Whether
or not they take salmon better than feather-wings do may be a matter
of opinion. Many of us have learned that it pays to fish hair-wings
almost exclusively. They are mobile while many of the feather-wings
are stiff. They breathe and pulsate in the current, and act alive. They
are juicily translucent while many of the feather-wings are opaque.
But sometimes one wants an opaque fly!

When hair-wing patterns were first developed, they were large
and bulky. Experience proved they should be smaller and dressed
more sparsely. I cringe when I see the hair-wings normally sold in
stores. They look like a paint brush going piggy-back on a hook!
The wings should be sparse, hugging the hook-shank, and no longer
than it. Whatever type of hair is employed should be reasonably
straight and fine enough to give breathing action in the water.

Experience also proved that some types of dressings work better
than others, and that very few patterns are needed—perhaps only a
dark one, a lighter one and a brighter one with a tinsel body. For the
darker ones, those with a colored butt and black body, tinsel-ribbed,
and with a black or at least a dark wing, are very effective, especially
on the Miramichi. The black body with yellow butt is nothing new.
Many British feather-winged flies have it, including the *Black Fairy*
and the *Jeannie*. Many fishermen favor flies with similar bodies with
red, green and orange butts, and which is more effective than the
others is a matter of opinion. The modern opinion generally is that
the butts should be fluorescent (and quite small). For a lighter fly,

that is, sort of a grey one, either the *Grey Rat* or the *Rusty Rat* would be hard to beat!

It was natural that anglers with a penchant for colorful hair-wings should cross them with such British classics as the *Jock Scott, Silver Doctor* and *Thunder and Lightning.* This has been done very successfully by using the classic's body (perhaps simplified a bit) and a hairwing of a mixture of the colors found in the classic wing. In North America, a great favorite is the *Green Highlander.*

Taking Atlantic salmon on the dry fly has become standard and successful practice in North America, especially under low-water and warm-water conditions, although we have had quite a time convincing our friends across the sea of the fact.

The history of catching salmon with the dry fly goes back farther than some may think. For example, in a letter written in April, 1906, the great American angler, Theodore Gordon, wrote: "A friend of mine took a 14-pound salmon on a dry fly tied like a *Coachman* but dry-fly style on a big Pennell hook. The line was slack, he broke his rod in striking the fish and was a long time killing it. This was on Restigouche and he got two more, a grilse and a small salmon, in the same way out of the same pools in three days."

George M. L. La Branche, in his *The Salmon and the Dry Fly* (1924) gives credit to Colonel Ambrose Monell for being the first angler in North America to take a salmon on a dry fly (which may be incorrect in view of the foregoing). He says, "Believing, as I did, that salmon do not feed in fresh water, I hesitated to introduce the subject of fishing for them with a floating fly. Divining, perhaps, what was in my mind, my friend (Colonel Monell) calmly announced that he had killed a fifteen-pound salmon two years before on a dry fly, and assured me that it was not an accident. He had seen the fish rising just as a trout would rise and, having failed to interest the fish with any of the wet flies in his box, he had deliberately cast across and upstream with a No. 12 *Whirling Dun*, floating it down over the fish, which took it at once. It was the taking of this fish, and the rising of six or seven others which he did not hook, that convinced him it would be possible to kill fish with the dry fly when the water was low." In the book, Mr. La Branche gives four favorite dressings of dry flies which are heavily palmered over silk or dubbing.

The greatest exponent of dry-fly fishing for salmon is Lee Wulff, author of *The Atlantic Salmon* (1958), who designed the *Grey Wulff* and the *White Wulff* (see index) in 1929. He says, "In the early thirties, it was unusual to meet another dry-fly angler and it was quite common when moving to a new river to find guides and fishermen who had never seen a dry fly fished and who were frankly doubtful that a floating fly would have any attraction for salmon."

In 1962, Lee fished Scotland's Aberdeenshire Dee and demonstrated his ability to catch salmon on the dry fly. He caught only one, but proved it could be done. Either salmon are much harder to take on the dry fly in the British Isles than in North America, or the British anglers are much harder to convince that it can be done consistently under favorable conditions.

Lee Wulff's series of flies were a valuable contribution to dry-fly salmon fishing because their bushy hair-wing dressings make them excellent floaters, even in fast currents. Many other floaters such as spiders, skaters and heavily palmered patterns have been developed. Their dressings and the methods of employing them to induce reluctant salmon to strike will be discussed as we go along.

Perhaps the greatest thrill in all angling is to cast a floating fly above a salmon lie and to watch it merrily bob along on the current until, with a mighty swirling swoosh, a great salmon rises up to take it. In wet-fly fishing, the strike of the fish cannot always be observed, and never can be observed as well as when he takes the floating fly on the surface. We will learn new ways of causing this to happen more often: ways that make salmon fishing more challenging, and a great deal more fun!

Nymph fishing for salmon is another relatively new field still being developed. Under suitable conditions—usually those of low, warm and clear water—salmon may take nymphs while refusing everything else. A little earlier in the game it was thought that exact imitations of nymphal life were necessary for best results. It has been proved that simple imitations are approximately as effective as more complicated ones. Wrap four or five strands of Peacock herl around a Number 8 hook to make a cigar-shaped body. Using a Number 7 or Number 8 hook, make a body of fine black chenille and wind on about two turns of a very narrow and soft black hackle at the head. This provides two nymphal imitations that seem to work as well as more complicated dressings. It is rarely necessary to go to sizes smaller than these. Although these simple dressings are effective, many anglers will think that more lifelike ones should do better. This book therefore includes six nymph patterns by the celebrated angler-artist Charles De Feo, of New York, and three by the prominent fly-dresser, William Kean, of New Jersey.

While discussing nymphs we should be reminded that there are three basic types of wet flies. The simplest is the fly-hook with a body which is, of course, a nymph. Next is the fly-hook with a body and with front hackle. Finally, there is the conventional wet fly with body and front hackle and also with a wing. There can be variations of these, such as a hook with a body and a wing, but no throat hackle, or a body with a palmered hackle rather than a mere throat hackle. There are times in salmon fishing when one of these stages in fly-dressing will work better than the others. There are also times when any one will be as successful as any other. Perhaps salmon fishermen should take greater advantage of these types, occasionally trimming off the wing of a wet fly and some or all of the hackle to see if such simplification works any better. In the next chapter we will see that there are times when nymphs can be amazingly successful.

While nymphs in part are low-water patterns, other uses for them will be noted later. The uses of nymphs in salmon fishing seem to be a North American method which has been neglected elsewhere.

Low-water patterns are small flies tied on long, light low-water hooks where the dressings occupy no more than the forward half of the shank. They have the advantages of the larger hook's greater hooking and holding power and, since the bend and barb of the hook is well behind the dressing, they hook fish that "rise short" more often than standard dressings do. Low-water patterns are very seldom used by experienced anglers in North America because of the popularity of small flies and nymphs. Colonel Drury writes that, in the British Isles, "Low-water long-shanked singles are 'out' and most experienced anglers now use flies directly tied on to medium long-shanked trebles, or tubes, or doubles." (Treble-hooks are allowed in the British Isles. Tube flies are discussed in Chapter IX.)

While any wet-fly pattern can be dressed in low-water style, there are favorites. In the classic patterns these include: *March Brown, Blue Charm, Logie, Silver Doctor, Silver Wilkinson* and *Thunder and Lightning*. Here also is where we run full circle with standard trout fly patterns which are popular for Atlantic salmon either in standard dressings or on low-water hooks. Trout fishermen who go salmon fishing and who have a shortage of salmon flies will find the following trout patterns to be among those which will be effective from time to time: *Black Gnat* (similar to *Black Jack*), *Blue Quill, Cowdung, Dark Cahill, Muddler Minnow, Professor, Quill Gordon,* and *Royal Coachman*.

In Canada and in Maine the first flies used for salmon fishing were either the standard British patterns or wet trout flies. The development of typical American-Canadian salmon flies came later, especially the development of hair-wing patterns. An important part of the development of North American salmon flies includes the bucktail and the streamer. Of course these long hair-wing and feather-wing baitfish imitations, in large sizes, were, and still are, used for black salmon in the early spring on certain Canadian rivers. Let's ignore that, at least for the moment, and examine their value for bright salmon fishing.

The idea, quite obviously, came from Maine, where they are outstandingly popular for land-locked salmon, the little cousins of the Atlantic salmon. Lee Wulff, in *The Atlantic Salmon*, says, "In the overall picture, streamer flies are not very effective for Atlantic salmon. Streamers have been tried out extensively. The consensus is that they are good for special occasions, poor producers for steady usage." While this statement is correct to an extent, Lee's book was written in 1958, and a lot has been learned since then!

The proficiency of streamers for bright Atlantic salmon has been underestimated to an almost unbelievable extent. Their value is bound to become more generally recognized. In this connection it is interesting to note that some of the most modern British salmon flies are little more than adaptations of the American streamer, especially where hook-length is concerned. This is true, for example, of the *Elver,* the *Tosh* and other patterns. In the next chapter we will see when and why streamers and bucktails can improve our success in catching salmon.

*(B. Schley)*

Fig. IV-1

HOOKED!

65

In looking back from the new to the old in salmon flies the age-old question always comes up: Why do Atlantic salmon take artificial flies when it is known (or presumed) that they do not feed in fresh water? Other authors have also been completely frustrated in attempting to research this question, and no one has provided a valid answer. It may help to ask what one means by "feed." If it means taking sufficient food for survival, we can agree that they don't. If it means rising to a hatch of insects, then they do feed, because salmon have been caught with their mouths and gills littered with insects. We have seen them rise up and take bits of this or that floating on the surface. We know they will strike at artificial lures and that they will take other things. They will strike from anger at little parr which intrude on their nuptial proceedings, which may contribute to the reasons why they strike at streamers or bucktails.

A salmon fly is a lure which is fished to provide the illusion that it has life but, in the angler's attempt to make it act lifelike, it cannot appear to salmon to look and act any way but abnormal. In Darwin's law of the survival of the fittest we may find a partial answer, but it does not have to do with feeding. We know that big fish prey on smaller fish and that they kill the weak ones, not always because they are hungry, but often because of the instinct to get them out of the way. This may be a partial answer, but it doesn't explain why salmon take nymphs or things that look like insects, or why they rise to a hatch. They may do it because they are bored, or perhaps because they think they might like the flavor. Anyway, it is fortunate that salmon do have this instinct because, without it, there would be no fly-fishing for salmon!

Another question to which there is no valid answer is why salmon will take one size and type of artificial on occasion, at the same time refusing to bother with the others. I have seen salmon become very obstinate about this—quite often. Also, I have seen salmon rip after a tiny fly and take it with a suddenness and ferocity that are astounding.

In this chapter about flies, let's face a few facts. One is that most flies are purchased to please the angler more than to tempt the fish. The fish couldn't care less how cheap or expensive the fly is, or whether it is a fancy concoction of rare feathers or the simplest hair-wing that can be put together. What the fish does care about is how the fly is offered to him, which probably is about ninety per cent of the problem. The rest is a matter of size, proportion, translucency, visibility and the mood of the salmon itself.

This brings us to the fact that most anglers (this one included) collect too many flies and perhaps that too many of these are improperly dressed. But who cares if a dark one, a lighter one and a bright one in a few different sizes will do the job as well as many boxes full? Part of the fun of angling is tying them, buying them, swapping them, giving them, admiring them, comparing them, trying them, owning them—and just enjoying them!

If this book could tell its readers exactly how to select flies for various conditions it probably would contribute to spoiling the fun of fishing. In common with others, I have participated in discussions over the years which have beaten the subject to death without arriving at anything more than generalities and personal opinion. There are a few general rules, however.

When rivers are high, large wet flies seem to do best, but what is considered large varies with the river. Flies as large as 1/0 are considered large on smaller rivers; on big waters they may be at least as big as 5/0. If waters are discolored the larger, brighter and more opaque ones should do best because they are more visible to the fish. Clearer waters suggest flies that are duller and perhaps more translucent. The smallest fly which seems to fit the conditions should be chosen.

When waters are low the same applies except for size. Sizes between 4 and 10 are popular: the lower the water, the smaller the fly.

While dry flies will be discussed in more detail later, they are most appropriate in warm, stale water (over 70° F.) under bright sky conditions. Dry flies are of sufficient importance to deserve a chapter of their own, and streamers and nymphs will be discussed in the next chapter because the ways of fishing them are more important than the pattern chosen.

Of course, we in North America approach the matter of fly selection somewhat differently from our fellow anglers in the United Kingdom. While researching this book its author has enjoyed fascinating and very helpful correspondence with friends overseas. One of the most accomplished salmon anglers in England is Colonel

FIG. IV-2

MODERN FLY BOXES CONTAIN
HAIR-WINGS, NYMPHS AND STREAMERS

Esmond Drury, whom I have the privilege of quoting from time to time. It may be of interest to note some of his remarks:

"The tendency in the United Kingdom is to reduce the number of patterns carried, and many old favourites are now rarely heard of. Hair flies are increasingly used and many old patterns now have the hair-wing equivalent. There is a strong tendency towards simplification of dressings, and body veilings with Toucan, Indian Crow, etc. are now rarely seen except on exhibition tyings. Very large (5/0 and upward) singles and doubles are rarely used. Their penetration characteristics were always bad and it required an almighty pull to bury the barb.

"There is a tendency to use darker flies more lightly dressed. There are some exceptions here. *Garry* and *Silver Doctor* still are popular for early spring and autumn but *Black and Gold*, *Brown and Gold* and *Yellow Belly* flies now are widely used for spring fishing.

"Articulated shank flies (*Waddington* and *Arctic*) are not very popular. I don't know why. I like them.

"Jungle Cock and other rare feathers are now gradually being regarded as non-essential and a relic of Victoriana. Many flies today look dull in comparison with those used thirty years ago, but they are more effective, I think.

"Kelson would have a fit if he could see modern salmon flies used by chaps who know their stuff: dark body, a bit of gold or silver tinsel and a few black and yellow hairs. Sartorially unexciting, but they do kill fish!

"When water is below 48° F., 2½- to 3-inch flies (hook lengths not including eye) are used mostly. Change to sizes 6, 8 and 10 as soon as water is above 48°. Sizes 5/0 to 6/0 are rarely used today. In other words, one uses a bloody big fly, corresponding to the appropriate minnow size, when water is cold or in flood conditions, and on a sinking line. One uses quite a small one, on a floating line, as the water warms up. Occasionally in low, clear water conditions a well sunk small fly pays off, but only occasionally.

"The *General Practitioner*, originally tied by me to circumvent a ban on the use of a prawn on a fishery where, in some pools, a prawn was the only thing one could fish, can be quite deadly in April and May when water is warm, clear and low. (It also is very effective in

Norway.) The *G. P.* can be fished like an orthodox fly or can be cast in above the lie and trotted down to fish which are lying in deepish water close in. I use a 14-foot rod on one pool where I fish. I cast in at the top of the pool and, unless I get a fish, I never take the fly out of the water, but walk it down 30 yards below me. The pool is 100 yards long and all fish lie in deep water on my bank, and close in. It takes an hour to fish it properly. I mostly use the large *G. P.* (size 2 hook, but 4 inches long) on a sinking line and the small one (size 6) for orthodox fishing, but sometimes fishing very fast by pulling through on a floating line. (The length of the size 6 fly, including whiskers, is $2\frac{1}{2}$ inches.)

"A new pattern, the *Tosh* is often a good fly in low water, where it breaks all rules. We tie it on a treble-hook. Body: black floss. Wing: mixed black and yellow bucktail, tied long and very sparse. That is all. The fly first was tied by hand by a ghillie at Delfur, a famous Spey beat, from hairs from black and yellow Labrador dogs!

"You ask my opinion about how experienced anglers select flies. This is a difficult question to answer. They seem to finish up by using smaller, duller, more scruffy-looking flies than the tyros, and generally catch more fish on them. The theory of bright fly for a bright day and dull one for a dull one is regarded as rot by most of the best salmon anglers today, and I would agree with them. Opaque built wing flies are mostly for ladies' hats, and translucence and mobility of dressing are the characteristics of modern flies for Atlantic salmon. Most of my friends think with me that there are two kinds of fly, one to catch anglers and one to catch fish.

"One often sees inexperienced anglers and ghillies holding a fly to the water to see how it looks, though Heaven knows what they are looking for. Short of diving into the river to have a look at a fly *from below* (I often did this as a boy, but not any more) the only way to get any idea of what a fish sees is to look at a fly against the light. Everything looked at in this way, in silhouette, looks dark except for material that is translucent, and on a dark day translucence doesn't show much. I don't honestly know why I pick this or that fly unless a ghillie has told me that a so-and-so is always used. In this case I put on something different because I think the fish are probably bored stiff by the so-and-so.

"I have caught a large number of salmon fishing a fly upstream to them. This is an effective method but rarely practiced; in fact, I *think* I started it. Why they seem on occasion to prefer it pulled downstream over them, rather than swimming across, I don't know unless it is that they think it a bit cheeky and that it is going to bat them on the nose—so they grab it instead.

"Experience and some experiments suggest that in low water the size of fly that we feel we should use is generally too large. I have often done better than others by starting with a fly that seemed too small. Number 10 is my favourite fly for low water. Most people would go for size 8. I only use 12's when fish won't come to a 10. Size 12 hooks, being very fine in the wire, tend to cut themselves out of a big fish in fast water. It is a case of sending a boy to do a man's work. A size 12 treble is not bad in this respect because generally two of the prongs take hold.

"When I use silver-bodied flies I like them on silvered hooks. I can't see the point of using a black one when the whole idea of the fly is to give flash. I would like gilt hooks for gold-bodied flies but I don't often use them, except a *Dunkeld*, and that only rarely. Gilt hooks are not readily available in strengths suitable for salmon.

"I regard flies tied on long-shanked flat singles (so popular in U.S.A.) as the most inefficient hooking instruments of the lot. They look nice but are poor hookers and, because of leverage from the long shank, bad holders. If the point is snecked (offset), their efficiency is increased fifty per cent. Atlantic salmon take a fly to chew it and spit it out. Any hook which does not have 360 degrees of penetration potential is inefficient. Both trebles and snecked singles have this. I prefer a treble as, if the original hold gives, there is generally a spare prong standing proud.

"I see from your colour plates (in *Streamer Fly Tying and Fishing*) that you almost invariably paint eyes on your flies, or use Jungle Cock. This may appeal to the angler but I doubt that fish worry about it very much. I doubt if a fish moves to a fly and at the last second rejects it because it doesn't have eyes. In the same way I doubt if a fish which moves to a *Silver Doctor* turns away at the last moment because what it wants is a *Silver Wilkinson*. A change of fly and of the size of fly may induce a take from a fish that has boiled at a previous offering, but who is to know whether a smaller (or sometimes larger) one of the original pattern would not have been acceptable?"

In September, 1969, the author fished New Brunswick's Miramichi River with the Reverend Elmer J. Smith. It may have been noted before that Father Smith has fished for salmon more often than any man I know, and his inquiring and experimental mind is always on the alert to fathom the idiosyncrasies of the salmon. Therefore, in an attempt to provide readers with additional authoritative comments on fly selection the author hitched up a tape recorder, fixed two glasses of moose-milk,* and asked Father Smith to provide suggestions. They apply particularly to the Miramichi River:

"If the river is of normal height and clear, and if you are fishing wet, usual fly sizes are 6, 7 or 8. Most of us have given up going below 8 when water conditions are normal just as we have given up using very light leaders. This is a take-over from trout fishing and not a valid transfer of technique to salmon fishing on the Miramichi. Size 7 is a happy choice. If, under these conditions, you fish a *Cosseboom, a Butterfly* or one of the *Butt* patterns, generally one will be as effective as another. Most flies which catch fish under these conditions on this river are on the subdued side, are sparsely dressed, and usually have a little fluorescent material at the butt. However, silver-bodied flies will work also under normal summer conditions, but they are not used as much as the more subdued flies. The old yarn about a dull fly on a dull day and a bright one on a bright day is just a theory which has no viable application to this river.

"After a group of fish have been fished over very much it is wise to try a change-over fly, one radically different, such as a streamer fly, or a simple nymph. The simple nymphs, such as ones merely with Peacock herl or black chenille wrapped around a hook, are very effective but not very popular. The name of the game is to know the water you are fishing: to know the lies so you can fish them properly and carefully.

"Now suppose there is a rain and a rise of water. In this case many fish may be moving, and previous conditions have changed. The lies

---

* Moose-milk is ordinary cold milk to which a jigger or two of strong, dark rum has been added. Stir the rum slowly into the milk. If it's done otherwise the milk may curdle, but it's good anyway! This is a traditional salmon angler's drink on the Miramichi.

of the salmon have changed. Fish will take during high water if it doesn't turn a reddish peat color, and even then you can get an occasional fish. Under these circumstances the best place to fish is where there is a bar so you can get the fly over shallow rather than deep water. Use a good-sized bright fly, but don't oversimplify what you will do. I have seen conditions of a four-foot rise of water when you could hook fish on a number 10. If you get your fly over fish they will take an unbelievable range of types and sizes.

"As the water recedes and clears up, the fishing will become better. Observe the lies where the fish are, and fish accordingly. When water is just beginning to rise this is a good time because water is not discolored and fish are moving. A *Cosseboom* of reasonable size is as good as anything else. If the water is high and clear, use a larger size.

"In the fall salmon often lie in ponds, in deeper water than in the summer, and they may not move quickly. When they are lying in (staying from half a day to several days in one place when water is low) a dry fly may work best. Clipped-hair bodied dry flies are very effective. Watch the water temperature. Regardless of whether the water is high or low, if it is real cold a large streamer is absolutely deadly. The important thing is that the water must be cold. Then, fish may take a number 10 fly, but they also will take a number 2 streamer. When fishing streamers, the likelihood of catching more salmon than grilse is much enhanced. In the fall the river has old fish in it, but it also has new, bright fish coming in. I don't know why it is that, when you fish a dry fly under such circumstances, you will catch more old fish than bright fish.

"When water gets to 70°, look for cold-water pools, the pools lying below cold-water brooks. When water is warm the tendency is for fish to go into cold-water pools. The water may be so shallow that the fish may have their backs out of it, but they are not very shy. If the fish haven't been jigged (and driven out of the pool) you can see them. I use my pattern called *The Priest*, or a simple number 8 nymph. By false casting I deliver the fly a foot or two ahead of and beyond the fish. I move it quite rapidly on the surface the moment it hits the water. I pull it across the salmon's snout. If he shows interest I usually catch him by waiting a minute or two and then repeating the cast. This works because there is very little current in these cold-water pools. If you fish the wet fly downstream in the orthodox manner the fish sees too much of it, and it won't fool him. If the fish shows no interest, move on and try another one.

"Why do some fish take, while others don't? The taking salmon is one which has rested and is ready to move. A fish which is ready to move always is the best taker. Therefore I think that, in cold-water pools, the fish you are most apt to get are those which have just arrived. The longer they stay, the less they are inclined to take until they get ready to move. If the cold-water pool has a run at the top of it, the fish in the run are ready to move and should be good takers. In cold pools the dry fly is effective but you will have to seek the fish that are good takers. There are times when these fish will respond to a fly, and others when they won't. If they won't they may take streamers or large classic patterns."

At this point evidently I felt that, while the good father was recording some important information, he wasn't answering a question which we both knew couldn't be answered by stating fixed rules. "When do you use a dark fly and when do you use a bright one?" I asked.

"The theory circulated by British writers," he replied, "of using a bright fly on a bright day and a dark fly on a dull day, doesn't necessarily work. If you have a dark fly with just a touch of fluorescence on it you have one of the best flies for salmon. As Henry Ford used to say about his cars—any color is all right just as long as it is black. The theory of the bright fly versus the dark fly is simple. On a bright day a bright fly sparkles, but it doesn't sparkle on a dull day. Salmon will respond to bright flies. In all the history of writing about salmon fishing the tendency has been to make too many rules. Salmon in every river behave differently, and they don't always take the fly in the same way. There are days when they just nip at it. If we try to oversimplify we would reduce the salmon to a mechanical animal and salmon fishing to a mechanical science. Perhaps an answer to fly selection and to success in salmon fishing is for anglers individually to study the subject and to decide on a program and a technique for inducing the fish to take the fly.

"What a salmon sees," he added, "is the overall bulk and proportions of a fly. We don't take enough advantage of hook sizes. It is easy to tie a number 6 fly smaller than a number 8, depending on the amount of dressing which is put on it. A slightly larger hook is to the angler's advantage. The larger the hook, the heavier the wire, and vice versa. Fine wire will pull out quicker than heavier wire. This is negligible with a small fish, but important with a big one. The longer shank the hook has, the more leverage it has. Short shanked hooks hold better."

(In the above comments the word "streamer" is used in its comprehensive sense. Bucktails are more popular than feather-wings although the latter in patterns such as the *Gray Ghost* and *Black Ghost* frequently are successful.)

In discussing fly selection it seems to the author that the opinions of any one man would be presumptuous, but perhaps the opinions of such experts as Colonel Drury and Father Smith will help readers to form opinions of their own. In wet patterns the author has admitted to favoring hair-winged flies over feather-winged flies, but tries the latter occasionally in case a less mobile pattern with a more definite silhouette might do better. He favors (in either or both types) a dark fly or two (with a fluorescent butt), a lighter fly or two, and one or two bright flies rather heavily tinseled—all these in a selection of sizes. In dry patterns, variety in size and shape seems more important than variety in color. We will draw some conclusions in Chapter VI and will see why dry patterns should include a few unusual ones. These, plus a very few bucktails and nymphs, should cover all normal requirements. No one can tell others exactly what type and kind of fly to use for any specific condition, but readers should be able to form opinions as we go along.

| APOLLO 11 | PRINCE PHILIP |
|---|---|
| Originated and | (*First Prize,* |
| Dressed by | *Fly Dressers' Guild,* **1969**) |
| Mr. Alex Simpson (A) | Originated and Dressed by |
| | Mr. Jimmy Younger (P) |

| GORDON | POPHAM |
|---|---|
| Originated by Mr. Cosmo Gordon | Originated by Mr. F. L. Popham |
| Dressed by Miss Bessie Brown (P) | Dressed by Mr. Colin Simpson (P) |

| | SALSCRAGGIE |
|---|---|
| COLONEL BATES | (or PALE TORRISH) |
| Originated and | Dressed by |
| Dressed by | Miss Megan Boyd (P) |
| Mr. Jimmy Younger (P) | |

NIGHT HAWK
Dressed by
Mr. Jimmy Younger (P)

| BEAULY SNOW FLY | NARCEA RIVER |
|---|---|
| Dressed by | Originated and Dressed by |
| Mr. Colin Simpson (P) | Mr. Belarmino Martinez (P) |

(NOTE: In descriptions of the flies shown in the color plates (P) indicates a professional fly-dresser; (A) identifies an amateur. Addresses of professionals are given on page 345.)

PLATE I

Exhibition Patterns and Exhibition Dressings
of Standard Patterns

76

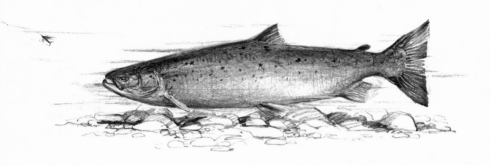

# V

# Wet-Fly
# Fishing Methods

People who fish for salmon often employ rather definite methods
of one sort or another which may be based on how high and cold the
water is, or how low and warm it is, often using wet-fly techniques
for the former, and dry-fly ones for the latter. Many of them will say
that if the water is colder than the air, or if it is below 50° F. or so, wet
flies are the ones to use, and that dry flies may be the answer when the
river warms to over 50° F., especially when it is low and clear. Some
would disagree with this and fish wet flies even when the water
temperature is 70°.

Often, anglers who are dogmatic about their tactics aren't as
successful as they might be because they fail to recognize that perhaps
the salmon are not operating under the same rules. They fail to
realize that salmon are unpredictable and also that there may be some
tricks the angler doesn't know. While high and cold water may indicate wet flies, and low and warm water may recommend dry flies, often
there are medial conditions when either method will be successful.

77

Under wet-fly conditions does one fish near the surface, or down deeper? Should he fish quartering downstream, cross-stream or upstream? What size and type of fly should he use, and what action should he give it? Under dry-fly conditions what should he do? When should he use large flies or small flies, feather-wings or hair-wings, bright flies or dull flies, streamers, bucktails or nymphs? No one knows all the answers, but there are methods for the various conditions which are recommended by experience. Let's combine the experiences of some of the world's best salmon anglers, and try to decide what makes sense!

Wet-fly methods probably will be chosen when streams are cool or cold and of moderate height. Salmon may be anywhere in the fishable water, whether they are lying in or are on the move. Under these conditions we can fish the simple way, perhaps using a dark or dull fly of average size for clear water and cloudy skies, an average-sized bright fly for sunny conditions, a larger fly when water is high and a more heavily tinseled one when it is discolored.

## BASIC WATER COVERAGE

The usual casting method, when we presume that fish are scattered here and there in pockets, near rocks and in other unseen lies, is to cast a short line quartering downstream at an acute angle if the current is swift and more nearly cross-stream if it isn't. We let the fly swing on a tight line, retrieving it for another cast after it has worked in the downstream position for a moment or two. We cover the fishable water, which may be on only one side or on both sides of our position. After retrieving the line we extend the cast by about a foot, and repeat the process, gradually extending line until we have all out that can be handled comfortably. Then we wade downstream for a few feet and repeat the process, with the short line gradually being extended on each successive cast, as before.

Near the end of this chapter it will be noted that salmon habitually seek certain locations while ignoring others. When such potential "hot spots" are observed it is obvious that they should be given special attention.

If this method of lengthening line causes us to delay the normal

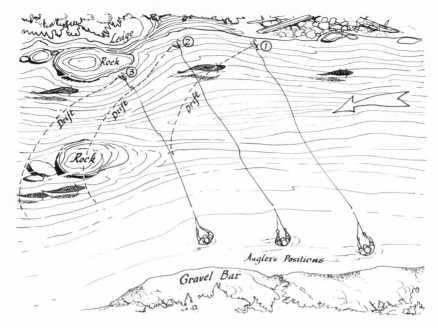

FIG. V-1

BASIC WATER COVERAGE

progress of anglers wading down behind us, of course it is polite to maintain a suitable wading pace. This may mean that, rather than extending the line during each pause, we would cast about the same length of line each time and progress downstream more steadily.

If we are in a boat we anchor at the head of the fishable water and cast in the same way until we have reached maximum casting distance. Then we pull the anchor to let the boat drift downstream nearly to where the previous maximum cast was, and we repeat the process.

In selecting the fly we remember that a heavily hackled one will tend to swim near the surface, while a sparsely hackled one will fish deeper. However, the depth at which the fly swims is more dependent upon type of line and length of leader. Most anglers think a leader longer than the rod is unnecessary, and, as we have seen, its tippet strength depends largely upon the size of fly used. With such a leader and a floating line the fly should swim only a few inches below the surface. This may be the most effective depth, especially if the water is fairly shallow. It should swim at a depth of a foot or two (depending on current) if the floating line has a sinking tip. For deeper fishing, as in deep pools, a sinking line is called for. If one should err in either direction, it is better to fish the fly too shallow, rather than too deep.

I know many salmon fishermen who use this common method exclusively, not seeming to realize that there are several others to employ if this one doesn't take fish. If it doesn't take fish, they may change the fly and try again. Usually, the choice of fly isn't the solution of the problem. The solution more likely is a change in its presentation.

## UPSTREAM FISHING

The first (but not necessarily the best) change in presentation is to reverse things by fishing upstream. The upstream method has been used for salmon very successfully in the British Isles by casting baits or lures (which are allowed there on many rivers) in a manner similar to the American method of "spinning." I don't know who first found this to be effective with the fly-rod and the fly, but it could have been Colonel Drury. Anyway, he sent me an amusing account of it:

"It was the proved effectiveness of this upstream minnow fishing that prompted me to try fishing a fly upstream for salmon. The water was gin clear and several fish could be seen lying in the tail of the pool. My host wanted a fish for the pot and I was assigned to get one by any fair means. My reward, if successful, was to be a large whiskey and soda. If I failed, I had to drink Coke, which I dislike.

"Thus bribed, I fished the pool down twice with a fly, but failed to do any good. Using the large *General Practitioner* (see page 288) I started casting to the salmon (I could see two of them lying together) exactly as though fishing a dry fly except that, as soon as the fly hit the water, I started to strip in line fast. On the second cast one of the salmon came up and grabbed the fly and was duly landed. It was only ten pounds, but it had earned me my drink.

"Since the river is so narrow that, in playing a fish, one is almost bound to scare the others, I decided to give them a rest and went to the house to claim my reward. My host was so delighted with the fish that he doubled the stakes for a second one. So, after about twenty minutes, I went back to the river and started again to fish upstream. On the third cast, bang! and I was into number two! This was a larger fish, and it took some time to get it under control with the little 8½-foot rod I was using, but eventually it came to hand. It weighed 18 pounds. Back to the house again and, two whiskeys later, back to the river, this time accompanied by my host.

"I did hook a third fish but was much too confident. In trying to land it before it was played out, it broke away. Since the stake was now up to four whiskeys, this probably was just as well!

"Fishing upstream is not a method of universal application. One cannot, for instance, cover a distant lie but, if it can be covered, it is well worth a try. Generally the fish seem to take best if the fly is moving fast. To achieve this one should either pull in line with the left hand or, if the current is suitable, make a downstream mend as soon as the fly lands in the water. This downstream mend throws a belly of line across the current, and the push of water on this belly will give the fly ample speed. Also, fish may take a fly that is coming down quite slowly and rather deep. The upstream method seems to be most successful in clear, low water which is not more than five feet deep. The only serious problem is line shadow in bright sunlight. It may be necessary to fish with a very long leader to avoid this. Hooking the fish is easy. They hook themselves, and stay hooked."

Let us note here that Colonel Drury used the upstream method at a time when normal downstream fishing tactics didn't work. Probably most anglers would agree that the upstream method should only be used as a last resort. However, it is a good one to remember because it can make the difference between a fishless day and a productive one.

## THE "GREASED LINE METHOD" (so called)

One of the classic methods which modern anglers will often find useful is the so-called "Greased Line" technique conceived by an English gentleman named A. H. E. Wood while fishing in Ireland in 1903. Mr. Wood learned that salmon which would not take normally presented flies would often take them when fished near the surface while drifting at a steady speed. He learned that his method made

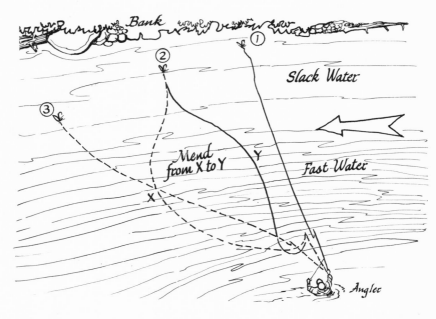

FIG. V-2

## FISHING THE "GREASED LINE"

1) Fly is cast normally to (1).

2) Drag sets in at point (2). To prevent fly and line from being pulled down-stream, mend line from (x) to (y).

3) Fly then will continue natural drift. Continue to mend line when necessary.

small flies practical; that they could be fished at a "taking angle" (broadside to the current); and that the use of the slack line allowed the fish to be hooked in the side of the mouth (the most secure place) without the necessity of striking because the fish would hook himself, or so he thought.

Of course, modern floating line manufacturing techniques make the greasing of lines unnecessary, but the name still persists for the method. It has been discussed in many salmon angling books of this century, and most of the writers have made it sound rather difficult— so much so, in fact, that most contemporary salmon fishermen shy away from trying it. In practice, the method actually is quite simple.

Equipped with a fly-rod having a floating line, a leader of average length, and a thinly dressed wet fly, the angler casts to a selected position directly across the river, or perhaps at an angle very slightly upstream or downstream. The object is for the fly to drift two or three inches below the surface broadside to the current and therefore pointing toward the angler. Of equal importance, it must drift at a steady speed in the current.

Normally, however, the current would immediately put a belly in the line which would cause the fly to whip around, not at a steady speed. This can instantly be prevented by mending the line (by flipping an upstream loop in it) and by doing this as often as necessary to maintain the fly's steady drift. In handling the fly we must be careful not to pull at it, which can be done by leaving some slack line in the water near the angler. The process is a deliberate one, without any jerking or twitching of the line. The fly is led downstream by keeping the rod-tip ahead of the line and by keeping the line as straight as possible. In a slow current the rod-tip can be kept low, but it should be kept higher in faster currents so any belly in the line is between the rod-tip and the water. This is done to give the fish a *side view* of the steadily drifting fly. A little slack line is kept in the hand for use as necessary. If the fly's drift temporarily slows, a little line is pulled in to keep it moving steadily.

In some cases the current where the fly lands will be moving faster than the current where the line is. In this case a series of reverse mends (downstream loops) is necessary to maintain steady drift.

When a fish comes up and takes the fly the rod-tip is lowered to allow the line to belly in the current and to put *no tension* on the line. The tendency to strike must be avoided. Handled this way, the salmon takes the fly in his mouth but does not try to eject it because it is not being pulled by the angler. The belly in the line gives a slight downstream pull on the fly which causes the salmon to head upstream, thus pulling the fly well back into the angle of his jaws, which is the most secure place to hook him. At this point, a downstream flick of the rod-tip should set the barb.

The part of Mr. Wood's theory dealing with hooking salmon on the "greased line" (or on the "floating line," as it now should be called) is included only for historical reasons because it is disputed by many later anglers who maintain that the way he thought salmon take flies is not the way they usually do it at all.

Following are modern opinions based on lifelong experiences in salmon fishing during which the ways salmon take flies have been observed very closely and very often. While some readers may debate parts of this next section, it would be rather difficult to refute the results of so much experience on:

### HOW SALMON TAKE FLIES (*and how to hook them*)

Basically, salmon approach the fly in three different ways. As indicated in these three drawings they may 1) rise and take it almost at once. They may 2) leave the lie to follow the fly and take it after it has well passed them. They may 3) leave the lie to follow the fly until it is hanging downstream and take it after lying momentarily behind it.

The most usual way is 2) to take or refuse it when it is well past the fish. In this case the fish may start moving for the fly, decide not to take it, and return to his lie—or he may start moving for it, and take it after it has swung past him. In the latter case when he moves to the fly he will be moving toward the shore from which the fly is being fished, and he will be moving *with the current*. This means that the fish takes the fly as he turns and starts *downstream*—not upstream, as Mr. Wood believed.

This action has been observed so often that it appears to be typical: anglers spending considerable time watching from a bridge what goes on while people are fishing the pool below. One who watches from above can see what really happens, and there is a lot more going on than most people seem to realize!

Such observations refute the long-accepted theory that loose line should be fed to the fish in order to cause the bag in the line (made by the current) to pull the hook into the back of the jaw. Since the fish is *not* going upstream at this point (but going downstream) the loose line theory more often than not prevents the angler from hooking the fish! It is true that a bag or belly of line in the current will tend to cause a salmon to move upstream, but this is *after* the fish has been hooked. Actually the angler has little control over where the hook becomes imbedded in the mouth.

In the case 3) of the hanging fly, a typical situation is that of the fly swinging across the current and reaching a hanging position in a current that is rather slack. The salmon hesitates and then darts

Angler's position

A. Fly presented
A-B. Fish follows by dropping back
in current and moving cross-
stream.
C. He nips at fly or —
Turns on fly and takes it.

Rock

Original Lie

FIG. V-3

HOW SALMON TAKE FLIES—1

toward the fly, but merely nips it. In instances such as this the fish either is not hooked or is hooked on the edge of the mouth. If hooked this way he frequently becomes "unstuck" because there is inadequate barb penetration. If one knows the fly is moving into a slow current to hang there it is wise to give added movement to the fly. However, when a fly hangs in a moderate current the fish is more likely to turn on it and become properly hooked. If possible, one should avoid hooking fish on a hanging fly even though it may produce rises. In order to prevent this try not to wade out so far that you are standing immediately above a lie, or a possible lie. The chances of securely hooking a fish on a swinging fly are much better than on a hanging fly, regardless of current conditions.

In any case, when there is less than a moderate flow the likelihood of good hooking will be improved by imparting added movement to the fly. Of course, there are many cases when a salmon will take a fly which is scarcely moving in very slow water, but the chances are that the fish will spit out the fly before the angler feels him and has a chance to tighten up enough to hook him securely. Even when a salmon's mouth is closed there is a considerable gap through which a fly can slip out. For this and other reasons many modern fishermen are using offset and double-offset hooks.

The word "striking" often is used because it is a familiar term used by trout fishermen who go fishing for salmon. Probably the word is responsible for more lost salmon than any other in angling literature. If one strikes, what happens? The angler strikes because something he sees (such as a boil) or something impeding the natural motion of the fly causes him to do it. There is a time-lag involved in this reflex, due to slack line, softness of rod-tip and other factors, which affords ample time for the salmon to take the fly. To strike then only risks insecure lip hooking or taking it away from him altogether. Under normal conditions the fish turns downstream as he takes the fly, and the current pushing against him provides added downstream velocity. Since the fisherman should keep his end of the connection fairly rigid (probably by pressing the line against the rod-grip with a finger) the connection tightens up sufficiently to properly set the hook. So striking can only do more harm than good because the desired result is already accomplished and a smart

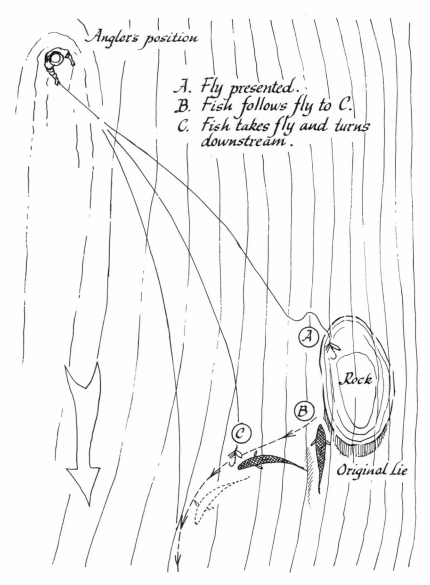

*Angler's position*

A. Fly presented.
B. Fish follows fly to C.
C. Fish takes fly and turns downstream.

Rock

Original Lie

Fig. V-4

**HOW SALMON TAKE FLIES—2**

87

Angler's position

A. Fly presented.
B. Fish rises and takes fly
   almost at once.

A

Rock

B

Original Lie

FIG. V-5

HOW SALMON TAKE FLIES—3

88

strike may only result in pulling the fly from the mouth of the fish. The finer the wire of the hook, the less tension is required to set it. A moderate flow will produce better tightening than a slack current. The best the fishermen can do is to "tighten"—that is, to be sure there is sufficient tension to make the barb penetrate. After the weight of the fish is felt the pressure on the line can be released and the fish can be played in the usual manner.

Of course, many anglers will say that they always strike and that they always catch fish, but there are times when the fish are so much "on the take" that it is nearly impossible not to hook them, no matter what one does. The anglers who say they always strike might pause to remember how many strikes have resulted in lost fish, many of which might have remained hooked by using the tightening process.

We have said that the angler has little or no control over where in the mouth the salmon is hooked, regardless of what Mr. Wood said about it. The "hinge" of the jaw is a good place. When a fish takes a fly, even when it is swimming properly with the barb(s) down, the hook may be turned sideways, downward or upward by contact with the mouth of the fish. Because of this the fish may be hooked in the hinge or in the lower or the upper jaw. Sometimes they are hooked in the nostril, which is as good as or better than the hinge. The worst place is on the edge of the mouth because the bone structure is so close to the skin coverage that it is difficult to get hook penetration. Fish often are hooked through a piece of mouth skin. Summer fish have tender mouth skin and they often break off. Autumn fish have much tougher mouth skin, and even the slightest hold may be enough to land them.

There are many different types of "connections" the angler can make with the fish in fishing the wet fly. For example, there is the sudden sharp jerk followed by the line going loose. This is caused by a fast-moving fish merely touching the point of the hook. There is no real penetration and there is nothing the angler can do about it. The fast jerk is caused more often by fast-moving grilse than by the rise of a salmon. Again, there is a heavy pull, after which the line goes loose. This usually is caused by a salmon taking the fly without the hook penetrating. There is the boil caused by a salmon turning on a fly near the surface of the water. He may take the fly or he may not, so you may hook him or you may not. If there are many boils to flies and no fish are hooked, the answer is to fish the fly a bit deeper. This can be done by using a line with a sinking tip instead of a floater; by extending the length of the leader; by using a more sparsely dressed fly; or by a combination of these methods.

## HOOKING A FISH AFTER A RISE

Now let's assume that a salmon comes to the fly, but that we don't hook him. A fish that shows interest in a fly is considered one that can be hooked, and part of the challenge of salmon fishing is to try to hook him. When he comes to the fly we know how much line

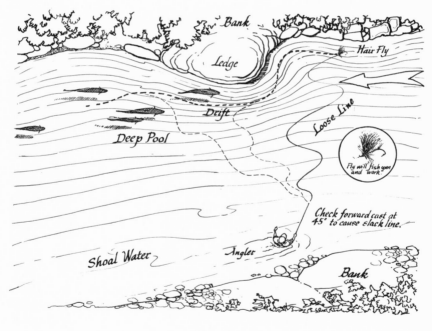

FIG. V-6

### FISHING "THE PATENT"

Cast a slack line up, across or down-stream. Allow hair-wing fly to drift without any pull from line, thus making it "work", or "fluff". Fish near surface, or deeper down.

is out and, because this measures his distance from us, we don't reel any line in or change our position. We mark the fish's location against something on the far shore. We let him rest for a few minutes, occupying ourselves meanwhile by filling and smoking a pipe, or by doing something else to pass the time.

While we have been resting the fish, it is possible that he may have moved upstream a few feet. Therefore we make the next cast to a point about ten feet above him, judging the exact location by the landmark and by the amount of line which is off the reel. If the fish is more or less directly downstream we would not cast the final ten feet of line. If this brings no result we continue casting, each time to a point a foot or so nearer his original position. If we have marked the spot carefully we should by this time have hooked the fish. If we haven't done so, and if we want to continue to work on him, this chapter gives several other tactics that can be employed.

Some anglers think that during this resting period the fly should be changed. That is a matter of opinion. If one changes the fly the purpose would be mainly to occupy time because, if a salmon comes to a fly once, he will probably come to the same fly again and this time will probably take it.

## FISHING "THE PATENT"

Another method in the salmon angler's bag of tricks is one which has more or less been cloaked in mystery but which is quite simple. It is called "Thompson's Patent," or merely "The Patent," and it has been referred to in the brief history of salmon flies in Chapter IV. There we noted that Colonel Lewis S. Thompson obtained some hair-wing flies from an angler who pioneered them, A. S. Trude, and that he tried them on Canada's Restigouche River in 1928. The colonel wrote about his experiences in the March, 1934, issue of a now defunct magazine called *The Sportsman*, and we may as well tell the story in his own words:

"Five years ago I was fishing in Jimmie's Hole: a celebrated pool on the Restigouche. At that time there was in that pool an old he-salmon that we got to know as the 'Hobby Horse.' There he was in the middle of the pool, and all at once he would start in on his hobby, rolling up to the top of the water with his big, broad back, and doing it for twenty times or more at short intervals, always in the same place. Not a fly would he ever look at. We would always inquire at night from the one who had fished the pool, 'Anything doing with Hobby?' But there never was anything doing with that scoundrel. I was fishing the pool one day, and there was the old Hobby Horse doing his cavorting around much more than usual, I thought. But the fly meant nothing in his life, as I fished on to the-drop below. I had on a 5/0 *Abbey* (see '*Red Abbey*' herein). A large salmon rose to it away over near the bank. I let the fly come on around. There was some more time to spare before the next cast, so I retrieved the fly and cast it away up the stream. As it floated down it looked like a large mouse. It drifted into the eddies and was then thrown out into the crystal-clear, mirrorlike surface of the pool. It was slowly coming down to the home of the Hobby Horse and, by gracious, here came that horse! He grabbed it, and had gone for his last ride. And that was the birth of a new way to take a salmon, and a way that I think is far superior to any other method that I know about. We call it 'The Patent.'

"I have always been trying something new or different and have called whatever it was a Thompson Patent. The method is simplicity itself. The fly is thrown so that it lights on the water at the end of a loose line. Throw it up or down stream, at any angle, or straight across. Instead of having the line out straight, the rod will be stopped at about 45 degrees and the line pulled up before the fly hits the water. The hair fly instead of having its hair all in a line as it would be on the end of a taut line is spread out in an A-shape, and it looks like no other fly on earth or in the water. You can use it on a dry (sinking) or a greased (floating) line. I prefer the greased line on account of the easy pickup. You fish this Patent as you would fish for trout. You must strike the fish, and you can see every fish that comes. That is all there is to it. Let the fly float of itself without any pull at all from the line. Whether the water is high or low, or dark or clear, the salmon will come to this fly and will take it."

Later experience with this method recommends using a sinking line, or a floating line with a sinking tip, to allow the fly to sink gradually as it drifts downstream. The obvious purpose of the method is to make the fly fluff up to give maximum life to the hairs in the wing as they encounter action in the current.

## FLUFFING THE FLY

This method of fishing a fly so it will "breathe" in the current reminds me of an almost fishless week on New Brunswick's Cains River when the water was low and clear and when very few fish were in the pools. On one of the days we selected a wilderness pool because a brook flowed into it and, considering the warm and low water, we surmised that fish should be lying below the brook where the water was cooler. Although it was early morning, and the pool was supposed to be a private one, we found three local rods already on it. Although they left when we arrived, the small pool evidently had been well fished. The only life we could see in it were two large grilse lying just over the lip of a riffle. My companions and I took turns fishing for them, with no result.

While sitting on the bank I tried to think of a trick that would induce some action. Remembering that in a previous book I had written of catching a large trout by fluffing a marabou streamer fly in front of him, I decided to try this tactic on the grilse.

After they had been rested for a while I waded well above them and worked the streamer down to them. When it was directly in front of them I began to twitch the rod-tip to work the fly in a fluffing manner. Nothing happened for several minutes. I had smoked a pipe and was about ready to give up when I noticed that one of the grilse, by increasing quivering of fins, seemed to be getting a bit agitated. Suddenly he struck the fly and was hooked but whether he struck from anger, just to get rid of the nuisance, or for another reason, is a question only he can answer.

I thought at the time that I had added a new trick to the communal bag, but this doesn't seem to be so. In some notes given to me by the Reverend Elmer J. Smith, who fishes for salmon almost constantly during the seasons, is a remark: "There are instances when a literally hung fly will be the most productive technique. Wave it in their faces!"

## THE RIFFLING FLY, OR PORTLAND HITCH

Riffling or skating a fly is a technique used in both wet- and in dry-fly fishing. In wet-fly fishing it can be done by skittering nymphs, streamers or bucktails on the surface, or by riffling a standard feather-wing or hair-wing. To do this one merely throws one or two half-hitches of the leader tip around and just back of the head of the fly. If it is a double-hook fly, the end of the hitch can be below the head—that is, the hitched leader extends down from under the rear of the head. If the fly has a single hook, the hitch can extend from under the head, but preferably it should extend out from the side so that, regardless of whether the fly is fished to the right or to the left, when the fly is facing upstream the hitch extension is on the side facing the angler.

This riffled fly should be skated on top of the water at a speed slow enough so that it will not throw spray and fast enough so that it will not sink. If salmon are in evidence the fly is riffled on the surface so that it can be led about a foot in front of them.

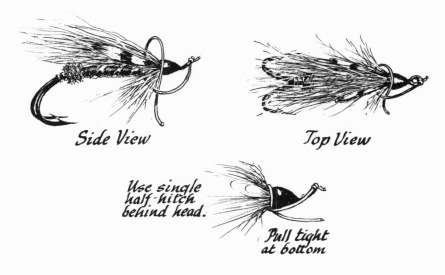

*Side View*                    *Top View*

*Use single half-hitch behind head.*

*Pull tight at bottom*

FIG. V-7

THE RIFFLED FLY

The name Portland Hitch came from Portland Creek, Newfoundland, where Lee Wulff had a camp for several years. Evidently at Portland Creek the riffled fly is used almost exclusively. In other places it is generally used when salmon have been fished over considerably, have observed all the styles in flies, and will respond only to a method which is new to them.

We have noted that before the days when the hook's eye was part of the hook an eye of gut was affixed to the tip of the iron. Sometimes these gut eyes deteriorated before the flies did, and the flies were expensive and often hard to come by. To utilize the hooks that had lost their eyes the leader was tied back of the head with half-hitches, with the result that the hitched fly swam differently. This difference often proved to be effective, and thus gave birth to a new method. At least, this is the explanation that appeals to the author!

## THE IMPORTANCE OF FLY SPEED

In discussing these various methods we note that in normal wet-fly fishing the fly should be fished at a constant speed. No belly in the line should be allowed which causes the fly to whip. When fish are lying in slack water the fly may not travel fast enough unless it is given added motion. Increasing the fly's speed can be done momentarily by lifting the rod-tip or by swinging the rod-tip upstream. It can be done more constantly by stripping in line, just as the speed can be slowed by lowering the rod-tip or by letting out line. In slack water the cast fly must be stripped in to give it adequate speed. Salmon may show interest in a fly which is being fished slowly and often can be made to take it if it is fished faster. Many anglers think that twitching the fly does no good. On some rivers the guides recommend it, especially while the fly is swinging in an arc after being cast quartering downstream.

In wet-fly fishing the speed with which the fly is fished can be a determining factor in success or lack of it. While traditional theories of fly speed may be subject to question, generally speaking it is true that in a strong flow the wet fly should be fished more downstream than cross-stream and that in a slow flow the fly should be fished more cross-stream than downstream. Experimentation is often rewarding because there are times when fishing a wet fly somewhat upstream will be productive, as we have seen in the discussion of previous methods. There are times when it is most successful to give the fly hardly any drift at all, and there are times when very fast stripping in of the line produces best results. Usually, one should not give the fish time to inspect the fly closely. He is more likely to take it when it is being fished fairly fast and he thinks it is trying to escape.

## NOTES ON FISHING DEPTH

Since a floating line is easy to pick up and to handle, and since it is more fun to hook fish on or near the surface, many anglers use the floating line, or one with a sinking tip, through habit, even at times when they shouldn't be doing so.

One of the maxims of salmon fishing is that, if the method we are using doesn't work, we should try something else. If other anglers have preceded us down a pool using near-surface techniques, and if we aren't doing very well, the solution may be to change over to a sinking line with the hope of hooking idle fish, the ones that won't bother to come up for a near-surface fly. Quite frequently very small flies such as number 10 will be better than larger ones, even low-water patterns or nymphs. On the other hand late in the season when both stale and fresh fish are in the river the stale fish often will be so interested in streamers, bucktails or other big flies that they will rush nearly across the river to grab them.

To get the fly down on as tight a line as possible we cast more downstream when the current is fast, and more nearly cross-stream when it is slower. Casting with heavy, sinking lines recommends selection of rods with plenty of power and butt action. Rods too stiff in the butt and quite soft in the tip won't pick up deeply sunken lines as well.

There are many instances when deep fishing will get results at times when surface and near-surface techniques won't. If the methods we are using, or those that others are using, are not successful, the experienced angler refuses to remain in the common rut. He is the one who tries something new, and he is often rewarded.

## THE HOW AND WHEN OF BUCKTAILS AND STREAMERS

Disregarding early spring black salmon fishing on the Miramichi or wherever it may be permitted, streamers and bucktails have been found very effective for bright salmon, especially under three conditions:

In summer fishing they are valuable as a "change of pace" fly. For example, there are conditions when a pool has been fished by a large number of rods. The rods have been taking fish, but suddenly the action slacks off. At such times these baitfish imitators prove effective because the fish have seen conventional patterns, which reminds us of the story of the successful neophyte related in Chapter I.

Streamer flies can produce excellent results during a summer rise of water. Under these conditions the water is often discolored, but the fish seem to have little difficulty in seeing and in being attracted to these large and colorful flies.

In bright salmon fishing the streamer or bucktail can be very effective in fall fishing when the water temperature is 50 degrees or lower. They will work in deep water, in shallow water, in broken water or in smooth water. Under such conditions they can outfish any of the standard patterns. The splash of a streamer, rather than flushing fish, seems to attract them. In this type of fishing the streamer can be fished with either a floating or a sinking line. When the water is very cold, the sinking line is preferred. Under all conditions the fly should be cast straight across the stream, allowing the current to make a considerable bag in the line and hence increase the fly's speed. Evidently working the fly does not increase its attractiveness to salmon although the author's opinion is that it helps to bucktail it occasionally in imitation of the erratic manner in which a baitfish swims. Fly sizes usually are numbers 2 or 4, on 3X long hooks.

Bucktails are preferred to the feather-winged streamers largely because of their greater degree of translucence and the greater degree of mobility of hair over feathers. More than two or three patterns varying from dark to bright are unnecessary. My fellow anglers on the Miramichi normally use only one, which is a compromise of coloration called the *Herb Johnson Special*, named for its originator, Herbert Johnson, of Yarmouth, Maine. It was originally dressed in 1960 as a Smelt imitation for land-locked salmon and big Brook Trout but it has had sensational success on Atlantic salmon. Since many other patterns suitable for salmon have been given in the companion book to this one, *Streamer Fly Tying and Fishing*, I shall give the dressing of only the *Herb Johnson Special* in this book:

## HERB JOHNSON SPECIAL

*Head color:*  Silver paint, with yellow eye and black pupil. The head is quite large. (Hook size: #2 or #4 streamer hook)
*Body:*  Black wool, fairly full
*Ribbing:*  Embossed flat silver tinsel (wound in reverse, toward tyer)
*Throat:*  White bucktail, as long as the wing
*Wing:*  A very small bunch of bright yellow bucktail, slightly longer than the hook; on each side of this two strands each of red and blue fluorescent nylon floss; on each side above the floss one strand of Peacock herl; over this a rather sparse bunch of brown bucktail dyed yellow. (All components are of same length, slightly longer than the hook. On a No. 2 long-shanked hook the dressing is 2 3/4 inches long.)

If two other patterns are desired, the author would select the *Gray Ghost* streamer for a dark one and the *Mickey Finn* bucktail for a bright one, but many others would do as well.

The interest in studying the uses of streamers and bucktails for effective salmon fishing is recent and is increasing as this is being written. Some of the expert anglers in the United Kingdom snapped up the idea about as soon as we did. Their bucktails are very sparse— only a dozen hairs or so, and are up to three inches in length.

One of several reasons why bright salmon may be interested in these baitfish imitations is interestingly brought out by Colonel Drury in the Autumn, 1969, issue of the *Flyfishers' Journal*. In an article on how salmon take flies in flowing water he says:

"In the autumn the situation is complicated by the fact that one may be dealing with two distinct categories of fish. There is the fresh fish which may, depending on conditions and water temperature, behave either like a spring fish or a summer one and there is the stale fish which, as the spawning season approaches may, particularly if a cock, come on the take again. When these stale fish are interested it is generally in a large fly, irrespective of water height or temperature, and they will often grab it with a ferocity that almost pulls the rod out of one's hand. To understand this 'killer' take one must remember that the male salmon parr can fertilize the eggs of an adult female salmon and that, if allowed to do so, this precocious youngster will take part in the nuptials.

"As the spawning season approaches, the cock fish do become restless and one can watch them chasing about in the pools. I suggest that they are beginning to feel jealous and to regard small fish as potential suitors for the favors of the hen fish, which they understandably regard as their special prerogative. They will kill these potential interlopers if they can catch them and this explains why a large fly which superficially resembles a salmon parr can be so effective. As the season advances still further toward spawning time all fish seem to lose interest in small flies to the extent that, one might almost say, 'They are on the parr,' but it is noticeable that the nearer it is to spawning time the less inclined are hen fish to take, but that the cocks when they take, take with an almighty bang!"

Sam Slaymaker, of Gap, Pennsylvania, developed three baitfish imitations of bucktails called *Little Brook Trout*, *Little Brown Trout* and *Little Rainbow Trout*, and their dressings have been given in *Streamer Fly Tying and Fishing*. I know of no occasion when they have been tried for Atlantic salmon but, in sizes 2 and 4, they should do very well.

## WHEN TO USE NYMPHS

We have seen that nymphs do not need to be intricate in their dressings, although many of us take more pleasure in using them when made that way. Under normal conditions of good flow, average temperature and reasonable height, when fishing a pool fished by many rods a simple nymph with or without hackle often is more effective than the fully dressed fly. This may be because the nymph is different from the types of flies usually used.

Nymph-like flies (which may be flies with the wings clipped off) also work well when salmon are "lying in" as they do for example in cold-water pools or in the tails of pools in the autumn. These fish have little motivation to move and usually are difficult to entice. Under such conditions nymphs can be deadly if they are fished properly.

In the summer, cold-water pools should be fished by false-casting the line and delivering the fly straight across stream. If the fish can be seen, as is often the case, the fly should be fished about one foot beyond and ahead of him. The rod should then immediately be raised with a slight tremor in the hand and with considerable speed so the fly is practically breaking the surface while it moves several inches across and ahead of the fish.

If the fish moves to the fly, we should be able to catch him. Take the fly away; cast it downstream; and wait half a minute or so. Repeat the process, and invariably the fish not only will take the fly, but will be solidly hooked.

The reason this technique is effective is that the fish does not get as much opportunity to see the fly as he would if the fly were being fished by normal wet-fly methods. Fish are penned in these cold-water pools because other parts of the river are too warm, and there is very little current in these pools.

In the autumn, when a number of fish are lying in rather slow-moving water ("lying in," or staying for several days or perhaps weeks) and are being fished over extensively, these nymph imitations are very effective when fished in the following manner. A long line should be cast straight across the stream. After several seconds, while the nymph sinks slightly, the line should be grasped just below the stripping guide and drawn moderately slowly until the pulling hand is straight down by one's side. The process is repeated until the fly has fished the water to be covered. If a fish should boil for the nymph and not take it he should be rested for a short period and then fished for again in the same way. No change of fly is necessary. A fish that shows can invariably be hooked.

Other conditions during which nymphs should be productive are as a change-over fly during normal summer conditions and during low-water conditions before fish have gone into the cold-water pools.

## "ON AND UNDER" TECHNIQUES

A method we use, mainly on the Miramichi, and often with great success, is one the author calls the "on and under" method. To fish "on and under" we need a fly like Maurice Ingalls' *Butterfly*, sometimes called the *Splay-Wing Coachman*, which is included in the American hair-wing patterns in this book. With its splayed wings, it can be fished both dry and wet. Initially we use it as a floater, and sometimes as a skittering fly. Eventually it will sink. Then it is used as a conventional wet fly, but a slight twitching or bucktailing action is given to it to make the divided wings open and shut as it moves. If salmon haven't seen this fly fished these ways very often they are quite sure to go for it, and it has proved to be perhaps the most productive fly (or method) used on the Miramichi. Certainly it is one of the best of the many angling methods suggested in this chapter.

## DAPPING THE FLY

Another method that gets results, if reluctant salmon lie near enough to use the trick, is to dap, or bounce, a wet fly over the lie. This bouncing method works best with a very long rod, and even when there is a strong wind on one's back to aid in flicking the fly over the desired position. The fly should remain on the water only for a second or two at a time so the salmon has only the briefest chance to see it. The timing should be rhythmic so the fish can anticipate the instant when the fly will reappear in his cone of vision. This rhythmic dapping should be maintained for a considerable period of time, if necessary. It is often a killing method of inciting action, and the action sometimes happens quickly. There are instances when a salmon, after having noticed the quick and regular arrival and departure of the fly, has suddenly erupted from the depths and taken the fly in the air as it arrived over his position and before it has landed.

This method works occasionally with wet flies of any sort but seems to be even more successful with dry flies, so it may be helpful to remember it as one of the tricks that can be used during the warm weather doldrums when a radically different trick is needed to produce action.

## EVEN TINY FLIES MAY DO IT!

When a friend phoned to report fishing results for the last week of a season on the Miramichi he said that the usual fall run of fish hadn't arrived and evidently few were in the river. Conditions were wrong; the water was extremely low; and only the occasional salmon was being taken.

"But Paul Kukonen stayed at the camp for three days," my informant said. "He didn't hook anything the first day but on the second and third he took five salmon and he lost several more. No one else even hooked a fish, and twelve rods were fishing."

Paul is a highly experienced angler and an old fishing companion, so I knew he must have tried something unusual. Of course I wanted to know about it, and before long we got together.

"I fished hard that first day," Paul said. "Now you know there are lots of tricks that can take salmon. I tried all the suitable ones, but nothing worked, although salmon were bulging occasionally. I decided to try very small flies, right on top. Of course these are a last resort because you have to use awfully light tippets, and it's pretty hard to hook fish on size 12's.

"Anyway, that night I tied some number twelve doubles, but I wanted them to look even smaller, so I dressed size 14 flies on size 12 low-water hooks. Teal wing, yellow hackle, and assorted colors for the bodies. The pattern proved to be unimportant. It was the size that counted.

"The pool was two hundred yards long. First I fished it with regular flies, and did nothing. Then I fastened a fifteen-foot leader tapered to four pounds onto a floating line, and I greased all but the front four or five feet of the leader because I wanted the fly to work barely under the surface.

"On the second or third cast I hooked a large salmon, but the leader broke. Then I hooked and landed an eleven-pounder. Then I hooked and landed a thirteen-pounder. After that I lost one of about twelve pounds. Another fish took, and I actually could feel the fly grating through his mouth, but it didn't hold. Finally I hooked and lost a very large one.

"On the third day I did even better, landing three salmon and losing several more. With these tiny flies it's awfully hard to hook them, and of course you have to handle them very carefully on such a light leader. But the trick worked. I had over a dozen salmon on during the two days, and landed five. All this time nobody else took a fish!"

We have commented on the fact that salmon flies as small as size 12 are rarely used because it is so difficult to hook and hold large fish with them. They may not be the answer normally, but this is an instance of when they were.

Readers who like to hook salmon during the frequent periods when they are more of a challenge than a bonanza may by now have realized that there are more in the Atlantic salmon angler's bag of tricks than the simple but too often used "chuck and chance it" method which started this chapter. Some of the methods take a bit of pondering if we are to learn them well enough from the book to use them effectively on the stream. As one who also enjoys fishing for trout, this author also knows that many of the methods learned for salmon are also applicable to them, so it is hoped that trout fishermen also will find uses for some of what this book contains.

Since many trout anglers also enjoy fishing for salmon it may be of value to remark that one can err in believing that trout techniques in general should be approximated in salmon fishing. Too many fallacious analogies have been drawn which have resulted in the transference of trout theory to salmon fishing. For examples: unlike trout, salmon are not particularly shy and seem little disturbed when anglers get close to them or make reasonable commotion near them. Leader shyness, which is a concern in trout fishing, is hardly applicable to salmon. Poachers who jig for salmon with large treble hooks and 40-pound monofilament are successful because they can throw the rig over a salmon and allow it to settle with the leader resting on the salmon's back without driving him away. Careful presentation of the fly is of lesser importance because flies with very large heads (making for the poorest kind of entry into the water) can be fatal in fooling salmon. The length of leaders and their diameters (but not their tapering) seem unimportant. If the leader is long enough to fish the fly at the proper depth and if the diameter of the tippet is such that it will enable the fly to fish naturally, that is all that is required. Leader color and line color are much more important to the fisherman than they are to the fish. The author believes in using the strongest leader tippet that will fish the fly properly because large salmon can't always be handled "with kid gloves."

But there is more to the salmon angler's bag of tricks than this.

Many new uses for the dry fly have been discovered, and we'll soon get to that! Before doing so, however, it may be well at this point to know how to presume where salmon should be found in rivers so we can spend less time working flies in unproductive water.

## LOCATIONS OF SALMON IN STREAMS

The trout fisherman who goes salmon fishing has things to forget as well as to learn because, for example, while trout frequent feeding lanes where the stream brings food to them, salmon, having no great desire for food, may be found elsewhere. Salmon do not seek hiding places as trout do; they often lie in plain sight and perhaps in shallow, gravelly water so close to the bank that the wading trout fisherman would be stepping where they were while casting where they aren't!

When one has the knowledge and ability to fish for salmon, perhaps the greatest question, more important than fly-dressing or fly selection, is where salmon should be found in streams. It is a question which, if treated at all in other books on salmon fishing, has been handled rather superficially. It is a question which can only be answered properly by the combined judgment of salmon anglers of many years' experience. Very fortunately the author has been given that kind of assistance in compiling the following data. It is a complex question to resolve because the answer is a variable one, dependent on several factors. It does, however, have valid solutions which we shall try to cover.

For example, it has to do with the size of the river and the volume and temperature of its water, also of how long the volume of water will last. If the river is a spate river it will afford lies only while there is a good run of water. The normal volume of water from non-spate rivers will move a more continuous run of salmon for a longer period of time. There is the factor of the physical conformation of the river bed and its depth. The accessible areas of some rivers are deep and without lies. If salmon run these rivers there may be no available places to fish for them unless it be on their return to the sea when they may be caught as black salmon, or kelts.

The matter of where salmon lie has to do with the bed contours of rivers because they vary, one from another, in their bed characteristics.

A large river with a moderate flow of water which is not too deep will afford characteristic lies in deeper places on shallow bars. The great torrential rivers may have few well designated bars but they will have quieter places where the salmon may rest. Some rivers may afford the best lies (or holding places) at the tails of pools which afford proper stream flow. The point of all this is that the kinds of lies salmon will use vary greatly from river to river. The salmon angler who is familiar with one river and its characteristic lies may become quite confused when he discovers that the rules he has learned do not apply to another river.

What then does one do when fishing on any given river? He takes time to study the stream and to figure out its characteristics.

Many salmon fishermen do not bother to do this. They depend upon the knowledge of the guides, who may not know much about it. In any event, dependence on the guides gives them part of the credit for catching the salmon, and it would be better if the angler could do the whole thing himself. An accomplished angler not only knows his tackle and how to use it. He is also able to select by himself the type and size of fly that seems best, and he has decided upon a plan which includes what method or methods he will employ and exactly how and where he will fish his stretch of water.

Perhaps the question of locating salmon in streams can best be answered by starting with where they should be under normal summer conditions, which include most of the fishing we will do. Then because the lies change under very warm conditions and again in the autumn when the water gets colder, these periods will be handled separately. We will ignore spring fishing, which is primarily for black salmon, a matter which has been touched upon before.

Since there are typical situations applicable to almost any river, drawings seem appropriate to help in making them clear. If one absorbs the meaning of the drawings, he will find that the conditions they represent will be encountered again and again.

Normal summer conditions generally are defined as when the temperature of water in the stream is 70° F. or below. Since this is a rather critical temperature, carrying a thermometer is very helpful. Some rivers will produce fish in the regular pools even when the water is above 70° but this is true primarily when there is a heavy volume. When this situation exists, fishing is best very early in the morning and very late in the afternoon or evening, not during the heat of the day. If the regular pools do not produce fish under such conditions, one would seek them in cold-water pools such as have been and will be discussed.

Under normal summer conditions fish like a *moderate flow* of water for their lies. What is moderate flow? We will soon see that it is caused by stream obstructions and by other things, but perhaps a quick way to discover it is to stand in a stream in a foot or so of moving water and to feel the water flowing around his boot. By placing a hand in the water outside the leg one will feel rapid water. By putting it immediately downstream of the leg one will feel dead water. Between the rapid water and the dead water there will be two "edges" where one can feel moderate flow. Any obstacle that causes moderate flow can provide a lie for salmon. A very good way to understand this better is to drift over a pool in a boat on a sunny day and see where the salmon are resting under conditions of moderate flow.

Since summer fish like moderate flow they are less likely to be in the deeper quiet water and will not stay in very fast water that has no current-breaking obstacles. One should not be fooled, however, by the *surface* speed of water. The water on the surface moves faster than the water beneath. The bed of the river itself acts as an obstacle to speed and therefore the narrowed tails of pools (where the water on the surface may be quite fast) will hold fish—more so if there are rocks or other obstacles in the tail.

This can be made clearer by some sketches of very typical situations.

Figure A shows a rock or boulder in a salmon stream. As we noted when we felt the water swirling around our boots, there are two "edges" or conditions of moderate flow trailing downstream from the rock, as marked by the dashed lines. These edges can be lies for salmon. How good they are depends on the size of the rock in relation to the depth of the water. As a rule a large submerged rock provides a better lie than a rock in shallower water. Rocks in shallow water tend to pile sand and gravel at their heads, so whether or not there will be a suitable lie just above this rock depends on how deep the water is. Of the two edges one may be better than the other, as

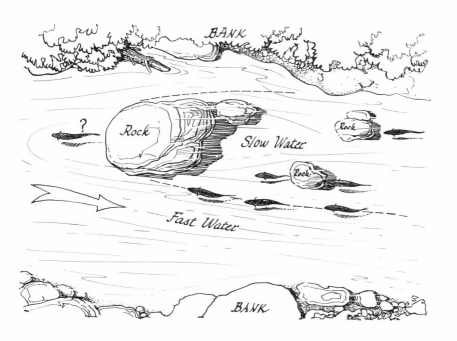

FIG. V-8-A

SALMON LIES NEAR A ROCK

determined by which offers more ideal flow and the best stream bed
conformation. Salmon may lie in the edge nearest the inshore bank
if the water is deep enough, but generally the best water is on the
offshore side.

Below this large boulder may be smaller rocks. Salmon may lie
in this "in between" water. Probably none will be in the water
immediately below the large rock because there the flow may be too
moderate.

A better lie is one where another big rock is immediately below
an upper one. In fact a combination of several rocks, as in Figure B,
may provide an ideal pool. Salmon will lie in such a place for the
same reason as in the preceding instance but, since the two or more
rocks provide more area of moderate flow, the place may harbor
more of them. The shoreward lines of moderate flow (marked "X")
may or may not be suitable for salmon, depending largely on the

107

MAR LODGE      DURHAM RANGER    SILVER WILKINSON

The patterns above were dressed by Hardy Brothers (P)


AKROYD      JOCK SCOTT      BRORA

The patterns above were dressed by Miss Megan Boyd (P)


**BLUE DOCTOR**
Dressed by
Mr. Colin Simpson (P)

**RED SANDY**
Dressed by
Mr. Colin Simpson (P)

**BLACK DOCTOR**
Dressed by
Mr. Belarmino Martinez (P)


**BLUE CHARM**
Dressed by
Mr. Colin Simpson (P)

**SILVER DOCTOR**
Dressed by
O. Mustad & Son (P)

**CARRON**
Dressed by
Mr. Geoffrey Bucknall (P)


**LOGIE**
Dressed by
Hardy Brothers (P)


**FIERY BROWN**
Dressed by
Mr. Colin Simpson (P)

**DUNKELD**
Dressed by
Mr. Alex Simpson (A)


PLATE II

Classic British Patterns

108

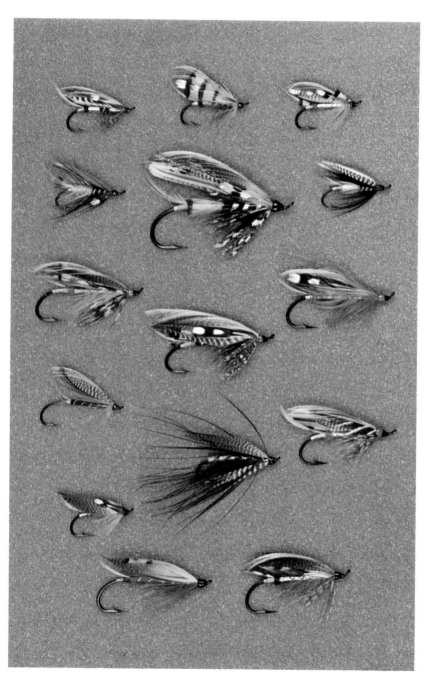

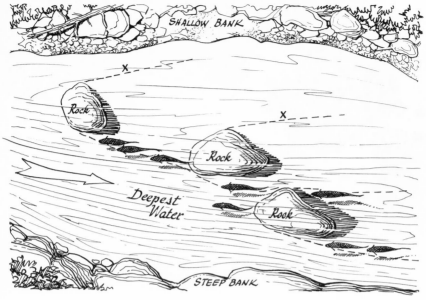

FIG. V-8-B

SALMON LIES NEAR A COMBINATION OF ROCKS

amount of depth and the relative desirability of the edges. Too many rocks or boulders may slow down the current so much that the position will hold no fish.

In fishing a wet fly on an edge lie it is better to present the fly just at the *inside* of the edge than to cast it well beyond it.

Salmon will not lie in eddies even if they seem to present an edge. If an angler hooks a fish in an eddy he may think that they stay there, but this evidently is not so. Very probably the fish has left his lie and has followed the fly into the eddy and has taken it there, rather than having been there in the first place.

On some rivers pools are made by one bar after another along the length of a large part of the river. A typical bar situation is shown in Figure C. The shallow water on the bar causes the fish to hesitate before going over it, so some may be nosed up in shallow water on the lip of the bar, and may take a fly there. In the shoal

109

FIG. V-8-C

SALMON LIES IN A POOL MADE BY A BAR

above the bar there may be little pockets (or depressions) in which salmon may lie. Pools made by bars often have rocks or boulders in the deeper water, and fish may lie in moderate flow areas below or near the rocks. The large rock to the right in the diagram indicates that fish may be in the edge of current on the channel side, but perhaps not on the right edge where it shelves into shallows.

Another situation frequently encountered is a ledge in a stream, which might look somewhat as in Figure D. If certain conditions exist, this could provide an ideal pool for salmon. The depth of water running over the ledge must be shoal. The water off the ledge must be of reasonable depth and afford a moderate flow. In cases resembling this salmon may lie in the deeper water right off the ledge and along it. They also may lie in the edges of moderate flow below rocks in the pool and possibly in the pockets just above them.

In some pools the flow of water will come from two different directions, as when a current flowing over a bar meets the main

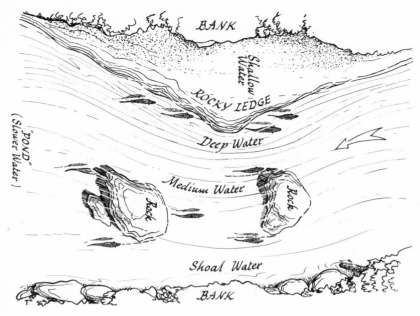

FIG. V-8-D

SALMON LIES NEAR A SUBMERGED LEDGE

current, as in Figure E, or when a side channel meets a main channel, as with a brook entering a stream, or a river rejoining itself below an island, as in Figure F. Regardless of how this happens, the places where the two currents meet provide "in between water" which is water of moderate flow and a good lie for salmon.

In Figure E, the deep current is entering the pool from the right while part of the same stream is running over a bar at the left. Where the two currents meet there is "in between water," indicated by the dashed line. This may be ideal.

In another similar instance, shown by Figure F, two currents join and form two places where there is "in between water." One is where the two currents meet, which is very similar to the preceding instance. In this case, this is also called "decision water" because salmon may pause there while deciding which of the two streams they will follow. The other place is where the water from the entering stream at the left swings outward around the bend of the

111

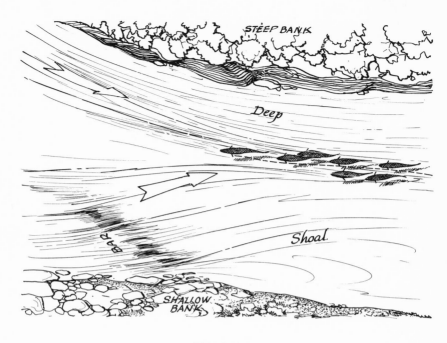

FIG. V-8-E

SALMON LIES WHERE TWO CURRENTS MEET

bank at the left. Here also is "in between water" because the strong current of the stream meets the water on the inside of the stream flow. If salmon travel up the inside they will lie on the edge made by the turn of the current toward the bank. Often this edge is rather close to the shore, so fishermen who do not understand the situation may wade where the fish are instead of fishing for them there. Fish will stay in all these places, perhaps for an extended time, if stream depth, rate of flow and other conditions are to their liking.

We should not be fooled by channels. Sometimes a side channel will be the *main* course the fish will take. If the flow in the main river becomes slow and that in the smaller channel remains brisk, the fish will run the smaller channel.

Salmon often will lie in the narrowed tail of a pool even when the surface water is very swift. Very often beneath this swift water there are submerged rocks which brake the fast water into moderate flow.

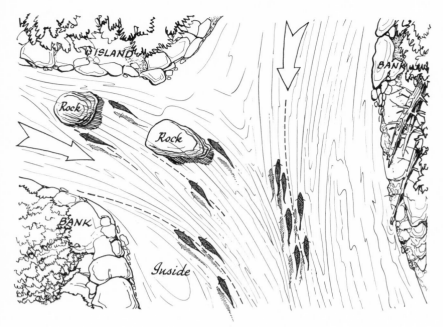

FIG. V-8-F

SALMON LIES NEAR AN ENTERING STREAM

Tails of pools which are at the heads of strong rapids may be ideal. We have learned not to judge current flow as it appears on the surface because it is what lies underneath that counts!

Any major obstruction on a salmon river, such as a small dam or even a counting pen, will impede the salmon's normal ascent of the stream. In such situations we should look for the first good holding pool *below* this spot. It is the habit of salmon, upon reaching such an obstruction, to turn back to the first good lie. Eventually they will pass the obstruction, but they seem reluctant to do so when they first encounter it.

If there is a good flow and depth of water along the shore of a stream and a protrusion is made into it by a rock, a large submerged log, or anything else that breaks into the flow, the downstream side of such a place may be a good lie for salmon. The obstruction makes an edge in the current, and fish will lie in the moderate water along such an edge.

113

There are stretches of water on many rivers that look hopeless. We are now speaking of long flat bars whereon there is a good uniform flow of water which, under normal conditions, may be about three or four feet deep. While there may be no rocks or boulders, the bottom of the river probably will have large pot-holes in the gravel and salmon often will lie in these protective holes. Even the rim of a big wagon wheel or a rubber tire lying on the bottom can provide a good lie wherein a salmon will rest. In the fall a burlap bag submerged in water of moderate flow and held in place flat on the bottom by four small rocks often will coax a salmon to rest over it, perhaps partly because this seems comfortable to him! If the salmon is caught, another one soon may take his place.

The lies of salmon change as the volume and depth of the river changes so, if the summer condition of moderate flow is lost, the places where salmon used to lie usually cease to be lies. We have seen fishermen doggedly fish a spot where they caught a salmon a week or so earlier, not realizing that the volume of the river had dropped and what once had been a lie is not one any more. Since the condition of moderate flow has been lost the angler is fishing barren water.

If there is a big rise of water and the lies where fish used to be have become obliterated, we should not overlook small back channels where, under normal conditions, there was little, if any, water. With the rise, such channels may have a moderate flow, and fish will run them.

In general, if there is a big rise of water, it is better to fish the shallower bars than to fish in the big pools.

One must learn to understand his river. On some rivers the fish will run primarily at night. On these rivers one has to fish over whatever salmon have stopped in the pool. There will be no more until possibly toward evening, when some fish will start to move.

On other rivers the fish may run all day long, regardless of whether the day is bright or dark. On these rivers a pool may be empty for a short or a long period and then suddenly fish will come in and all anglers are busy! When this happens and one is fishing a good pool it is better to stay there than to move from one pool to another.

We have seen that 70 degrees is a critical temperature. When warm weather and probably lower water make the stream's temperature reach or exceed 70 degrees, normal summer conditions change, and the salmon move into colder water, which is more to their liking. By colder water we usually mean "cold-water pools," which can be a stretch of water below a spring-fed brook, a spring sending cold water from the bank of the stream, a spring feeding into the river in any other way such as bubbling up from the river bed, or even a pool in the spring-fed brook itself.

Most of these pools have a rather slow current. If they have a narrow section where the water flows more swiftly, and if there are suitable lies in it, the fish will take best in this faster water. There may be faster water where a cold brook pours water into a pool. In such cases the salmon will work right up into this current and will take flies in such a place better than they will elsewhere.

Most cold-water pools contain rocks and other obstacles, and salmon should be found around these, but under these cold-water conditions they may be anywhere. It is now less a question of their finding conditions of moderate flow than it is of their finding the most available oxygen. If these conditions prevail in certain places, fish will lie in them even if they are so shallow that parts of their backs are out of water!

Many experienced anglers think that when salmon lie in cold-water pools this provides the most challenging angling because it requires more skill and thorough knowledge of various angling techniques in order to coax them to take a fly. Usually this is the most difficult area of salmon fishing. Unfortunately when salmon are in the shallow cold-water pools they are at the mercy of poachers, who too often jig for them there. If a pool has recently been jigged for salmon the remaining fish in it may be impossible to take with a fly.

We have discussed elsewhere in this book techniques for fishing in cold-water pools. We should add that, under such conditions, if there is a sudden rise of water and if the fish begin to move, the fishing can be fantastic!

A final condition in fishing for bright salmon has to do with their habits in the autumn, just before the close of the fishing season. Normal summer conditions may not prevail if the water becomes quite cold because, in addition to their usual lies, under conditions of moderate flow the salmon will also seek deeper, slower water. Thus, in the fall there may be more potential lies than there are in the summer. Fall fish may hold "lower down"—that is, in what are called "ponds," which are the deep, quiet stretches below the pools. They may work up into the pools from time to time, but such movements usually are in the early morning or in the late afternoon or evening.

Fall fish also will run even into small brooks, so it is possible then to catch salmon in a trout brook! Some pools that are poor for summer fishing may be productive in the fall, so perhaps pools could be classed in three ways: those which are good in the summer; those which are good in the fall: and those which are good at both times. The trick is for anglers to learn to understand the water they are fishing. The basics that apply to normal summer conditions also apply to those in the fall.

One who returns to the same stretch of river year after year should remember that large rivers which are not very deep may be affected by ice. Thus, lies may have changed and places which were hot spots a season ago may be hot spots no longer. Some pools may have been ruined, and good new ones may have been made. There may be good fishing in a place that formerly was no good. This may be a warning to people who are considering spending large sums of money to buy or to lease pools on such rivers.

## TIDAL WATER FISHING

Anglers always seem to have been of the opinion that Atlantic salmon would not take flies either in salt or in brackish water. The increasing number of fishermen on public streams induced a few of them to experiment with the idea of getting away from crowded waters and enjoying more sparsely populated areas. These few made the happy discovery that salmon would take flies in such places, flies even as small as 10's! In such waters there is no "fly only" rule, and adept fly handlers found to their surprise that flies could be as productive as big Dardevles or other forms of hardware.

In areas where public salmon streams are crowded this discovery has caused anglers to spread out, thus improving the fishing for all concerned. Flies that are productive on the upper stretches of any given river seem to be equally productive in tidewater; this includes even dry-flies. In North America we don't yet know how productive shrimp and grub imitations could be but there seems to be no reason why some of the British patterns described in this book shouldn't turn out to be killers.

Salmon rarely will be caught on all tide conditions, and the best time of the tide on one river doesn't mean that this is the best on others. The key to this depends on the presence of suitable "lies" where fish will congregate and rest for a while. These places may be in pools, near breakwaters, or other locations where depth and the speed of tidal flow is to their liking. A good "lie" at one time of the tide may be no good at another because the ebb and flow constantly changes conditions.

Thus, a good deal of experimentation is necessary to discover where the lies are and the time or times of the tide when they are occupied. Quite often local anglers are able to chart such knowledge, so the tip to visitors is to obtain information from someone who knows and who will be honest about it. There are tidal areas in some rivers where many good lies have been located. Some rivers have no fishable places at all.

## ADDITIONAL SUGGESTIONS

It is unnecessary to tell experienced stream fishermen that, when fighting fish as large as salmon, it is important for the angler to work his way below the fish whenever possible, so that the force of the stream is in the angler's favor, thus making the salmon fight the stream flow as well as the power of the rod.

When a salmon jumps we should try to remember to drop the rod-tip momentarily to give slack line so that the fish, while jumping, won't fall on a tight line and thus break loose. As soon as he returns to the water, raising the rod-tip again will resume tension. This is known as "bowing to the fish" and it is a technique or safety-measure used on all large jumping fish, such as Tarpon. Experienced fishermen usually can sense when a fish is about to jump, and can be ready for him.

Perhaps no comments are needed about landing salmon, although I have seen guides, who jab nets at fish and who try to net them before they are ready, who could use a comment or two. The angler is in charge of his fish, and if he has reason to consider his help incompetent, he should tactfully instruct whoever is helping him on the landing procedure he desires. Experienced guides know how to rest the net on the bottom, and experienced anglers know how to lead the exhausted salmon over it so that, when the fish or at least the forward half of it is over the net, the helper only needs to quietly lift it to get the fish safely in the bag. One would think that all guides (or ghillies, as they are termed in the British Isles) would know this, but unfortunately some of the guides foisted off on Americans are local men in need of employment who seem to take pride in remaining abysmally ignorant about catching salmon.

When possible, most of us like to beach our fish (to "grass" them is a term used overseas). When the salmon or grilse is so tired that he has difficulty remaining upright, the angler selects a smooth spot on the beach and leads the fish to it. Then, by slowly walking backward under as much tension as seems reasonable, he will cause the flopping fish to work himself onto land. Once there with line reeled in about to the leader butt, the angler can grab the salmon around his body just above the tail and either lift him or push him to safety.

An alternative to netting, when beaching is impractical, is the use of a tailer, which is a device employing a wire noose which can be slipped over the salmon's tail and triggered to snap the noose tightly around it. Gaffs, even if allowable, should be avoided except where they have to be used.

## TRACE YOUR TROPHY!

After a large salmon is caught we may not want to have it mounted, but we might like to keep a record of its shape and size. To make a memento of the occasion lay the fish on a section from a roll of wrapping paper and carefully trace around it with a long pencil. If the paper becomes slimy, the outline can be traced on another paper. Then, with the fish in view, draw in parts such as

FIG. V-9

THE AUTHOR SHOWS ONE OF HIS TRACINGS

gills, eyes, mouth structure, fin rays, etc., making the tracing in color, in pencil, or in ink as elaborately as desired. Letter in under the drawing the weight, where and when caught and by whom, fly used, and other data. Roll up the tracing and keep it for a souvenir. Few people realize how big a large salmon really is. An accurate drawing provides interest for many years to come!

## ON CARRYING SALMON

If salmon are to be kept in best condition they should not be carried by the gills. In his book, Mr. Kelson shows a good way, still used to hand-carry big fish. All one needs is a suitable length of

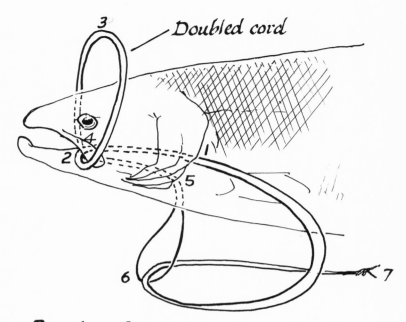

**Doubled cord**

1 Pass looped end of doubled cord through gill.
2 Out corner of near side of mouth at 2.
3-4 Over nose 3- and in far corner of mouth at 4.
5-6 Out far gill cover at 5 - form loop at 6.
7 Other doubled end of cord is passed through
  this loop and after forming loop around
  tail - pull taut.

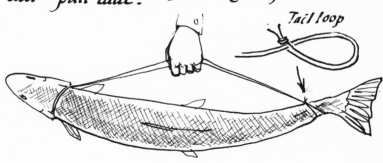

Tail loop

FIG. V-10

A WAY TO CARRY A LARGE SALMON

120

strong cord (like parachute cord) with the two ends tied together to form a loop. One doubled end is passed under the gill-cover, then out of the mouth at the lower corner, over the nose, and in at the mouth at the opposite corner and under the opposite gill. The other doubled end of the cord is then passed up through this end, under gills, and after a loop is formed at the other end, it is looped around the tail and pulled taut. This way of stringing a large salmon makes it easy to carry without being dragged on the ground.

It is always handy to carry one or more such cords. Another method is to loop the cord around the tail (only) as above and perhaps to make a half-hitch around the tail afterward. The salmon then can be carried on a stick or pole. Two fish can be so looped, one on each end of the doubled cord, and carried together.

Since salmon are not fatty fish it does no good to open and clean them when they are caught. This can wait until they are being prepared for the table.

# VI

# Dry-Flies and
# Low-Water Tricks

Dry-fly fishing for salmon began to be a practical method in the early 1920's mainly through the pioneering efforts of inquiring American anglers such as Colonel Ambrose Monell, George M. L. La Branche and Edward R. Hewitt. The bivisibles and other heavily palmered flies they used then have largely been supplanted by more efficient and more productive floaters, and the techniques for dry-fly fishing have been improved so much that, if they were living today, these experts would have to restudy the subject in order to catch up!

Dry-fly fishing for salmon evolved from dry-fly fishing for trout, which largely means casting the fly upstream and across. It is not very sportsmanlike to use this method when the man wading behind the dry-fly man is fishing a wet-fly downstream. On public waters, or other waters where many rods are fishing, the two conflicting methods cause difficulties.

Partly for this reason anglers experimented with new dry-fly methods and reaped an unforeseen bonus or two. If the dry-fly is fished across and downstream, with a reasonable amount of slack line shot through the guides, the fly will float freely for a time while the slack line is being used up. Of course during the float the line can be mended as need be.

When fishing upstream and across the slack line is being increased but, when fishing downstream and across, it is being decreased. When fishing downstream and across with a wet-fly in a reasonable flow we know it is not necessary to set the hook because the line is sufficiently tight so that this is done for us. Therefore in fishing downstream and across with the dry-fly the question of when one should set the hook has been answered. When fishing by this method it is not necessary to set the hook at all because, in approximating wet-fly conditions by removing excess slack line, the fish will set the hook himself. Slack line is being used up during the float and all that is necessary on the strike is to pull out whatever remains of it, if any.

A second bonus when using this method is that, when fishing some of the modern dry-flies which have tails, such as the Wulff patterns, the *Rat Face*, the *Irresistible* and others, it is much easier to cause the fly to float tail first downstream. This is the most effective way to fish this type of fly because the salmon takes it hook-end first, and he should be hooked solidly!

A frequently used method is the "curved" or "loop" cast which is made with the rod held almost horizontally. After a false cast or two to gauge distance the fly is directed a few feet beyond the chosen point and, just before it lights, the angler pulls back on the rod slightly. Since any action given to the rod-tip while the fly is in the air has an effect upon the behavior of the line and the fly, this tactic of pulling the rod back will throw the fly off-course and cause it to drop downstream on an upstream curved line. This has an advantage if the fly is directed to a slower current than the midstream current, and salmon often lie in the slower current beside the faster one. The faster current will use up the upstream curve of the line, meanwhile allowing the fly a free float.

After casting the dry-fly by whatever means is employed the angler lowers the rod to the horizontal and keeps it pointing toward the fly. This provides maximum float and also makes it possible for the angler to raise the rod slightly to tighten on the fish and set the

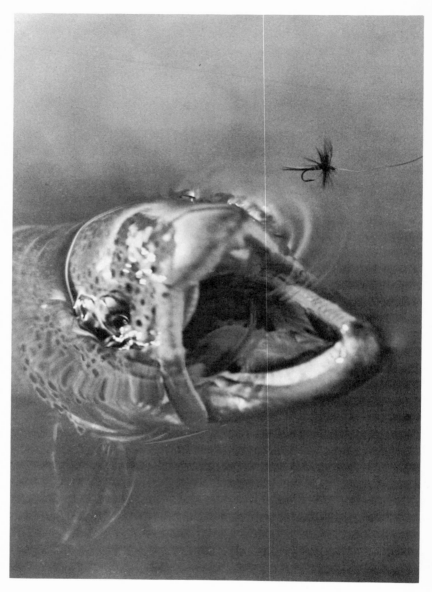

(*W. Meinel*)

Fig. VI-1

A RISE FOR A DRY FLY : SUCKING IT IN!

124

hook without causing the rod to be too near the vertical where there would be loss of control. After casting the dry-fly and lowering the rod the angler usually pulls it backward a foot or so before the fly lands. This provides a wavy effect in the loose line and leader on the water, which allows a longer float. If, during the float, a belly starts to come into the line on the water, it can be partially reduced by mending the line——that is, by lifting part of it and flipping it upstream, meanwhile perhaps letting out a little more slack.

Another tactic in obtaining a longer float is to use a tippet section on the leader which is considerably longer than what would be used in wet-fly fishing. This length is whatever the angler wants it to be, and whatever length he can handle easily, usually two or three feet but sometimes as many as six. Since this length causes the improperly tapered tip section to fall in a wavy form or in coils it provides a longer float while the current straightens it out. Some anglers approve of this; others don't. Since salmon are not very gut-shy, the strongest tippet section can be used which can be handled properly and which the size of fly can accommodate.

Another trick that La Branche and his cronies didn't know about is called the "Half and Half," which is casting a bug-type floating fly with a decided drag. Cast the fly across stream and allow the current to put a bag in the line. This causes the fly to whip, to travel at high speed, making a wake. It is a tactic usually new to salmon, and it frequently incites one to chase the fly and to grab it solidly while it is dragging. We have seen that a dragging fly is usually the wrong way to fish but, with a large and bushy dry-fly (and sometimes with a streamer), this can be very effective. It disproves the often-held theory that a dragging fly won't take fish!

When is it most productive to change from wet-fly fishing to dry-fly fishing? If the water is not very cold, very high or very discolored, one answer is that the dry fly is productive under a wider range of conditions than most of us might think. Some recommend fishing a dry-fly when the water in the body of the river is warmer than the air but, if anyone considers this a rule, he should consider it a rule to be broken.

When the mainstream of the river becomes warm (and thus usually low) we have seen that salmon move to cold-water pools

Fig. VI-2

A ROLLING SALMON

below cold-water brooks in the summer, or in to the tails of pools in the fall. This is an ideal time for the dry-fly, but many of us think that the time to use the dry-fly is under any reasonably warm and low-water conditions especially when we are not having much luck with wets. Then, one can fish the dry-fly in the orthodox manner and, if this doesn't work, he can try some tricks——tricks that often take fish when people who don't use them remain fishless.

If one raises a fish one time or more to a dry-fly and the fish doesn't take, or if one knows where a fish is that can't be made to rise, a trick is to cast the fly above and beyond the fish in such a way that the fly can be drowned by pulling it under the water. The fly should be pulled underwater so that it moves right in front of the salmon's snout. Many a fish has been taken by this method when other techniques have failed.

The dry-fly principle that the fly must float right over the fish's head is not true when applied to salmon. If the fly is cast over his head and he doesn't come for it the trick then is to cast above and beyond, allowing the fly to float only a very short distance. The fly then is picked up and cast back, allowed to float briefly; and the process is repeated, again and again if necessary. Some anglers do this in a very rhythmic manner, so that perhaps the salmon anticipates the moment when the fly will arrive again over his cone of vision. Part of the principle is not to let the fish see the fly too long at any one time, and casting in front of and a bit beyond him rather than directly over him sometimes is referred to as "taking him off his lie." One side may be tried and then the other. It is a principle similar to that which George La Branche applied to Brown Trout, that of "making a hatch," and very often the fish will come for the fly with an exciting surge!

Another trick is to skitter the fly, one also discussed under wet-fly fishing but, this time, using a large dry one. We can go it blind if we don't know where the fish are, by using it anywhere where salmon are presumed to lie. We can do it better if we can see the fish. In this case the fly is cast on a tight line a few feet beyond and ahead of the lie of the salmon. It is immediately pulled into a skittering action with a wake so that it passes directly in front of the salmon. Another method when the location of fish isn't known is to cast it across stream and immediately to pull it fast and steadily in with a speed that leaves a wake on the water.

While orthodox patterns in the larger sizes such as the *Wulffs*, *Irresistible* and *Rat Face* are good for these purposes, several special patterns are made specifically for them. François de B. Gourdeau's *Bottlewasher* is one, and its counterpart in hair-body is another called the *Bomber*. Lew Butterfield's *Whiskers* will do the job, and so will Harry Darbee's *Skater*. These are enough and, if this book should show many more, it merely would confound the issue. If one or two don't work by any of these various methods, it's time to go in and enjoy the happy hour.

These big and bushy flies are rather hard to sink. They will float jauntily on strong currents and can be dried quickly by a false cast or two. Using a waterproofing dressing to make them float longer is an individual decision that may not be a good one because, after letting them float for a while, we may want them to sink so we can fish the remainder of the cast wet. The *Bomber* often is used this way. Drift it or skitter it over the salmon. If they don't respond, work it in front of them again at a lower level!

Frequently salmon will come to these big floaters but won't take them.·After resting the fish for a few minutes, try him again in the same way. If this doesn't work, at least we have located and interested the fish (which perhaps we couldn't have done by usual methods) and probably we can hook him by casting for him again after changing to a smaller dry-fly or to a wet-fly. The maxim is that, if we can cause the fish to show interest, we should be able to catch him. Sometimes this requires many casts and several changes of flies.

While salmon frequently take the big, bushy flies, the big ones often are used as "locators." They make a salmon show his position. When whatever fly is used makes him show his position, the usual procedure is, if a large dry-fly is used, to try to tempt him with a smaller one, then perhaps with a wet fly, or by using one of the other methods we have discussed. If the fly that tempts him is a wet-fly, it is worthwhile to switch to a dry one. Dry-flies are good under a broad range of conditions, but especially when a fish has been located. Since one can cover more water faster with a wet-fly, many anglers use it initially, switching to the dry-fly when the position of a fish is known. Salmon often will take very small flies. Don't give up trying to tempt a good fish until the smallest sizes have been tried.

When should we use a dark fly, and when a bright one? Older books have indicated that on very bright days all colors are very visible, and a light fly may be as good as any. They have said that when skies are overcast or if the water has an oily, glistening look, a dark fly should be more visible, probably a nearly black one.

In North America the expert consensus is that this question should not be oversimplified. On some rivers, for example, one particular pattern of dry-fly seems to work best regardless of whether the day is dark or bright or whether it be in the morning or evening. Very large dry-flies work better on some rivers than on others. At the same time on the same river large flies may be more effective than smaller ones, and it seems that certain types of dry-flies will work better one year than another. There seem to be no fixed answers. One has to size up not only the river he is fishing but also what appears to be the specific taste of the fish at the time. For example, a *White Wulff* may be the best all-around fly for a given river under almost any dry-fly conditions. On another river the same may be true of the *Rat-Faced MacDougall* or the *Irresistible*. It is also true that on the same river any number of patterns will work well at various times. This is one of the fascinating things about dry-fly fishing. While the factors of fly selection may be complex, they generally can be solved. Then, the reward is all the more enjoyable.

There are practical aspects to be considered, however. Toward evening it is more sensible to fish a fly the fisherman can see and therefore can fish it properly, than to use a dark fly which theoretically should be better but which he can't see as well. For example, many, many fish have been caught close to dark on the *White Wulff*.

Experimentation always is in order. Father Smith, an acknowledged expert as well as a practical experimenter, ties an all-yellow fly in the Wulff manner. He has used it on New Brunswick's Miramichi, on Maine's Narraguagus and on many other rivers, and reports that on some occasions when salmon are in the rapids and under many other conditions this is the only fly the fish would take.

This reminds me that, while preparing this book, many people submitted flies with the recommendation that "this one took fish when everything else had failed." Inspection of these remarkable "creations" indicated that nearly all of them were inconsequential "bastards" which probably were used during a sudden lucky period when the flies formerly tried would have done as well, or even better. Sensible experimentation, however, often does get results!

Workable sizes of dry-flies vary a great deal. Salmon often will show for a big, bushy, palmered fly tied on a long-shanked number 2 streamer hook (like the *Gourdeau's Bottlewasher*). Salmon often will take a floating *Bomber* tied on a number 2 black Japanned low-water hook. However, the sizes used most often are numbers 4, 6 and 8, and there again a dry-fly tied on a short-shanked number 4 hook may in overall size be smaller than one tied on a number 6 regular-shanked hook.

Finally, there are occasions when salmon will refuse to come to anything but very small and lightly dressed dry flies such as numbers 12 and 14. Of course fewer fish are hooked and landed when using these very small sizes, but it is more fun to use them when necessary than to get no strikes at all.

In reading the older books, mainly by British anglers, these authors seem to have come up with some very pat answers (such as as the "bright fly—bright day and the dark fly—dark day" theory). Many of us think that some of these theories are misleading and should be disregarded. This may not answer the unanswerable question, but it seems to make sense to a great many very successful anglers.

Some of the principles, such as dragging a dry-fly for salmon, may be surprising or even upsetting to the dry-fly purist who usually fishes for trout. Perhaps the answer is that two different types of techniques are involved, and we have noted that trout fishermen going for salmon must forget some of the things they learned while fishing for trout. In trout fishing, "matching the hatch" is a time-honored precept. In salmon fishing, this matching business should be forgotten. All that seems to be needed is a vague representation of something that will interest a salmon because it seems to be alive or because it is something acting differently from anything he ever has seen before.

There are times when nothing seems to work. A trick of last resort is to try the kind of popping bug ordinarily used for bass. The late Ray Bergman (who before his retirement was fishing editor of *Outdoor Life* magazine) reported that on an occasion when no one could catch anything he tried a popping bug and popped it on the surface over a spot where he could see a salmon. He related that, after refusing everything else, the salmon took the bug. If this indicates anything it may point up the fact that, when the going is tough, the name of the game is *experimentation!*

# V I I Atlantic Salmon Fishing in North America

Until late in the eighteenth century most of the large, unobstructed streams along the North Atlantic from Ungava Bay in Labrador to the Hudson River in New York State abounded with Atlantic salmon. The ravages of dams, pollution and over-fishing so greatly decimated the salmon stocks that no salmon worth mentioning now exist any-where except in the State of Maine. While efforts are being discussed to restore Atlantic salmon fishing in some of the other New England states, the battles with obstructions and pollution have just begun and constructive results, if any, are more talk than tangibility.

Salmon fishermen often dream of trying new rivers in new places. Where shall we go—to Maine, New Brunswick, Nova Scotia, Quebec, Newfoundland or to Labrador? What flies and other tackle should we take; what can we expect of the fishing; where should we go; and what will we find when we get there? Let's take a quick trip through these areas starting, quite logically, in Maine, a state which is seriously doing something about improving the sport of fly-fishing for salmon.

131

FIG. VII-1

THE NARRAGUAGUS RIVER IS ONE OF MAINE'S
REHABILITATED ATLANTIC SALMON STREAMS

## MAINE

Veining outward to the coast, several Atlantic salmon rivers can can be located on maps between the city of Bath and the New Brunswick border. The principal ones are the Sheepscott, Narragua-gus, Pleasant, Machias, and finally the Dennys.

The restoration of salmon fishing in Maine is a tribute to the state's officials and scientists, who know on which side the public's bread is buttered. Very fortunately it is not on the side of the com-mercial fishermen, who nevertheless profit from the program. The State of Maine realizes what officials in provinces to the north find convenient to ignore: that a salmon caught by a visiting angler can be worth hundreds of dollars to the local people in money spent locally by visiting sportsmen. It realizes, on the other hand, that one taken commercially brings only a tiny fraction of that amount, and that not to the people generally, but only to the few who catch and ship it. For this reason, commercial fishing for Atlantic salmon is radically restricted. The salmon is regarded as a valuable sport-fish and of course should be so regarded, to a much greater degree, every-where else.

This restoration program was started in 1948 by the appointment of a Commission to supervise it. The Commission first concentrated on the most easily reclaimable rivers, which are the five mentioned. Dams which impeded migrations of salmon were torn down. Strict anti-pollution measures were set and enforced. Water control facilities were built to insure steady stream flow in times of drought. Hatcheries were built to provide constant plantings of smolts with the hope that many of them would return to their rehabilitated rivers as mature fish.

Of course all this is a continuing process, but very fortunately steady improvement is being noted. Several hundred adult fish return to these rivers every year and, somewhat dependent upon rainfall from year to year, the number on the average is increasing.

In Maine, a fishing license costs very little, and the angler need not hire a guide. Tactful conversations with friendly local anglers can brief visitors on where the action is. Black salmon fishing is permitted in the early spring. Only unweighted flies with single hooks are allowed. Rods eight and a half or nine feet long are appropriate. Favorite flies are simple hair-wings adapted from the *Black Bear* such as the *Belfast Killer*, also the *Cosseboom*, and the *Butt* patterns in sizes between 2 and 8 (depending on water conditions). The dry-flies and fishing methods described in this book can be very successful during low-water periods. We have discussed tidal water fishing for salmon, and this can be enjoyed on some of the rivers. In tidewater, double hooks are permitted, and flies can be weighted. Maine salmon average from medium to fairly large size. Fish of between 15 and 20 pounds are usual, and occasionally larger ones are caught.

Perhaps one should not try to forecast the times when the best salmon runs occur but, depending on stream flow and other factors, the fishing normally is good on the Dennys, East Machias and Narraguagus Rivers from mid-May through the first two weeks in June. The Machias River's best runs usually extend from late June through the first two weeks of July, with smaller runs in the fall. The Sheepscott provides a small run from early July through the remainder of the fishing season, which currently opens to angling on April 1 (the Dennys opens May 1) and closes on October 15. Lack of rain may hold salmon in the tidal areas, but they can be fished for there.

The future of the Maine salmon fishery may prove to be better than the present. The vast Penobscot River system, which once abounded with salmon, is being reclaimed. As this was written, all but one dam have been removed or installed with fishways, and pollution is gradually being decreased. On this river, in the city of Bangor where Hiram L. Leonard once made his famous fly-rods, is the famous Bangor Salmon Pool, just above the Bangor Dam. This was a famous salmon fishing spot at the turn of the last century, and those who read this in later years may find it to be so again.

Salmon fishing in Maine offers various fringe benefits which should be remembered especially if one arrives at the wrong time. Motels, hotels, guest-houses and camping spots are abundant and provide comfortable bases for operations. The rugged coast dotted by quaint towns is fun to explore, and excellent seafood is an added inducement. Fresh-water fishing abounds in Maine for bass, trout, land-locked salmon and other species, some of this in remote wilderness regions. Salt-water fishing for a wide variety of fish is nearly always available, and Striped Bass are a prime favorite.

Since Maine abuts New Brunswick and is convenient to Nova Scotia either by road or ferry, salmon fishing trips can be extended to those areas if desired.

### NOVA SCOTIA

Under ordinary conditions in salmon fishing one gets about what he pays for. What he pays can be as much as several thousand dollars a week in a relatively few places, more reasonable amounts usually; and sometimes one can enjoy excellent fishing on a very low budget. The size and abundance of the fish, the degree of exclusiveness and comfort of the location, and regional fees for guides, beats and other such requirements help to decide the cost.

In Nova Scotia the cost is quite reasonable. The license fee is low; no guides are necessary; the waters are open; and living costs are moderate. Perhaps there may be too many fishermen on the streams when the salmon are running and perhaps some of the local citizens may monopolize the best spots on the pools, but those are the chances one has to take when he wants to fish reasonably.

There are about thirty salmon rivers in Nova Scotia. Most are small rivers which can be waded. These include such famous ones as the Medway, St. Mary's and the Margaree. The salmon average between ten and fifteen pounds, but some of them are in the twenty- to thirty-pound class and bigger ones occasionally are taken. Along with the salmon are many grilse, but these provide good sport with eight- to nine-foot rods, which are adequate even for the larger fish.

There are spring and fall runs of salmon, with good fishing in June and usually better action in September. In June many of the rivers have runs of large sea-trout, which add to the fun.

Since anglers in Nova Scotia cling to old traditions more than those in some other places, British classic feather-wing patterns are used quite often, but their use declines as the efficiency of the simpler patterns becomes better known. These classics include *Thunder and*

*Lightning, Black Dose, Silver Grey, Jock Scott, Black Fairy, Brown Fairy* and the *Durham Ranger,* although not necessarily in the order named.

Year by year the simple hair-wings become more and more popular. These include several of the Quebec patterns, including the *Rusty Rat, Silver Rat* and *Cosseboom.* One often sees the *Ross Special* and the *Black Bomber.* Popular dry-flies include the *Wulff* patterns (especially the white one), *Irresistible, Rat-Faced MacDougall* and *MacIntosh.* We have also seen why a few streamers or bucktails sometimes are needed to get action. Two good ones are the *Herb Johnson Special* and the *Mickey Finn.*

The usual hook sizes are 6 and 8. When waters are high the more visible 2's and 4's should do better. During spate conditions the best sizes may be as large as 2/0. Then, Harry Darbee's *Spate Fly,* which was originated for these waters, should do well.

Nova Scotia has so many inns, motels and other accommodations that finding a place to stay should present no difficulty even if the trip is taken on the spur of the moment. The Nova Scotia Travel Bureau in Halifax publishes lists of these, together with maps, booklets and other information. The Margaree Salmon Association has a small angling museum at Margaree Harbor, on Cape Breton Island, which is well worth visiting.

Maps indicate that in 1967 there were 327 trap nets, 320 gill nets and 16 drift nets surrounding the small peninsula of Nova Scotia and its Cape Breton Island, or a total of 663 places where salmon could trap themselves before reaching their rivers. Although this figures to only about one net for every two miles of coastline it should be remembered that the nets are placed in or near the estuaries of the rivers and in other places which are directly in the migratory routes of salmon. They are not placed along the coast in positions where salmon usually do not travel. It is also commented that, even though rivers are well patrolled, there is always a problem with illegal netting and poaching with spears, jigs and other such devices.

Paradoxically, the people of Nova Scotia seek and need the tourist dollars which visiting anglers could provide in much greater abundance in return for better fishing. Of course, the commercial fishermen of Nova Scotia need to make a living but certainly they and everyone else there would profit vastly more if better sport fishing were insured, even at the expense of buying many netting rights and thus reducing the commercial exportation of Atlantic salmon. Unfortunately, this "penny-wise and pound-foolish" attitude is not peculiar to the good people of Nova Scotia. It is an international malfunction of elementary economics which anglers should vociferously call to the attention of everyone who has anything to do with it.

## NEW BRUNSWICK

Although there are other famous salmon rivers in New Brunswick the one with the most stretches open to the public is the Miramichi, and it is the river most often visited by Americans. It is actually a giant river system, composed of the main river, which is the Southwest Miramichi, and many tributaries including the Northwest Miramichi, the Little Southwest Miramichi, the Cains, Bartholomew, Dungarvon, Renous, and Sevogle (the latter containing little, if any, public water). All empty into Miramichi Bay, near the city of Newcastle. Perhaps the best way to learn what is public (crown) water and what isn't is to study the map mentioned in the footnote on page 14.

While this map shows vast stretches as public water, this is not accurate, because many fishing camps and individuals own many of the pools and they are rather strict with visitors who fish them without permission. There are, however, many pools and stretches available to the public, and some of these are among the best on the river. Owners or lessees of private waters often allow others to fish them and after a considerate angler knows his way around a bit a telephone call or two or a personal visit is all that is needed to obtain permission to fish as many spots as desired. Sometimes these friendly liaisons can be extended almost indefinitely!

If one is starting from scratch, so to speak, perhaps the best idea is to write the New Brunswick Department of Lands and Mines (Fish and Wildlife Branch) in Fredericton for a list of fishing camps. After hearing from a few of these one can be selected. During the trip a little browsing around should indicate whether or not it is the most acceptable one and, from there on, more permanent relations can be established for future years. Fishing camps on the Miramichi are

Fig. VII-2

THE MIRAMICHI RIVER AT BLISSFIELD, NEW BRUNSWICK
The near shore is public (crown) water and sometimes is crowded. The water along the far shore is privately owned.

not overly expensive, as such things go. The trick is to find one having access to good pools and compatible with our way of doing things.

New Brunswick law says that licensed non-resident anglers must be accompanied by a licensed guide but, when wading or fishing from the shore, a party of as many as three people can all employ the same guide. Qualifications for a guide's license in New Brunswick are not very strict and depend mainly upon casual proof that the guide is still breathing. While some of the guides are very efficient,

138

by and large they are an ignorant bunch who seem to glory in knowing as little as possible about salmon fishing. To the accomplished angler, this makes little or no difference if the guide is willing to carry equipment the sport doesn't want to lug around, and if he isn't sound asleep on the beach when a salmon needs to be netted. But to the tyro this can present a problem, a problem we hope this book will help to solve. Anyway, the guide should be able to take his sports to the water assigned by the fishing camp, or to show them other good places to fish. If he can do this and pole a boat without tipping it over, that is about all that can be expected.

The Miramichi is a friendly river, easy to wade in most places, and usually with a solid gravel bottom containing very few rocks. It meanders through wilderness stretches and through farmlands dotted with small homes, all providing scenery that adds greatly to the fun of fishing.

On most of the rivers the fishing season starts on May 15 and extends to the end of September, some of the rivers remaining open as long as a month later. As this was written spring salmon (black salmon or "kelts") can be fished between April 15 and May 15, but this period may be shortened.

The best bright salmon fishing starts after the first of July. Currently the law says that commercial fishermen must raise their nets during the first two weeks in July and must stop netting for the season after September 1. Thus the best time for summer fishing should be the last two weeks in July. Usually there is a slump in August and good fishing in September. This normally increases in tempo until the close of the season.

The Miramichi is known as a grilse river because, on the average, one takes nine or ten grilse for every salmon. However, when the fishing is good most anglers consider this to be an advantage because one may catch as many salmon in the Miramichi as on many other rivers with the added inducement also of hooking grilse. The grilse are strong, lively fish usually averaging four pounds or better, and they can put on an exciting display of aerial acrobatics. When the grilse are running, light fly rods are in order and, if one doesn't mind risking the loss of a fish or two, it is fun to see how light one can go. Salmon in the Miramichi don't run very large, usually in the vicinity of ten to fifteen pounds. However, once in a while a really big one is hooked, and many in the thirty-pound class have been caught.

The most productive flies on most stretches of the Miramichi are the simple *Butt* hair-wings in sizes between 4 and 8. These include the black bodied, winged and hackled flies with butts (usually fluorescent) in yellow, orange, red and green, with green the most popular. A squirrel tail winged red-butted one does well, and the (green) *Cosseboom* is a perennial favorite. Every fly box should include a few *Butterflies* (*Ingalls' Butterfly*), fished as described in the text.

The most popular dry-flies are the *Wulff* patterns (especially the *White Wulff*), the *Rat-Faced MacDougall* and the clipped deer hair *Bombers* (also fished as described in the text). These can be alternated with the *Whiskers*, which many fishermen use almost exclusively. Flies as small as 10's and even 12's are used during low-water conditions. Also, a bucktail in size 2 or 4 such as the *Herb Johnson Special* is excellent for high water and as a "change of pace" fly.

A man who plays baseball better than almost anybody and who is equally accomplished as an angler is Ted Williams, whose signature also is a guarantee of excellence for Sears & Roebuck sporting goods. His favorite river is the Miramichi, where he has a camp and owns some water in the vicinity of Blackville. I asked him what flies he preferred and was a bit surprised to have him say he used some of the British classics occasionally. "I definitely like a *Black Dose* over a *Jock Scott* and a *Dusty Miller* over a *Silver Grey*," he said. "I like a *Silver Rat* much better than a *Rusty Rat*, but my favorite salmon fly is what they call a *Conrad*, with a fluorescent green butt." (This is the one first mentioned above.) He added, "My favorite size is a 7—anything smaller than an 8. I like double hooks because I feel that they lead better. My leaders are tapered to 7 or 8 pounds test, and I use an eight-and-a-half-foot rod for all the salmon fishing I do on the Miramichi. However, I can well understand using bigger, more powerful rods when the river conditions, fish and fly necessitate heavier equipment."

Once I watched Ted hook and land a large salmon in Swinging Bridge Pool, and the way he did it proved conclusively that he knows exactly what he is talking about!

Fig. VII-3

A BIG ONE ON THE MATANE

141

## QUEBEC

The beautiful Province of Quebec offers visiting salmon anglers almost any variety of fishing desired, from the very expensive to the least; from boisterous, brawling rivers to placid wadeable ones; from fishing near roads and civilization to seeking the big ones in the remoteness of forested wilderness stretches. Here, as in most other regions, the most successful anglers are the ones who know their tackle and who have done their homework, because big salmon are not as abundant as they used to be and often require a degree of skill and knowledge for their taking.

A favorite river which is kinder to the angler's pocketbook than most others is the famous Matane, which people from the States find most convenient to reach by driving north through the town of Matapedia on Route 6 to the village of Amqui and from there down the river to the city of Matane. After leaving Amqui and crossing the bridge over the river one sees signs on the right pointing to Matane Park, a reservation where camping is allowed and where twenty-eight marked pools are reachable from the road which borders about twenty miles of the river. Each pool is marked by a neat little sign bearing in French the word "Fosse" and the number of the pool. The one marked "Fosse 65", for example, points to pool number 65. Maps of the river showing its numbered pools are available without charge from the Park Service in New Carlisle, Quebec.

On arrival at the river one usually drives downstream to Matane, perhaps to seek accommodations or provisions but usually to find out how many salmon are in the river. Near the bridge going into the city there is a counting pen where salmon running upriver are tabulated. A government office nearby provides the daily tally. Since there are eighty-three pools in the stretches of the river which are open to fishing, if the tally says there are, for example, a thousand salmon in the river there would be an average of about a dozen in each pool. Since, in fact, some pools may be barren or nearly so and others may contain an abundance of salmon, the trick obviously is to find the good ones on which there are few, if any, fishermen.

A favorite pastime is to relax on a high bank and watch others fishing a pool. The salmon often can be seen, and the methods being used by the fishermen are subject to interesting debate. All too often, it seems, the fishermen use the same method over and over without trying some of the many different tricks they should know and use. After failing to raise a fish they finally give up. Then someone else wades in and, using a different method, succeeds in hooking a salmon.

Nine pools upriver from the city of Matane are open to licensed anglers without charge. A daily permit (available from the Park Service or locally) is required for the others. The cost (as of 1970) is four dollars for Canadian residents and ten dollars for non-residents, a daily fee usually considered well worth the improved fishing it helps to pay for. (Costs of daily permits are the same on all rivers unless otherwise stated.)

The best fishing on the Matane usually is from the latter part of June through the month of July, mainly because there are larger fish in the river at that time. Later on there are runs of grilse, and some anglers prefer later fishing for that reason.

The Park Service publishes maps and other information on the rivers, or those parts of them which it controls. Basic data on these (traveling on Route 6 clockwise around the Gaspé) is as follows:

*Matane River*

In addition to the preceding comments, it should be added that there is no restriction on the number of rods, and that guides are available although not necessary.

*Cap Chat River*

This can be fished on daily permit. There are seven beats which give each rod approximately five pools. One can fish the river by wading, and guides and canoes are available.

*Saint Anne River*

Here, each of three stretches is handled differently. There are five beats on the lower part of the river which can be fished on daily permit. This stretch is wadeable, and guides and canoes can be hired. The river flows through the beautiful Gaspé Park, described previously. There is a comfortable hotel in the Park (also a campsite) and two beats are reserved for guests on daily permit. The canoe trip down the river is well worth the investment because one travels through rough water in the wilderness and can fish many pools on the day-long trip down. Only two boats are allowed on the river each day, each accommodating one rod and being handled by two guides who pole down the rough stretches, one man in the bow and the other in the stern. This costs about $55 per day, usually on a weekly basis.

*Dartmouth River (near Corteral)*

Five rods may fish on daily permit.

*St. Jean River*

There are three beats on the lower part of the river, with two pools for each, fished on daily permit. This part of the river is wade-able. In addition, four rods who reside at the lodge on the river can arrange for fishing by the week at a cost of $85 per day (in 1970) including all expenses.

*Port Daniel River*

This is limited to two rods per day on daily permit, and the river can be waded.

*Little Cascapedia River*

Here, four rods residing on the river at Camp Melançon can fish by the week at an all-inclusive cost of $60 per day. In addition to salmon there is excellent sea-trout (Square-tail, or " Brook Trout ") fishing.

*Matapedia River*

Each of the four sections is handled differently. The Bridge Pool in the city of Matapedia accommodates two rods on daily permit, but this is reserved for residents of the Province. The St. Alexis section (four miles west of Matapedia) can be waded on daily permit with no restriction on the number of rods. The MacDonnell section (above the previous one) is fished from boats. Four rods are permitted here on a weekly basis at a cost (currently) of $40 per rod per day plus $15 for guide and boat. As described before, each rod has a large pool all to himself and each one rotates the pools to fish a different one each half-day. The fish are big (usually in the twenty- to thirty-pound class) but usually are not numerous. However, a know-ledgeable angler should do well under average conditions. Finally, between Salmon Lake and Causapscal there is open fishing for Quebec residents only, and only a provincial license is required.

*Mitis River*

This one begins in the Seigniory of Lake Mitis (Metis) and is fished on the lower stretches by daily permit. One should inquire about the opening date, which is set when enough salmon have reached the upper waters.

Five rivers also are open to public fishing on the north shore of the St. Lawrence. These are:

*Little Saguenay River*

This is reached by going to St. Simeon and traveling north on Route 16. Three rods can fish on daily permits, and the river can be waded.

*Escoumins River*

This is reached by Route 15 and is east of Tadoussac. The details of fishing this river are not complete as this was written, so inquiries should be made to the Park Service.

*Laval River*

Here there is a four-rod limit, and the fishing is on daily permit.

*Moise River*

This river accommodates fifteen rods, also on daily permit.

*Romaine River*

Currently there is no restriction on the number of rods. A daily permit is required.

In giving this information the author purposely has refrained from commenting much on the relative productivity of these rivers, and the best times to fish them. Productivity varies from year to year and, while the best times usually are between late June and August, some of the rivers offer excellent fall fishing; but this also is subject to change. Rather than provide information which might later prove erroneous, it is suggested that readers correspond with the Park Service of the Province of Quebec at its office in New Carlisle.

One also may wonder why famous salmon rivers such as the Grand Cascapedia, Restigouche, York and Bonaventure are not mentioned. It is because all or nearly all of the fishing on these rivers is privately owned by various clubs and individuals and thus is not open to visiting anglers unless they are lucky enough to get invitations. While some of these proprietors may take paying guests, any attempt to discuss such arrangements would be too involved and transitory for inclusion here.

There are nine small salmon rivers on Anticosti Island, which is in the Gulf of St. Lawrence. The biggest and best-known is the

Jupiter River and all or most of them have good runs of salmon. While these rivers are privately owned, visiting anglers can arrange to fish them by writing to the Consolidated Paper Company, Ltd., Post Office Box 69, Montreal. A fly used here, which also is a high-water favorite in Newfoundland, Labrador and on the Gaspé, is the *Potato Fly* named for the Patate River on Anticosti. It has no tail, a body of light blue floss ribbed with flat silver tinsel, a wing of white Polar Bear hair, and a yellow hackle throat applied collar-style after the wing has been put on. Favorite sizes are 2, 4 and 6.

Big flies in sizes between 2/0 and 6/0 or so are rarely used on Quebec rivers except occasionally during high water on very big streams such as the Grand Cascapedia and the Restigouche. Big rods are required to handle them, and big rods are no longer very popular unless fishing conditions require them. Thus, sizes generally are confined to 2, 4 and 6 with 8's and 10's being occasionally used during warm weather, low-water periods.

We have given the favorite patterns for Quebec rivers before but it may be convenient to readers to have them repeated here. The *Rusty Rat* is used twice as much as any other, and honors for second place are divided between the *Silver Rat, Green Highlander* (usually hair-wing) and the *Black Dose*, in that order. The *Silver Grey* and *Silver Doctor* place well among the runners-up, and the favorite dry-flies are *Rat-Faced MacDougall, Grey Wulff* and *White Wulff*, also in that order. The *Cosseboom*, either dry or wet, is also popular. All the others are used only occasionally, although there may be favorites on specific rivers. The guides employed on government controlled waters (as above mentioned) are asked to report on fish caught and on the names of flies used to catch them. The information given here has been drawn from these reports, which include several rivers over the years 1964 to 1970. It is provided merely as a matter of interest because there are many other patterns which, on the leaders of competent anglers, could do as well.

## NEWFOUNDLAND AND LABRADOR

It seems sensible to discuss these two vast, relatively remote areas, largely wilderness, together because their characteristics for salmon anglers are quite similar.

Newfoundland is a jagged island over 40,000 square miles in area, containing about one hundred salmon rivers including several well known ones such as the Humber, Grand and Little Codroy, Gander, Serpentine and Portland Creek, the latter made famous by Lee Wulff, who had a sporting camp there. Some of these rivers primarily are grilse rivers (especially those on the eastern side) and most of them contain salmon which make up in quantity what they lack in size.

A trip to Newfoundland should be arranged by flying, probably to Gander, after making arrangements with one of the fishing camps there. Lists of these can be obtained from the Newfoundland-Labrador Tourist Development Office, Confederation Building, St. John's. Rather than select one on the basis of whatever is offered in print, it would be preferable to find anglers who have been there and seek recommendations from them.

Many of the rivers can be reached by road, including those mentioned. Others are available by float plane or by railroad. Those which are easily accessible may be fished considerably by local anglers. Salmon enter some of the rivers in early May, in others as late as the end of June or early July. The peak period is about the first week in July. Non-resident anglers must employ a guide, but he can serve two people. The non-resident season's fishing license is $30.

System 8 or system 9 fly-fishing tackle is appropriate and, since there are many grilse, smaller trout rods between seven and eight feet long are suggested. In addition to standard fly-hooks, low-water hooks are very popular with flies tied on them either in regular or low-water style. The characteristics of wet-flies used in Newfoundland are that their dressings are very sparse and that they are usually on light wire hooks. Sizes as small as 10's are often used.

Among the popular patterns are the *Black Dose*, *Green Highlander*, *Mitchell*, *Portland Colonel* and *Silver Grey*, plus others recommended for Quebec. The *Blue Charm*, both in regular and low-water dressings, is popular in sizes from 6 to 10. For high water, large hair-wings such as the *Cosseboom* and *Brown Bomber* are handy in sizes from 2 to 6. In dry-flies, the *Wulff* patterns are used extensively, and here again the *White Wulff* usually is the favorite. Spiders, skaters, and a few of the big "commotion" flies such as the clipped-hair *Bomber* would make up an excellent assortment, perhaps including a streamer or bucktail or two.

These same flies (and tackle) are the ones usually used in Labrador. Most rivers there are unrestricted and are open to anyone holding a valid license. The Forteau River, most southerly of those in Labrador, has runs of salmon in the ten- to twenty-pound class, as does the Adlatoc. The Eagle River has excellent runs of fish, but they are mostly grilse. Other good rivers are the Pinware, St. Marys, Sandhill, Big, Little Bay and the Hunt's.

After making arrangements (as suggested for Newfoundland) with a sporting camp or an outfitter, one would fly to Goose Bay Airport and be met by a float plane there. Outfitters lease or own a river or a section of it, and they usually build one or more camps on it. There is good trout fishing in June and July, but the season for salmon is short—primarily only the months of July and August. The peak salmon period for southern Labrador is the first week in July, for northern Labrador, the last week in July. For this reason, accommodations cost about $60 per day, plus air fare for flying back and forth. The bush pilots who ferry exploration and mining parties often explore for salmon in their spare time. They usually know good sections of rivers and will drop off campers in such places to try the fishing.

Arctic Charr, which are like big, boring Brook Trout and which fight somewhat like Bluefish, stay in the estuaries and come and go with the tides in June, July and August, making their spawning runs in August and September. Since they are an Arctic fish they are found in the northern rivers only. Anglers usually use spinning gear for them because they do not take flies readily.

Sea-run trout (Square-tail, or Brook Trout) averaging two or three pounds are bountiful in many of the rivers and at certain times many may be caught in the seven- to eight-pound class.

Labrador is the last frontier of salmon fishing in North America and those who go there usually think that the abundance of salmon and other sport-fish makes the long trip and its cost very worthwhile. Salmon, however, do not escape the harassment they are exposed to farther south. In 1967 there were 1,764 gill nets strung between the Quebec border and Hopedale, which is about halfway to Ungava

Bay. From Hopedale to Ungava Bay little is known about the salmon rivers, but this information is sure to come to hand shortly and commercial interests are sure to take advantage of it if they are allowed to. In Ungava Bay there are three important salmon rivers (and 51 gill nets). This presumably is the most northerly range of the Atlantic salmon in North America.

# VIII Salmon Fishing around the Atlantic

Many salmon anglers (this one included) itch to break the fetters of responsibility and travel to far-off places to enjoy new people, new scenery and new experiences on salmon rivers. While I have visited some of the countries to be discussed, my salmon fishing experiences in them have been too meagre for authoritative discussion. Fortunately good friends in many countries have come to the rescue, and the following, for the most part, is provided by them.

If anyone really is ideally qualified to write this chapter it would have to be the famous American fly-fishing expert and author, Joe Brooks, who has been my fishing companion on many (but altogether too few) occasions. One of Joe's most popular books is *A World of Fishing*, which is listed in this volume's bibliography among those most highly recommended on salmon flies and fishing. In his book, Joe takes his readers on fascinating fishing trips almost everywhere but, in the present context, his descriptions of salmon fishing in

various European countries are of the greatest interest to salmon
anglers generally.

Having left North America in the last chapter we now circle
eastward, passing Greenland, which has no salmon fishing worth
mentioning, to arrive in Iceland, where evidently it is superb.


## ICELAND

This island, about as large as the State of Maine, is much warmer
than its name might indicate. The Gulf Stream brings it a temperate
climate with summer temperatures averaging in the 50's (F.). The
country is mountainous, with peaks and glaciers from which pour
at least fifty salmon rivers. The best of these are mostly in the north
and west coasts, with a few to the south. Eastern rivers are rather
cold for salmon, although many have good sea-trout fishing.

Travel on the island is mostly by an excellent air network, because
there are no railroads and the roads are poor. However, the best of
them are easily negotiable by hired automobiles and the others by
Land-Rovers or other vehicles built for rough terrain. Since accommodations are few, arrangements should be made in advance. Trips
can be planned by corresponding with the Iceland Tourist Information
Bureau (161 Piccadilly, London W1V ONR).

Usually the rivers are fast and rocky, with numerous falls and
rapids. Some are clear; others have the typical milky color of glacier-
fed streams. The salmon are not large, but they are numerous,
averaging in the five- to fifteen-pound class but with occasional fish
of between twenty and thirty pounds or so, especially in some rivers.

Johann Sigurdsson, of the Tourist Bureau, discusses one of the
most popular streams, which is the Laxa in Kjos: "This is one of
Iceland's best salmon rivers and an outstanding one for fly fishermen,
situated about 24 miles northwest of Reykjavik. The total fishing
area is 12½ miles and the total number of rods (allowed on the river
at one time) is nine. 1,609 salmon were caught last year (1969) in
the three months' season of June, July and August. The average size
is approximately seven pounds. Fishermen are accommodated at a
nearby boarding school which offers all modern facilities, with a
housekeeper and staff.

FIG. VIII-1

SALMON FISHING ON ICELAND'S LAXÁ RIVER

"The cost of the fishing is £35 ($84) per day during the high season from July 4 to August 22, which includes board, rooms and fishing permit. In the low season the cost is £30 ($72) per day."

Few people who admire Bing Crosby's performances on television and in motion pictures realize that he is an excellent angler and a dedicated conservationist. Hearing that he had made a salmon fishing film on the Laxa for the "American Sportsman" series, I asked him how good the fishing was.

"Last July (1969) we flew to Reykjavik," he said, "and took a charter plane from there to the northern part of the island to fish the

152

Laxa River. The landing strip, of rolled lava rock, was near a little town called Husavik. The Laxa is a big river which occasionally splits into smaller streams which swing back and join the big stream farther down.

"Even though it was July the weather was very cold, but clear and sunny. The salmon population was considerable. We hooked four or five fish a day and landed half of them. They are very active, and strong fighters. The biggest caught was twenty-four pounds and my biggest was eighteen.

"Most of the standard salmon flies are productive, but by far the most consistent was the *Blue Sapphire*. The smaller fish jumped a lot, a great deal like Steelhead on the Pacific Coast. Accommodations were excellent but we had a little difficulty sleeping because the sun never set and they didn't have any shades on the windows.

"An amusing thing happened after we finished our filming on the Laxa. We flew back to Reykjavik and that day the members of a fishing club on a river that runs right through the city told me they had a rod for me, if I wanted to fish their river.

"I was fishing up and down the river and finally found myself just below a bridge, not far from the sea. I was busy selecting flies and casting to different rises, but saw Bud Boyd taking a movie of me.

"The camera was pointed at me, but at one point he panned straight up in back of me and kept grinding. I looked up, and there were about a thousand people on the bridge, watching my activities. Not a sound came from the group, and traffic was tied up for about a mile on either side.

"At this moment I hooked a fish and, after an exciting twenty or twenty-five minutes among the rocks in the stream, which was quite fast at that point, succeeded in landing him and gaining a lusty round of applause from the spectators.

"I like to think this was my most successful performance, in show business or any place else, and it is comforting to know there is a film to prove it. Candor compels me to admit, however, that it was a little salmon of only about nine pounds."

One can use spinners or bait on Iceland's rivers, but fly fishing is growing in popularity. Rods of between eight and nine feet are ideal. Salmon are not very selective as to fly pattern but, in addition to the *Blue Sapphire* and *Crossfield* (which are Iceland patterns), the familiar British classics in sizes from 2 to 8 still hold sway. These include *Silver Doctor, Black Doctor, Thunder and Lightning, Silver Grey, Silver Wilkinson, Jock Scott, Sweep* and *Blue Charm*, among many others.

## FINLAND

Northwest of the U.S.S.R. and east of Norway and Sweden are the 130,000 or more square miles of rugged country which is Finland, reputed to offer the greatest Atlantic salmon fishing bargains in the world. Salmon occur in three Finnish rivers: the Tenojoki, the Naatamojoki and the Torino. "Joki" means river, and in conversation is generally dropped from the name, so the Tenojoki is the Tana, or Teno. The Naatamo is a quantity river with plenty of salmon in the ten-pound class, but only a small proportion of big ones. The Torino produces few fish due to hydroelectric projects. The Tana, which flows along the northernmost tip of the country, dividing Finland and Norway, is the river usually referred to by salmon anglers. In it, yearly records usually exceed forty-five pounds and fish in the twenty- to thirty-pound class have been common. The river also holds large numbers of small grilse.

Waters become ice-free in early May in southern Finland and about a month later in the north. Although salmon fishing is permitted from May 1 through August 30 the best period is between June 15 and August 15. The waters, being partly in Finland and partly in Norway, are governed by a Finnish-Norwegian committee which has set up specific regulations covering the Tana. The fishing fee for aliens is approximately $3.50 (15:00 FMK) for a 24-hour day, the day counting from noon to midnight. One may fish the river for ten days per season, a period which can be broken into not more than two parts. Those not living in the community must use flies only; residents can use plugs and hardware.

Fishing licenses are issued by local police. Guides are readily available but, since they speak only Finnish or Swedish (or both), visitors may have to resort to sign language. The guide will charge about $15 per night (most of the fishing is done then) and owns half of all fish caught, regardless of who catches them. Boats are of the long "Norwegian" variety and, because of rapid water, the rowmen do not like to have more than one fisherman in a boat at a time.

The rocky, swift Tana has few places adaptable for wading or for casting from shore. Most of the fishing is done by trolling; the Lapp guides work the channels and midstream riffles with two lines out, while the customer uses one or two fly rods. The guide rows back and forth across the current in a series of drops, allowing his lures and the angler's flies to work 50 or 60 feet downstream where he has reason to believe that salmon are lying. When a fish is hooked the guide hands the busy rod to his sport and reels the the others in.

Guides are very fussy about fly pattern, size, style and the knot used in attaching fly to leader. They will change flies, trim them, reknot them and test them in the current until they are satisfied. In an article in *Field and Stream* (February, 1970) Al McClane reported, "Despite their own preference for plugs, Lapps are extremely critical about the flies used. The fly must be sparsely tied, which eliminated our expensive assortment of Norwegian and British patterns, as well as our modern Canadian patterns (mostly too small). They will take scissors and trim a *Green Highlander* naked as a jaybird, or suggest that you buy some locally tied Teno flies, which we must confess are not only unique and beautiful patterns, but perfect swimmers. They are not only works of art, but designed with slender wings and sparse hackles for perfect balance."

Arno Adlivankin, who fishes the Tana a great deal, obtained some of these specially dressed Finnish patterns for possible use in the color plates of this book. Unfortunately a miscreant somewhere intercepted the shipment but, if replacements can be obtained in time, some of them will be included. In spite of Al McClane's comments, others report that most classic patterns of "big" salmon flies are good, those being mentioned including the *Silver Jock Scott*, *Dusty Miller*, *Black Doctor* and *Butcher*. We will see in the account of Norwegian fishing that North American flies such as the *Rats* and the *Muddler Minnow* are good there, and what is a taker on one side of the river should be all right on the other. Guides quite often can be rather opinionated, usually without very good reason!

Accommodations in Finland are very reasonable——cheap, in fact, considering the fishing. There is a modern, comfortable hotel in the village of Utsjoki, which is located right on the Tana. All services generally expected are available; the food is reported to be excellent, and daily rates for a double room (as this was written) are in the neighborhood of ten dollars! Flying from place to place within Finland is inexpensive and low-cost transoceanic excursion rates are available. Taken all together, Finland seems to offer one of the world's best buys in salmon fishing. Information can be obtained from the Finnish Travel Information Centre, 56 Haymarket, London, SW1, England.

## NORWAY

Harboring the world's best Atlantic salmon pool and many of the world's finest Atlantic salmon rivers, Norway for hundreds of years has been a mecca for anglers who seek the "big ones." There are nearly a hundred salmon rivers in Norway, including such important ones as the Aaroy, Alta, Aurland, Driva, Flaam, Karasjok, Laerdal, Namsen and the Vosso, also the famous Malangsfoss Pool, which is on the Maals River in northern Norway.

Salmon between twenty and thirty pounds are common in the Malangsfoss, and fish of over forty pounds cause little more than casual excitement. The Malang waterfall, seventy feet high, thunders into the neck of the giant pool, which is shaped more or less like a bottle. In the rocky pool the summer level of the water is about thirty-five feet. While very large flies (up to 7/0) are used with sinking lines on long rods, there are no tackle restrictions and, due to the depth and speed of the water, deep trolled hardware is more popular. Fishing usually is done from boats in a manner similar to the methods described in the section on Finland. Fishing rights for a party of between four and six (usually for six days) cost about $150 per day per person. There is a comfortable lodge on the pool, with guides, boats and other conveniences readily available.

Joe Brooks, in his *A World of Fishing*, gives a 45-page account of Norwegian angling which everyone interested in fishing there should read. The Norwegian National Travel Office (Scandinavia

House, 505 Fifth Avenue, New York, N.Y. 10017) is generous in providing booklets, folders and other material. One of their best booklets, *Angling in Norway*, contains 96 pages of information.

Leigh Perkins, president of Orvis, wrote one of the most interesting accounts of Norwegian fishing for the December, 1969, issue of *Orvis News*, describing his experiences in fishing the Alta River. Parts of it are quoted with his permission:

"The Alta is probably the most legendary of all salmon rivers. It lies in the land of the Midnight Sun 300 miles north of the Arctic Circle in a beautiful setting. The average weight of all salmon taken is over twenty pounds and it has been restricted to fly fishing since 1862 when the Duke of Roxburghe first leased it. There are 27 miles of excellent water restricted to eight rods. Only the prime time is leased, the last week of June and the full month of July. There are three camps. The lower, or the new, camp, has four comfortable double bedrooms, dining room and kitchen. It is only a twenty-minute drive from the airport where you land in a jet. The upper two camps, Sautso and Sandia, are reached by river boats. They each have two double bedrooms and each accommodate two rods. The method of fishing is out of a unique Norwegian Karasjok River boat manned by two ghillies and powered by a 20-horsepower outboard. The river is slightly larger than the Restigouche and is a reddish tea-color, no silty glacial water. The temperature of the air and the water is surprisingly high. We saw noon at 75 degrees and midnight as low as 40 degrees in spite of the fact that one can actually see the sun at midnight. The water temperature was about 58 degrees during the third week of July.

"We fished the Alta at the lower camp between July 15 and 22. We had beautiful weather, and six out of seven days we had 24 hours of bright sunlight. We found the accommodations and food excellent, with all the salmon and trout we could eat, plus whale meat and reindeer steak as well as more common fare thrown in for variety.

"The schedule is an unusual one. Dinner is at 7:00 P.M. with the fishing starting at 8:00 P.M. The ghillies pull up on the bank for a midnight snack and light a fire to make coffee and cook sausages, then we continue to fish until 3:00 A.M. After an hour of cocktails and postmortems we go to bed at 4:00 A.M. and arise at noon for a one o'clock breakfast. The afternoon can be used for trout fishing, sightseeing or just relaxing. We found it quite easy to adapt to this schedule.

"I found the fishing unique, compared to any Canadian or Scotch salmon fishing I had ever done, in that once a fish was located he could invariably be encouraged to take a fly. One of the great luxuries of the Alta is that each rod has a beat of about four miles an evening, and there are always some pools holding taking fish. The Norwegian ghillies are very tradition-bound and insist on telegraph poles for rods and huge flies. While I don't feel qualified to talk for all seasons, my experience would indicate that the flies should be slightly larger than the ones used on the Restigouche because of the reddish tint of the water and the poorer visibility. The ghillies insist on double-hook flies, preferably 3/0 to 5/0's. I found that I had more strikes on smaller flies, double-hook 2's, primarily. I had the bad luck of losing three good salmon in a row on small flies with a small rod which convinced the ghillies beyond all doubt that it was impossible to hook a big salmon on a fly as small as a 2. I was convinced that it was my lack of skill and lack of luck that lost the fish as I was later able to land a large Alta salmon on my light rig and No. 2 hook as I have done many times before on the Canadian rivers.

"I recommend heavy leaders testing to about 17 pounds as there is no need for light tippets in the colored water. I found the wet tip line ideal although it was well to have a high density sinking line and a floating line along. There were some pools that one wanted to fish deep and other fishermen in our party seemed to do quite well with the floating line.

"For a rod, I prefer an eight-and-a-half-foot, 4 3/4-ounce, Battenkill with a System 8 line while using the small flies. I do not recommend this rig for anything over a size zero double hook as an 8-weight line just will not carry the fly comfortably through the air. A better all-around choice would probably be any of our Orvis Shooting Star rods, eight and a half through nine and a half feet, all of which take a System 9 line and can handle flies up to 3/0.

"Like most fishermen, I'm probably extremely prejudiced but my favorite fly was the *Muddler* salmon fly on a double number 2 hook. Taking a consensus of the other rods, the top takers were *Thunder and Lightning, Lady Amherst, Green Highlander, Durham Ranger, Silver Grey, Blue Charm, Black Rat, Silver Rat, Rusty Rat* and *Red Abbey.* Although Norwegian sea-trout do not run in the Alta until after the salmon season, we did catch a few Grayling, Arctic Charr and Brown Trout. This of course, is the reason for the lighter rods. Grilse were plentiful and actually outnumbered the salmon during our week.

"The grand total for seven nights fishing with seven rods was 59 salmon with an average weight of slightly over twenty pounds. Five salmon were over thirty pounds and one magnificent forty-six-pounder was caught by Everett Kirchner. We also took 77 grilse between three and six pounds. Unlike any of the canoe fishing I have experienced in Canada for salmon where one fished a series of drops while held by an anchor, the method in Norway is for the ghillie to row upstream holding his boat in position and moving you across the water as he sees fit. This method seems very strenuous, but the ghillies are strong and one is able to cover a lot more water more rapidly by this method.

"Looking back over the history of the Alta, there are some fantastic statistics. There are record dates of fish taken back as early as 1567. The Duke of Roxburghe took 39 salmon in a single night in 1860. The Duke of Westminister took 36 on a single night in 1906. The best record recently was 15 salmon in one night by the Duke and Duchess of Roxburghe. The all-time record was killed by the Earl of Dudley in 1951—a sixty-pounder. For the last two years the salmon fishing has been off due to excessive netting and long-lining. Last year they put a stop to netting in the fiord below the Alta and there is hope that the International Commission for Northwest Atlantic Fisheries will eliminate the commercial fishing for salmon in the high seas altogether. In any event, the Alta is still the best salmon river in the world that we know of and it certainly produces larger fish than any other. It is easy to get to, about a $2\frac{1}{2}$-hour jet flight from Oslo. The cost is high, but you get what you pay for; it costs approximately \$3,000 per week per rod. The Orvis Company is in a position to make bookings for anglers."

Leigh's account of his week on the Alta conforms so closely to the experiences of those on other rivers in both Norway and

Sweden that including more of them seems unnecessary. Other rivers usually are less expensive and probably will hold smaller or fewer fish, but angling methods on them are very much the same except that there is less boating and more wading or bank fishing on the smaller and less rapid streams.

One of England's foremost salmon anglers is Arthur Oglesby, who has provided some of the photographs used in this book. One of his favorite Norwegian streams is the Vosso, in which he has caught many salmon exceeding thirty pounds, topped by one weighing forty-six and half pounds. He suggests that visiting anglers who want to consider fishing in Norway should correspond with Haraldsen Tours, of Kronprincesse Marthas Plas 1, Oslo. Mr. Odd Haraldsen controls some excellent stretches on the Vosso and in other rivers and can make complete arrangements for transportation, lodging and fishing.

My friend and fellow member in the United Fly Tyers Club, Yngvar Kaldal, of Oslo, has provided information on flies commonly used all over the Scandinavian countries. Classic British patterns still are used but are declining in popularity. Best patterns are *Black Doctor, Black Dose, Durham Ranger, Dusty Miller, Green Highlander, Jock Scott, Mar Lodge, Silver Doctor, Silver Grey, Silver Wilkinson* and *Thunder and Lightning*. Patterns indigenous to the region are *Namsen, Peer Gynt, Sheriff, Shrimp* (*Chilimps*), *Ola* and *Ottesen*, plus many others. Low-water patterns are very popular for their purpose and include *Blue Charm, Logie, Silver Blue, March Brown, Orange Charm, Lady Caroline* and *Brown Fairy*.

Fly sizes for extra high or heavy water are between 5/0 and 8/0, but these very big flies are not considered as necessary as they used to be and they require powerful rods of ten feet or more to handle them. For high water or big rivers, flies between 1/0 and 5/0 are used. The average, particularly for smaller streams, is between size 4 and 3/0, but American anglers will prefer them in the smaller sizes. Low-water patterns usually are between 6 and 10.

More and more hair-wing flies are being used and almost all are American, Canadian and British patterns. These include the *Rusty Rat, Silver Rat, Black Rat, Cosseboom, Orange Blossom, Grizzly King, Red Abbey, Orange Charm* and *Akroyd*. Leader tippets

(*A. Oglesby*)

FIG. VIII-2

ARTHUR OGLESBY WITH A SALMON
OF 46½ POUNDS CAUGHT BY HIM ON THE VOSSO RIVER
NEAR BOLSTAD, IN NORWAY

should be no stronger than 20 pounds, and those in the 10- to 12-pound range are sufficient for the smaller rivers. Dry flies are being used more and more, and of course are of American origin.

American anglers fishing abroad will use rods not over nine or nine and a half feet long except when using big flies in extra high or heavy water. Then those between nine and a half and twelve feet are recommended, partly to cast the big flies and partly to help hold the line up in the fast currents. Continental anglers gradually are coming around to American practices both in rod sizes and in fly sizes and selection. The fancy feather-wings die hard in some areas, but the common sense and efficiency of the simpler and more productive hair-wings are gradually becoming apparent.


## FRANCE

We may jump from the Scandinavian countries to France because very little of interest to salmon anglers lies in between. By their own admission the people of Denmark have so abused their rivers that their salmon fishing is negligible. As the disgraceful Danish situation is discussed in the Epilogue of this book and elsewhere, there is no point in dealing with it further.

In France the salmon situation is rather bad also. Dams and pollution have ruined most of the rivers, and fishways, if they have been built, are inefficient or neglected.

Between Avranches and Granville are three short, narrow and fairly deep rivers named the Sienne, the See and the Selune, which altogether yield only a few hundred salmon per year. There are a few small rivers on the northern coast of Brittany, but they are of very minor interest. The Elorn meets the sea on the western end of the Finistere and lies parallel to the railroad between Paris and Brest. It contains a few pools suitable for fly-fishing, but most of them are overgrown with vegetation. Also flowing into the Bay of Brest is the Aulne: part of this (at the lower end) is a canal and can be fished from the bank.

In these rivers the salmon are small, rarely exceeding ten pounds, and they are few in number. Fly-fishermen have to compete with the hardware set, and salmon also are taken by even more uncouth practices. The trouble quite obviously is that the French authorities have neglected the salmon fishing to the extent that those wishing to fish a fly in these areas must be rather hard-up for other places to go. The best season, at least in the lower reaches of the rivers, is between the middle of March and the middle of April.

Continuing south we come to the Loire, a river nearly ruined by dams and by trap-nets. It has a fork upriver called the Allier which offers fair fishing upstream from Vichy. This beautiful stream, with its source in the Auvergne mountains, has been partly reclaimed, but a dam forming a lake made for boating purposes impedes or prevents the upstream migrations of salmon.

The Adour River, which meets the Atlantic at Bayonne, has two tributaries: the Gave d'Oloron and the Gave de Pau. The former is called the best salmon river in France, but the latter has been dammed and holds no salmon. Fish enter the Adour in February, and are large although not numerous. Smaller salmon and some grilse follow, swimming upriver late in March and providing good fly-fishing after the mountain snows have melted early in June.

Fly-fishing tackle is System 8 or System 9, depending on fly sizes used. These are large, between sizes 2 and 4/0. Classic patterns popular elsewhere on the Continent are used here, and smaller hair-wings are becoming more and more popular.


## SPAIN

In Spain the salmon fishing is a great deal better. On the northern Atlantic coast there are about sixteen salmon rivers, of which eight produce sizable catches of fish averaging about eleven pounds. These, listed in order with the most prolific river first, are the Sella, Cares-Deva, Narcea, Ason, Pas, Eo, Navia and the Canero. This order of listing does not, however, name them in order of choice for the fly fisherman.

In Pravia (Asturias) lives a very expert salmon angler and one of the world's most accomplished fly-dressers, named B. Martinez, who has a tackle shop there which specializes in salmon flies; his crafts-manship is such that his patterns are sought not only by anglers who fish for salmon in Spain, but by others who collect beautiful flies to

frame or otherwise to treasure as art objects. Sr. Martinez was kind
enough to send me several original patterns for this book. He wrote
me several letters in Spanish and we have tried to translate them:

"I list the numbers of salmon caught in each of our principal
rivers last year and the number captured might have been considerably
larger if we had not been limited in the quantity we were allowed to
catch.

"Of all the salmon rivers in Spain the one that has the best
conditions for fly-fishing is the river Narcea, which has many beautiful
stretches and which is considered the best river in Europe for this
kind of fishing. Beginning in 1968 there is celebrated along its waters
an International Festival of Salmon Fishing. This is exclusively with
flies, and the entire river is ideally suited for fly-fishing.

"Fly-fishing on the Narcea generally starts by the end of April,
according to the lowering of the waters. The flies mostly used are of
the English type, including the *Jock Scott, Green Highlander, Dusty
Miller, Silver Wilkinson* and so forth, in sizes between 5/0 and 2.
Smaller sizes are used as the river recedes and the season advances;
this terminates on July 18.

"After this river there follows in order of importance for fly-
fishing the river Cares, which is also very beautiful but more turbulent, and with stronger rapids. This is excellent for fly-fishing,
especially toward the end of May.

" The river Sella, despite its good salmon virtues, is the one least
suited for fly-fishing, and the greatest number of fish taken are taken
with artificial lures or with natural live bait.

"The river Eo has characteristics like the Narcea River. It is much
less rapid and has good pools in the shorter stretches. It is excellent
for fly-fishing from March to May.

"The Canero is a smallish river, and not very good for fly-
fishing."

Senor Martinez notes that in 1968 1,349 salmon were taken from
the Narcea, 1,869 from the Cares, 2,041 from the Sella and 408 from
the Eo. In his list of fly patterns he modestly does not include his
own originations, but he sent half a dozen very beautiful ones to me.
These are the *Eo River, Esva River, Martinez Special, Naranxeira,
Narcea River* and the *Silver Martinez*. Evidently these are very

popular in France as well as in Spain. Some are good enough to be classed as Exhibition Patterns and, if readers desire a few very handsome flies for framing, they surely should be included.

The salmon fishing season in Spain extends from the end of the first week in March to July 18. Some of the best stretches are controlled by a department of the Ministry of Agriculture, which undertakes the upkeep, stocking and patrolling of the various runs. In some cases the number of rods on these stretches is limited, and a permit in addition to a fishing license is required. Licenses and special permits are inexpensive, and arrangements can be made in advance by contacting the Servicio de Pesca Continental, Caza y Parques Nacional, General Sanjurjo, 47, Madrid. As in other cases, if a fisherman from another country wants to fish for salmon in Spain it would seem sensible to correspond well in advance with a prominent angler there, such as Senor Martinez.

## BRITISH ISLES

In England, Scotland, Wales and Ireland little, if any, productive salmon water is open to the general public. Non-tidal riparian rights are controlled by individual landowners, many of whom have held title to their waters for many generations. Some of these owners will lease stretches for a period of time, but their agents have no trouble in doing this even years in advance.

Visiting anglers, however, can make arrangements for fishing because many hotels control stretches of salmon rivers and make these available to guests. Fishing clubs, angling associations and syndicates also often control water and allow visitors to buy a "ticket" to fish it. Tickets usually are very inexpensive but, if many are given out, one may find the water a bit crowded. Certain waters, however, can be reserved for a fee of $50 (more or less, depending on how good the water is) per day, thus affording exclusive use of them during the reservation period.

Lists of "fishing hotels," with descriptive data, are provided by the British Travel Association, 680 Fifth Avenue, New York, N.Y. 10019, or 64 St. James Street, London, S.W.1. A firm which handles accommodations and arrangements is Paton, Grant & Woodward, 7 Bury

Fig. VIII-3

JOE BROOKS HAND-TAILS A FIFTEEN POUNDER
ON SCOTLAND'S OYKEL RIVER

166

Street, London, S.W.1. Other similar organizations handle such things regionally. Many of these fishing hotels are quaint and comfortable, especially the ones in more or less rural areas. The trick, of course, is to find one with the desired characteristics and to plan the trip for a time when the fishing is good. A river which may have an excellent run of salmon at one time may be barren of them, or nearly so, at others. The good hotels are booked full well in advance, particularly during the best parts of the season. Hotels usually will provide copies of "best records" detailing tallies of how many fish were caught daily each week of the season during the past few years. Fairly reliable conclusions, subject to weather conditions and other factors, can be drawn from these. A useful booklet entitled *Where to Fish* is published by *The Field*, 8 Stratton Street, London, W.1.

The fishing season in the British Isles generally starts in February, when there may be a good deal of snow water, especially in Scotland. The best period usually is between March 15 and May 15 but, because some of the rivers have summer runs of fish, good salmon fishing can be found here and there all summer long and well into the fall. Fish run up various rivers at different times. For example, the river Tweed gets fresh runs of small salmon all season from February through November, with larger fish (up to thirty pounds or so) later in the season. On the other hand there are rivers which are good only in the summer, others which peak between March and June, and others where the fall fishing is best. Therefore, finding a suitable location where one can go fishing is one problem. Arranging for such a location when the fishing is good is another!

Rods of twelve feet or more in length are habitually used by British anglers, but Americans think they are not necessary except perhaps to handle big flies on sinking lines in heavy water. Americans would use rods from eight and half to nine and a half feet long, and more and more British fly-fishermen are realizing the logic of these.

The favorite flies used in the British Isles vary so much from region to region that it would be almost impossible to provide a general list which makes any sense. This book contains over a hundred patterns of British hair-wing and feather-wing flies. All of them are currently popular in one place or another and, of course, many local favorites have had to be omitted.

FIG. VIII-4

FLY FISHING FOR SALMON ON THE AWE RIVER
IN ARGYLLSHIRE, SCOTLAND

In general, all the classic patterns mentioned in this book are popular and, while others are used, these seem to be enough. As we have noticed, these classics gradually are giving way to hair-wings like the *Yellow Dog* (*Garry*), *Hairy Mary*, *Stoat's Tail* and reduced or hair-wing versions of some of the classics. Low-water patterns like the *Logie* and *Blue Charm* are still used. Shrimp or grub imitations like the *General Practitioner* and *Usk Grub* are very popular on occasion. American hair-wings like the *Cosseboom* and the *Rats* are sneaking in very effectively. Tube flies are used a great deal, and have been discussed elsewhere. Treble-hooked flies are popular, as well as doubles and singles. Spinning also is very popular, especially during high-water periods.

During average water conditions, hook sizes 6 and 8 would be appropriate. In high or discolored water the sizes might be much bigger. For example, as this is being written, a letter arrived from Megan Boyd, saying (in March) that she is very busy dressing several dozen *Yellow Torrish* flies in sizes 7/0 and 8/0 for use in the snow water on the Brora. Whether or not the Scottish anglers need them that big is not for us to decide.

In late spring and summer when the water is clear and exceeds 48 degrees or so, fly sizes go as small as 10's and 12's (the latter only under extreme conditions). Usually the flies are lightly dressed and used on floating lines, but occasionally (as has been discussed before) they are fished well sunk. In the autumn, sizes 4 and 6, or perhaps larger, are popular, of course depending upon the fishing conditions.

Americans who plan to fish in the British Isles might remember that, while it is both fashionable and comfortable to dress rather casually at home, this is not considered correct on British rivers. There, one usually goes out wearing a rather tweedy jacket and probably wears a tie!

Fly-dressers and anglers who are interested in fishing in the British Isles should profit by subscribing to *Trout and Salmon* Magazine, which is the only British periodical that covers all aspects of British angling thoroughly. The publication carries excellent articles, fly patterns and fly-dressing information by leading anglers. It is published monthly by the East Midland Allied Press, Oundle Road, Peterborough, England.

# PART TWO
# Atlantic Salmon Flies

**GREEN HIGHLANDER**

**GREEN HIGHLANDER** (HAIR-WING) **GREEN HIGHLANDER**

(REDUCED) Dressed by (HACKLE-WING)

Dressed by Mrs. Carmelle Bigaouette (P) Dressed by

Mr. Harry Darbee (P) Mr. Geoffrey Bucknall (P)

**GREEN HIGHLANDER**

(CLASSIC PATTERN)

Dressed by

Hardy Brothers (P)

**DUSTY MILLER** **DUSTY MILLER**

(CLASSIC PATTERN) (REDUCED)

Dressed by Dressed by

Hardy Brothers (P) Mr. Harry Darbee (P)

**DUSTY MILLER**

(HAIR-WING)

Dressed by

Mr. Colin Simpson (P)

**BLACK DOSE** **BLACK DOSE**

(CLASSIC PATTERN) (REDUCED)

Dressed by Dressed by

Hardy Brothers (P) Mr. Harry Darbee (P)

**BLACK DOSE**

(HAIR-WING)

Dressed by

Mrs. Carmelle Bigaouette (P)

**THUNDER & LIGHTNING** **THUNDER & LIGHTNING**

(SHEATH-WING) (HAIR-WING, DEAN VERSION)

Dressed by **THUNDER & LIGHTNING** Dressed by

Mr. Geoffrey Bucknall (P) (CLASSIC PATTERN) Mr. Alex Simpson (A)

Dressed by

Hardy Brothers (P)

**SILVER GREY** **SILVER GREY** **SILVER GREY**

(SIMPLIFIED) (CLASSIC PATTERN) (REDUCED)

Dressed by Dressed by Dressed by

Mr. Philip Foster (P) Mr. Colin Simpson (P) Mr. Philip Foster (P)

PLATE III

Classic Patterns and their Simplifications

172

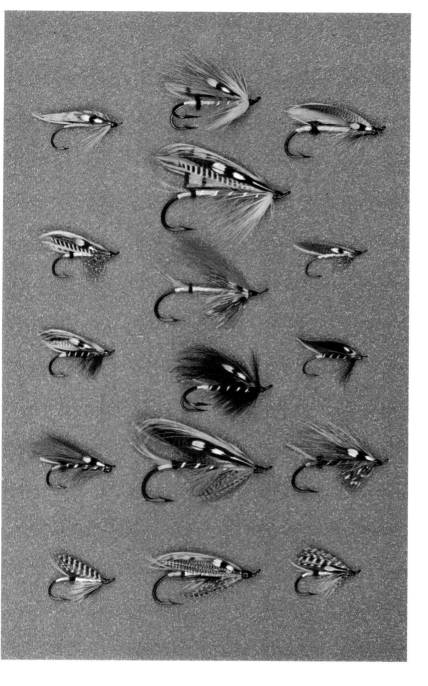

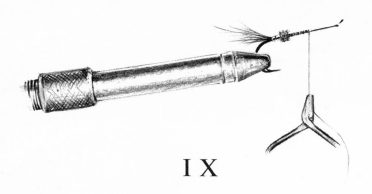

# I X

# Notes on
# Dressings and Patterns

For the dressings of complicated classic fly patterns readers are referred to the works of Kelson and Pryce-Tannatt, especially the latter, who know infinitely more about the subject than this author does. In modern times we see no need for complicated patterns, except possibly for exhibition dressings which few of us have the ability to attempt. We dispense with them here because they are a book-long subject unto themselves; because they would be of interest to only a tiny fraction of those who read this; because they are covered admirably in other books; and because modern, simpler patterns have made them more or less obsolete.

## DRESSING A CLASSIC PATTERN

In going from the sublime to the simple in fly patterns, however, it may be of interest to know how an example of the classics is put together. Therefore, in Chapter XIII we give the dressing of the *Black*

*Doctor* because it has the same wing as the *Silver Doctor* and the *Blue Doctor*. The other parts of the other two flies are different, and are included in the notes on the *Black Doctor*. In this fly the wing is composed of thirteen different bits of feathers; each is applied twice. In Pryce-Tannatt's instructions these are listed in such a bewildering string of names that the uninitiated will wonder what goes where. Semi-colons divide these feathers into four different groups, and that's the secret of the thing!

In nearly all classic dressings the wing starts off with strands of Golden Pheasant tippet and sections of Golden Pheasant tail (sometimes plus something else), married together with the first-mentioned feather at the bottom and the other(s) laid on in order given to the top. This is the foundation of the wing, on which everything else is built. Next, on each side of the foundation, is a "sheath" of other feather sections (in small flies, perhaps only one fiber of each), also married in order given and applied so they veil, but not entirely conceal, what's underneath. If there is an outer sheath, it is applied similarly and usually is a bit shorter to show the tips of the underfeathers. Finally, such dressings usually end up with Mallard, which is applied as a roof over the wing ("edging the top of the sheath") to keep everything else together so the components won't be splayed out. The wing's undertip should edge the curve of the tail, and the topping should enclose the wing's top and should end at the tip of the tail. (In this book the author does it the hard way and calls the "topping" a "Golden Pheasant crest feather," which it is.)

## ADJUSTING THE CURVE OF TOPPINGS

Since Golden Pheasant crest is used as a tail and topping on many simple patterns and since it's rather hard to find ones on a crest that fit exactly, this suggestion may be helpful: to give toppings a perfect curve, wet *similar-sized* toppings in *cold* water until saturated. Lay them individually around the outside or inside of a glass vial or cylinder having the correct diameter (curvature) and allow them to dry completely without touching them. When dry the feathers will have a perfect curve. If the right sizes of glass are selected for tails and toppings for various sizes of flies the tails and toppings will "crest" perfectly. They should not be cut in order to make them meet.

With that, let's bid a nostalgic adieu to Mr. Kelson's complicated creations and progress to patterns modern anglers consider more sensible. One has only to scan the color plates in this book to realize that salmon flies don't have to be complicated to be pretty—if beauty is what one is looking for. Among other innovations presumably this is the first book to show North American anglers the favorite modern flies of British and Continental anglers, and vice versa. Hopefully, each will get some ideas from the other. Undoubtedly our *Rats* and *Cossebooms* will invade the British Isles and American anglers will be using shrimp patterns and flowing heron hackled flies to catch more salmon with!

## CONVERSION OF CLASSICS TO SIMPLER FEATHER-WINGS

As one who has dressed his own flies for many years and has associated with clubs and individuals who do the same thing, the author once tried to dress some of the British classics mainly to see if he could do it. He couldn't, at least in a manner he considered satisfactory.

The dressing of British classics is an art form wherein one must have expert personal instruction just as surely as he must have it if he wishes to excel in music or in painting. We used to have a very few experts such as Alex Rogan and Elizabeth Greig, but these artists, who learned their craft in the British Isles, are no longer available. If there is anyone in North America competent to teach classic dressings properly, this author doesn't know of him (or her). And if such a teacher should become available, very few pupils would devote enough time in steady practice to become proficient in the art.

My good friend, Alex Simpson, of Aberdeen, Scotland, is a dedicated fly-dresser and angler and he is fortunate in having a fifteen-year-old son who follows in his footsteps. Alex was wise enough to engage the most expert teacher he could find for his son,

Fig. IX-1

COLIN SIMPSON, AN EXPERT AT 15,
USUALLY DRESSES FLIES WITHOUT A VISE.

176

Colin (and there still are numerous experts in Scotland). To show what an apprentice there has to go through, it may be of interest to quote from a letter from Alex:

"His (Colin's) teacher has drummed into his head that fly-tying is an art, and that the finished product must be a work of art. Other dressers have been taught at night classes, twelve lessons of two hours each. After attending these classes they think they know everything about fly-tying, whereas an apprentice fly-dresser has to serve his time for *five years*.

"Colin spent his first four months with his teacher tying tags, tips and tails *only*, and the tails had to be straight or he had a telling off! After studying these for four months he spent a month dressing butts; a month making plain bodies; and another month learning how to make multi-bodies of wool and floss. A month was spent on ribbing, and there still is a lot to learn. Then a month on body hackles; a month on throat hackles; a month dressing flies with plain wings; and another learning how to 'marry' wings without dressing the hook. That was his first year's work, and 'graduation' (from the apprentice class) is four years ahead!"

It should be obvious why this author desires to pay a tribute to a young man so dedicated, and why he is pleased and honored to include several of Colin's flies in this book.

Since almost none of us in the United States can (or will) afford the time to do things this way, the alternative in imitating the classic patterns (if this is what we want to do) is to take shortcuts. In dressing feather-wings we can do so by using hackles instead of the more intricate married strips necessary in preparing mixed-wing and built-wing patterns. A prominent English expert, Geoffrey Bucknall, explained how to do this in the December, 1969, issue of *Trout and Salmon*, so it may be helpful to learn it from him:

"Many amateur fly-dressers find it difficult to make mixed- and built-wing salmon flies, which involve the marrying of several strips of feather of different colour, perhaps from distinctly separate birds. This new method of winging avoids the problems of marrying without loss of the effect of the mixed colours in strips.

"The body is made in the normal way. If we take the *Silver Doctor*, you fashion the tail section, silver body and hackles in normal fashion, none of which is difficult for the beginner. Now for the wings:

"The tippet underwing can be tied in if desired, simply a pair of Golden Pheasant tippets back to back or even in a bunch to lie flat. Now the coloured, married strands of goose or swan are replaced by hackle-points in the same colours. These are put on in pairs, the second and third pairs going over and slightly above the lower pair, first yellow, then red, and finally blue. The bottom pair is the longest, the succeeding ones shorter to give the curved back of the wing. These are not long, as in a streamer fly, but occupy the same length as the normal wing. For lightly dressed irons and low water, this is all that is necessary but once these points are in position the wing can easily be built up for the fully dressed pattern by folding a strip of teal, mallard or Summer Duck over the wing to roof it so that it divides equally on either side. A topping then finishes the fly.

"This completes the wing for the simple mixed-wing fly but, for the overlapping built-wing of the *Jock Scott*, for example, you can add a further pair of grizzled brown hackle-points; then fold a strip of mallard over the top as a roof, topping off in the usual way.

"A glance through the lists of dressings will show the right combinations for various patterns. The first one I gave will suit all flies with an 'inner-wing' of yellow, scarlet and blue. This covers the various *Doctors* and odd patterns like the *Mar Lodge* and *Silver Grey*, but for the *Green Highlander* you would simply build up a series of points of green, yellow and orange.

"Finally, the method of 'roofing' a fly, as described, by folding a strip of mallard, teal or pintail over the inner wing is both simple and effective. The strip of feather is torn from one side only of the parent feather, first being straightened to align the tips. Care must be taken to divide this strip evenly as it is folded over the inner wing, but a glance from above insures this."

## CONVERSION OF CLASSICS TO HAIR-WINGS

On the presumption that the British classics had color schemes which made sense, many of these also have been converted to hair-wings. The same bodies (often simplified) are used, and the wings are of natural or dyed hair mixed to provide similar color effects. Some of these adaptations are of American origin but, if the parent fly was British, it is included here among British hair-wing patterns. Dyed Swan or Goose is imitated with dyed Polar Bear or bucktail; brown Mallard with brown bucktail; brown Turkey with brown Squirrel tail; Pintail or Teal with Grey Squirrel tail, etc. These hair-wing adaptations, of course, are easier to tie. They also are less inclined to become mangled in use, and their greater translucence and mobility are in their favor. For these reasons it would seem that anglers who still prefer the Victorian feather-winged classics do so more from tradition or misconception than from genuine need.

In addition to the three *Doctors*, the author illustrates and gives the dressings of a very few other classic patterns to show the original complicated fly and the simplified hair-wing and reduced patterns which have evolved from it. These include the *Black Dose, Dusty Miller, Green Highlander* and *Silver Grey*. The inclusion of these few complicated classics may also interest fly-tyers interested in attempting exhibition dressings.

## IDENTIFICATION OF FLY PARTS

Fly-dressers quite often use different names to identify parts of a fly, perhaps calling a throat a beard, a tip a tag, a cheek a shoulder, etc. To avoid confusion this drawing gives the names of parts as used in the 200 or more dressing instructions which follow. The tag always is of tinsel, its purpose being partly to provide glitter and partly to act as a firm base or support for the tip or tail. The tip, immediately forward of the tag, is very small and usually of floss. The butt always is immediately forward of the tail, thus distinguishing it from the tag and the tip. If any elements are not called for in a pattern, they are left out of the dressing instructions. The listing of elements is in order of their application. Sometimes, for example, a collar (one or more turns of a hackle at the throat) should be applied before the wing and sometimes after (as in the *Cosseboom* patterns). If it is applied before the wing, usually the fibers on top are pulled or pressed down and tied in to splay outward and downward to make a flaring throat and to leave room for positioning the wing. This

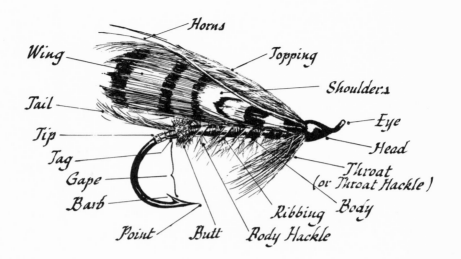

FIG. IX-2

NAMES OF PARTS OF A SALMON FLY

method and the application of a bunch of hackle fibers under the hook (as a beard) are two ways of applying a throat and often are substituted, one for the other, at the discretion of the fly-dresser. Usually, however, the dressing instructions specify the method preferred by the originator, and that is the way it should be done.

## IMPORTANCE OF CORRECT PATTERNS

While the dressing instructions are mainly of interest to fly-dressers, they also should be valuable to anglers who buy their flies because these specifications tell them whether or not they are getting correct patterns. When sending away for flies tied to order the purchaser can order them "tied by the book" and thus should get patterns dressed the way they should be. Often professional fly-dressers with the best of intentions innocently use incorrect patterns, thus sometimes delivering an order which displeases the customer because it is not exactly what he expected. Discriminating anglers want flies dressed exactly true to pattern and, since it should cost no more in time or materials, professionals should be meticulous about this. Two of North America's most popular types of flies are those in the *Rat* and *Cosseboom* series, but invariably they are tied with black heads when they should be red; and other more serious errors also are made.

To help readers avoid such errors the author has tried to get to the source of each fly, and to provide exact instructions for dressing it just as the originator did. While this was possible in most cases, it wasn't possible in all of them. Many old British patterns, for example, are dressed a bit differently in different regions, so the most logical prescription had to be accepted.

## STYLE IN FLY DESIGN

The greatest errors, however, are in style rather than in detail. Professional and amateur dressers alike invariably overdress their flies—a matter previously mentioned which bears repetition. In nearly all North American patterns and in most foreign ones dressings should be sparse; the wing should set low on the hook (nymph-style); and the dressing (except in streamers and similar types) never should extend beyond the bend of the hook. Salmon often nip at flies, and the idea is to help them get hold of the iron!

This is illustrated in Figure IX-3 wherein "A" is a fully dressed feather-wing and "1" is a fully dressed hair-wing. In these we should note that the tag and tip (if any) are directly over the barb of the hook. We have seen that when smaller flies seem appropriate the fully dressed fly is tied in a size smaller on the same size of hook, as sketched in "B" and "2." The idea here is that the angler thinks he will do better with a smaller size of fly, but he still wants the larger hook because of its greater hooking and holding ability. Carrying this one step farther into the low-water types, as in "C" and "3," the light-wire hook remains large while the dressing occupies no more than half of the hook's shank. Some anglers prefer very small flies, such as 10's and 12's (or even smaller) under low and clear

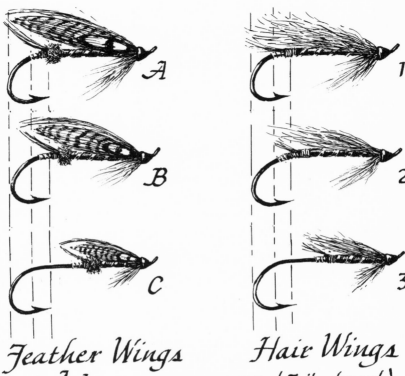

Feather Wings          Hair Wings

A-1.. NORMAL DRESSING (Fully dressed)

B-2.. SMALLER FLY ON SAME SIZE HOOK

C-3.. LOW WATER DRESSING

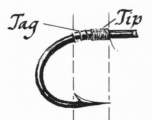

Tag          Tip

NOTE:
In a fully dressed fly
the tag and tip are di-
rectly over the barb of
the hook.

FIG. IX-3: STYLE IN FLY DESIGN

conditions, but most of them think these tiny hooks in the jaws of large fish cause too many pull-outs. Hence the low-water patterns. The choice, of course, is up to the angler.

## USE OF FLUORESCENT MATERIALS

One of the most important mid-century innovations in salmon flies has been the introduction of daylight fluorescent materials now being used in many modern patterns. This was pioneered for salmon flies in England by the well-known firm of E. Veniard, Ltd. and in North America by various anglers on the Miramichi. Daylight fluorescent material (D. F. M.) has the property of glowing when exposed to light rays, thus acting as a reflector. There is much to indicate that salmon respond to it, either because they are sensitive to ultra-violet light or because D. F. M. helps them to see flies from greater distances, especially in deep or discolored water.

D. F. M. is available in a wide range of silks, monofilament, wools, hackles, furs and other fly-tying materials. Best colors are white and pastel tints of blue, yellow, lime green, orange, scarlet, pink and grey. The darker the shade, the less the fluorescence. Since the material is not active when no light is present, it is of less value on very dark days or before and after daylight. This suggests that flies for such periods should contain a greater amount of D. F. M. than flies used in bright sunlight.

We have experimented with D. F. M. extensively on the Miramichi and this author is one who considers it virtually a necessity on hair-wing patterns such as the *Butts* described in Chapter XI. There, we use flies with black or brown hair-wings, black body ribbed with tinsel, and a butt of D. F. M. of one color or another. Some anglers are particular about the color; others think it makes little or no difference. When I dress these simple flies I like to add a strand or two of D. F. M. silk mixed into the wing (as well as using it for the butt) because this has seemed to be more productive. However, even if the amount of D. F. M. is regulated by the amount of daylight we should not suppose that if a little is good a lot is better. Only a suggestion is needed. It seems that salmon are not attracted to flies that have too much.

## HERON HACKLED SPEY FLIES

One idea that North American anglers should find valuable is the adoption of the British method of using flies with long, flowing hackles such as black and grey Heron, used chiefly in Spey flies. A leading exponent of this is the famous English angler, Geoffrey Bucknall. In an article in the August, 1969, *Trout and Salmon* he says:

"It would be a mistake to assume that Spey flies should be confined to the river that gives them their name. They are uniquely designed for effectiveness in fast rivers. Indeed, they need a fierce flow to give them full play, but there are many rivers in this category and even more pools on otherwise quiet rivers. The lesson is that not only do we need flies of various sizes and colours, but we should carry flies of different style to suit changing conditions on any given river.

"The family of flies have only two difficulties in their manufacture. The first problem lies in the number of ribbing materials which, with the usual Heron hackle, have to be tied in at the end of the body and wound up the shank. A normal Spey fly has three tinsels, a narrow flat and fine oval being wound in the usual direction with the remaining oval or flat reversed. To avoid an ugly bunching at the tail of the fly these materials are spaced out as they are tied in, leaving two turns of the body wool between each tinsel. Between the last two tinsels I tie in my Heron hackle by the butt. I also tie the reversed tinsel last, over the hackle to protect it.

"The other problem lies in winging, for although these are usually simple strips of brown Mallard feather, they do not sit on top of the hook shank in the usual wing position. They have to sit lower down on the shoulder of the hook shank, and this is tricky to manage without splitting the wing or bringing part of it below the shank.

"The usual procedure is to tie in the further wing, then reverse the silk to tie on the matching nearer strip. I find it better to tie both wing slips in together, and if care is taken the wings can be held in the normal upright position. Then the pressure is eased slightly while the wings are worked gently down on to the shoulders of the shank. The turns of silk are brought over the wings in the usual way, and after a little experience perfect results will be obtained.

"A minor problem is doubling the hackle, but Heron folds over easily once the butt has been tied down firmly to the hook. Moisten the long fibers and they can be stroked backwards into the doubled position. As in all salmon flies, stripping one side of the stalk denudes the fly of its share of working parts, and it is a sloppy expedient.

"Spey flies are drab, with a thin body and long flowing hackles. The body hackles are usually Heron, black or grey, with the tail and throat fibers from the body feather of the Golden Pheasant. The wings are low and slim, clinging to the body when wet, and they are also from a soft, flowing feather such as barred Mallard or Teal. When Mallard is used the grey roots of the feather are deliberately left showing in the wing, unlike most sea-trout and salmon flies using this feather.

"The Spey flies used to be tied on the old Dee hooks, long in shank, fine in wire, but these were so close to the low-water irons that they are largely superseded by the latter. This tells us that these patterns are good for the greased-line conditions, and there's a type of streamy water that screams out for a *Lady Caroline*.

"The *Lady Caroline* is, perhaps, the most popular of the family. The body is made by intertwining two strands of light-brown wool with one of olive—thin strands, that is. A flat gold tinsel is closely followed by a fine silver oval. The grey Heron hackle is doubled and wound and the third tinsel of flat gold binds it down in reverse direction to give a cross-stitch effect with the other two tinsels. The Golden Pheasant breast feather is used for the tail and throat hackle and the narrow strips of brown Mallard complete the fly.

"My own favourite is the *Grey Heron*, which is almost a Spey version of the *Jeannie*. The body is in two sections, the rear third of yellow wool and the front two-thirds black. The ribbings are flat and oval silver with flat gold reversed rib over a grey Heron hackle. The throat hackle is speckled grey Guinea Fowl and the wings are of brown Mallard. The throat hackles should be tied in as a beard or false hackle to allow the wings to hug the body.

"If you want a brighter Spey fly, try the *Carron*, with its body of orange wool ribbed over the black Heron hackle with flat silver tinsel and red floss silk, with fine oval silver in reverse. The throat is Teal and the wings are of brown Mallard. These three make up my

FIG. IX-4

THE "GREY HERON":
AN EXAMPLE OF HERON HACKLED SPEY FLIES

repertoire, but I add a concocted cross-breed called the *Black Heron*, based on a black body and hackle, silver ribs, Guinea Fowl wing and Teal throat hackle, with a red tail.

"These Spey flies hold their own among passing fashions. Their great quality lies in the mobility of the long, flowing hackles at a time when fly inventors seem preoccupied with colour. I rate them highly against heavier, solid tubes and hair-wings on elongated trebles. They are, for me, the best flies to use in low, clear, though fast, water. They are also popular among certain North American addicts. I use them for sub-surface fishing and I've no experience with their effectiveness as a deeply-sunk fly, though my reading leads me to conclude that they were used as such in days of yore.

186

"I can't say how many commercial tyers are still making Spey flies, but they are well within the reach of the home tyer with many simple household materials. That combination of shrimpy feelers, dull colour, slim line and maybe just one spot of brightness—say red or orange—and the line sings!"

Eric Taverner, in his important book, *Fly-Tying for Salmon*, discusses Heron feathers as follows: "Upon the head and the shoulder of the heron grow the long-fibered black hackles and upon the breast and rump of the same bird soft grey hackles, which are a special feature of the flies named after Aberdeenshire Dee. These hackles are very mobile and are extremely long in the fiber; the beginner who is laying the foundation of his collection of feathers will probably be surprised at the size of the hackles suitable for these patterns."

*Spey* strip-wing patterns (such as *Lady Caroline*) have long, flowing, mobile body and throat hackles, horizontal Mallard wings and their wool bodies criss-crossed with tinsel. They are designed for fast-water fishing. *Dee* strip-wing patterns (such as *Akroyd*) are lightly dressed to sink rapidly in cold-water fishing. They have shorter hackles than Spey flies, horizontal, separated Turkey tail wings, (usually) Seal's fur bodies, and are tied on longer-shanked low-water type hooks. The two types have much in common, including mobile hackles and wings.


## ARTICULATED HOOKS

We have noted that the long shanks of hooks such as are used on streamer flies and bucktails provide leverage which works a hole in the part of the salmon's mouth where they are embedded, thus sometimes causing them to pull out. To a large extent this difficulty has been avoided by the "articulated hook" (one having joints or articulations) such as the "Cebrit" brand available in England. This is a heavy-iron jointed hook wherein the short-shank rear part has a ringed eye joined to the forward part which consists of an upturned eye and a short shank on the rear end of which is a vertical ring permanently linked with the ringed eye of the rear part. This of course provides a longer fly with much less danger of pull-outs due to

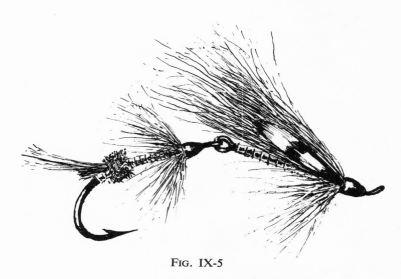

FIG. IX-5

AN ARTICULATED HOOK

leverage. The heavier hook fishes deeper and its jointed construction provides added movement to the fly. During the year following its invention the British inventor claimed sixty-one salmon hooked and sixty landed. Colonel Drury has observed that articulated hooks are not yet as popular as they should be. North American anglers who wish to try them should check their legality in regions where they are to be used.

## HOW TO DRESS TUBE FLIES

Another British development which, because of more restrictive fly-fishing regulations, will have less application to North American salmon fishing (unless used with a single or double hook) is the "Tube Fly" with the treble hook. An author in the September, 1959, issue of *Trout and Salmon* says, "Perhaps the most important advance which has occurred in salmon fly-fishing since Wood introduced the greased line method is the appearance of the tube fly. Armed with a treble hook it swims better, casts better and hooks far better than the

188

FIG. IX-6

A TUBE FLY (with extra tubes)

traditional fly. It has often been said that the tube fly is no good for greased line fishing because it tends to skate over the surface of the water. That is true of the unweighted plastic tube. The difficulty ceases to exist if one can vary the proportion of plastic to metal within reasonably wide limits in the construction of the fly."

Tube flies are tied on plastic or metal* tubes whose bores are no larger than necessary to allow them to slide on a leader tippet. One or more (usually two) dressed tubes are strung on the tippet and a short-shanked treble, double or single hook is attached to the end, this being partly concealed by the dressing on the sliding tubes. While anglers in the British Isles use and prefer treble hooks, North American salmon anglers usually must be content with doubles or singles, although the trebles will be ideal for other species of fish wherever their use is permitted. The tubes are cut just long enough to allow application of the dressing, usually a quarter or a half inch long, but sometimes considerably longer.

* Metal tubes being "weighted flies" may be illegal in many areas of North America.

189

The tubes can be cut from the empty ink refills of ball-point pens, although the bore is a bit too large; from fine metal or plastic tubing; from used hypodermic needles; from the tubing of electric wiring used in motor cars; or they can be made from small feather quills. Lips can be made on the ends of plastic tubes by holding them briefly in the center of a small flame; this helps to prevent the thread windings from slipping off. To tie them, slide the tube section on to the shank of an eyeless hook which is placed in a vise, or over a darning needle of a size which allows the tube to jam on it so that it will not turn or slide while being dressed. Of course metal tubes (such as copper) are used when weight is needed to sink the lure, while plastic ones are chosen for near-surface fishing. (A source for such tubes is model-making shops.) Since two tubes are generally used, one can be light, the other heavy. The interchangeability of dressed tubes also provides variety in color combinations.

The tubes are dressed as one dresses the body of a fly: by winding thread from front to back; tying in silk and/or ribbing; and applying the dressing forward, where it is tied off at the front end. (Colored tubes may not need dressing.) Prepare hair as one does when applying a hair-wing for a fly. Place a little varnish where the hair is to be tied in, and lay a very small bunch of the hair at the head of the tube. Tie this in with a turn of thread and then loosen and turn the tube toward you to tie in the next bunch beside the previous one. Continue this until the tube is covered with hair extending considerably longer than the tube. Bunches of hackle and feather sections can be applied similarly, two feather sections being applied on opposite sides of the tube to simulate wings. Care must be taken to keep the head of the tube as small as possible to prevent a bow-wave and to facilitate the entry of the fly into the water. Each bunch of hair should be trimmed when applied, rather than all at once. Palmering a hackle beside the body tinsel can be done, but applying a hackle as a collar makes too large a head. The winging usually is quite long, at least for rear tubes, because the winging should partially conceal the hook. Soft hair such as squirrel is preferred for slow water, stiff hair such as bucktail for fast rivers. If added weight is needed to make the lure fish deep, a round or cone-shaped metal bead can be strung at the head of the assembly (see preceding footnote). Sometimes a small extension of rubber tubing or something similar is pushed over the end of the tube so the eye of the hook also can be fitted into it for greater rigidity and to prevent foul-hooking the hook on the leader while casting. One does not normally tie a tube fly all at one time. It is more convenient to do several bodies at once and to let them dry before applying the winging. A convenient way to dry the tubes is to string each one on a vertical pin pushed through a piece of cardboard. Sometimes tubes are bound with wire or lead to facilitate sinking for deep fishing. Tube flies are fished like other flies. When a fish is hooked the tube is free to slide up the leader, so it is rarely damaged. Sets of light and dark colored tubes both in heavy and light weights provide a selection for varied uses, and two or three dozen of them can be carried in a small matchbox.

The variables in tube flies are weight, color and length of body. When water is high and cold and a large orthodox fly would be used, the composite tube fly would be made up of three or more half-inch sections of heavy (copper) tubes armed with a size 6 hook, or larger. When water is low and clear, and an orthodox fly such as one on a size 6 low-water hook would be called for, the composite tube fly might be one heavy and one light quarter-inch section armed with a size 8 or 10 hook. Both sections could be light-toned, or one light and one dark. In high- and cold-water conditions in quiet parts of a pool the heavy sections might snag on the bottom. In this case one would substitute one or more light plastic tubes. Selections of tubes in weight, color and number vary between these extremes.

Here are a few British tube fly-dressings which should give American anglers an idea of how to simulate any American fly pattern in tube design:

*Hairy Mary:* Tube: white or clear. Hackle: light blue. Wings: Grey Squirrel

*Blue Charm:* Tube: black. Body: Flat silver. Hackle: light blue. Wings: Teal

*March Brown:* Tube: black. Body: Oval silver. Hackle: Pheasant. Wings: Pheasant

*Jock Scott:* Tube: yellow. Body: $\frac{1}{2}$ yellow, $\frac{1}{2}$ black floss ribbed oval silver. Wings: Gallina with red, yellow and blue Swan fibers.

*Black Doctor:* Tube: red. Body: black floss ribbed oval silver. Wings: Pheasant and brown Mallard on two sides; red and blue Swan on the other two sides

*Silver Grey:*      Tube: black.   Body: flat silver.    Wings: Grey Teal on two
    sides; yellow and blue Swan on the other two sides
*Logie:*            Tube: yellow.   Body: $\frac{1}{2}$ bare yellow tube; $\frac{1}{2}$ red claret floss
    ribbed oval silver.   Wings: light blue hackle fibers and yellow Swan
*Jeannie:*          Tube: yellow.   Body: black floss ribbed oval silver.     Wings:
    black hackle fibers and brown Turkey
*Shrimp:*           Tube: yellow.   Tail: bunch of Golden Pheasant red breast.
    Body: black floss ribbed oval silver.   Wings: Golden Pheasant red breast and
    white hackle

Historically it is verified that tube flies were originated about 1945
by the noted fly-dresser, Mrs. Winnie Morawski (Colin Simpson's
instructor), when she was working for the tackle firm of Charles
Playfair & Company, of Aberdeen. At first she used sections of turkey
wing quills with the pith scraped out and with the shanks of the
strung treble hooks inside the quill sections. She dressed orthodox
flies (body dressing, wing, hackle, etc.) on these. A doctor named
William Michie, when visiting the shop, suggested using sections of
surgical tubing instead. Later the treble hook was left on the outside
so the tube could travel up the monofilament line, out of harm's way,
when a fish was hooked. Also the wing later was dressed around the
tube, instead of in only one place, as described above.


## FLY-DRESSING TIPS

Since this book tries to omit as much as possible of whatever has
been published in others it gives a minimum of instruction on the
techniques of fly-dressing. There are many excellent books on that
subject, some of the best of which are listed in the bibliography.
However, there are a few tricks of the trade rarely if ever called to the
attention of fly-dressers, so it might help to mention some of them:

Alex Simpson, of Aberdeen, who has dressed several flies for this
book, writes that he has trouble scraping off herl to make herl bodies,
because many herls break in the process. In connection with his
business of checking ship cargoes he noticed the attractiveness of
plastic ropes which are laid in orange, blue, hot-orange, yellow, olive
and other colors. He takes a thread of a piece of rope; places it on a
hard surface; and pulls it under a knife-blade whose top edge is held
sloping away from him. By slowly drawing the thread toward him it

becomes flattened, like a quill. He reports that these flattened threads, in appropriate colors, make excellent simulated quill bodies and are useful for ribbing and other fly-dressing purposes.

Because so many fly-dressers have difficulty in equalizing hair-ends for hair-wing flies it may be helpful to repeat an easy way of doing it. Cut off the hair needed for a fly; remove underfur, and drop the hairs tip-first into a small container such as the top of a lady's lipstick. Tap the container on a hard surface and immediately all hair-ends are of the same length.

To straighten hackles that are loose and have become twisted, tie a dozen or so at the quill base with thread so all are right side up. Hold them under cold water until they are saturated. Stroke them with index finger and thumb until all are lying even. Wet them again; check their alignment; and place them on several layers of newspaper, right side up. When so placed, pull the bunch slightly toward you to be sure all are straight. Allow them to dry completely and then hold the bunch by their quill bases between the thumb and index finger of the right hand and smartly strike the right hand on the left. This will make all the fibers take their natural shape, and every feather will be perfect.

All wet salmon flies will be stronger and will last longer if they have a tag of three or four turns of oval tinsel. While flat tinsel is sometimes used, it should be used only on flies which have no floss tips. The floss can slip over the flat tinsel, but oval tinsel holds it firmly in place and prevents it from fraying. The tinsel supports all that goes on afterward. Using oval tinsel or wire is especially important in dressing double-hook flies tied in the traditional manner. If flat tinsel were to be used it would be twisted out of shape as it is drawn up between the two hooks. Fine wire makes a very subtle tag on small and delicate flies and is often used on larger fancy flies and exhibition patterns.

In using herl for bodies of wet salmon flies the body will be stronger if four or five strands are twisted only a few times around the tying silk, with the twisted herl and silk wound on together. If one herl breaks it can be snipped off without harming the body.

Dry-flies for salmon, such as the Wulff patterns, will float longer if kapok is applied as a base before the body is dressed.

Hair used for winging salmon flies should be reasonably straight to provide the sleek, nymph-like look that seems to get best results. The fine hairs of Squirrel tail provide excellent mobility for small flies. Bucktail and Polar Bear do the same for larger ones. Polar Bear is a favorite because of its sheen.

It may do no harm to repeat that amateurs and professionals alike invariably overdress salmon flies. The mark of the expert is the *sleek look*. Too little hair and hackling is far better than too much!

## NOTES ON FLY PATTERNS

In planning this book it seemed that it would be most helpful to separate European patterns from North American ones and in both cases to describe hair-wing and feather-wing patterns in separate chapters, also to separate British patterns from those few used almost exclusively on the Continent. There is information about each division that applies to that category alone, and the identity of the information might become lost if everything were grouped together. Presumably this is the first book to examine the broad expanse of modern Atlantic salmon fly patterns and angling techniques all around the Atlantic wherever this noble gamefish swims. In being comprehensive it has been necessary to be somewhat restrictive, so the author hopes to be excused if somebody thinks that something important has been left out. Of course, the author will be criticized by anglers and fly-dressers who can't locate their pet patterns. Undoubtedly the pattern is in the book, if it is any good, but probably it will have been described as a basic pattern rather than an adaptation or variation under another name. All has been included which the size of the book permits. If local adaptations and variations could have been included the only result would be to clutter the book with trivia and probably to throw many of its readers into a state of relative frustration!

## EXHIBITION PATTERNS

In diminishing the importance of the British classic patterns the author realizes that many anglers like them because they are pretty, and many fly-dressers like them because they are a challenge. Dressing these complicated patterns properly is a great deal more of an art than the uninitiated might presume. While acknowledging the efficiency and common sense of modern simplified patterns the author wonders why we shouldn't also exalt the art of salmon fly dressing by doing Exhibition Patterns which are made to enjoy rather than to fish with. Evidently the British Fly Dressers' Guild promotes competitions, thus allowing its members to display the extent of their art, and perhaps the American Federation of Fly Fishermen and American fly-dressing clubs should do the same. For this reason the author has included a few Exhibition Patterns such as *Apollo 11*, *Prince Philip* and a fly named for him, the latter two dressed by Jimmy Younger, great-great-grandson of the famous angling author and fly-dresser, John Younger, and winner of the 1969 fly-dressing competition sponsored by the Fly Dressers' Guild. Jimmy dresses flies for the royal family and is considered about the best in the business but, with very young men like Colin Simpson coming along, Jimmy had better watch it! Readers who note the artistry of Colin's craftsmanship, which graces some of the color plates in this book, will realize that the ancient art is a long way from being dead. At the moment that I write this Colin Simpson is not quite fifteen years old! Also, he ties flies without using a vise.

## FLY PATTERNS OF THE FUTURE

American fly-dressers and anglers and their counterparts in the British Isles owe a lot to one another and can learn much from one another. Why don't we take advantage of the gracefully flowing Heron hackles used in Spey flies, and of the excellent British shrimp or prawn imitations, for example? Why don't the British do more with streamers, dry flies and nymphs? We also can learn from their angling methods, and they can from ours.

Examination of the modern patterns in this book should make us realize that what we now know is only a step toward what should be learned in the future. If, for example, salmon will rise to bits of foil torn from cigarette packages tossed off bridges, why shouldn't we use mylar tubular piping for fly bodies, and why shouldn't we include thin strips cut from mylar sheets to provide a touch of flash in hair-wings and in feather-wings? Salt water fly-fishermen know that these embellishments are notably effective. Synthetic hair, dyed in all colors, has been developed which has more strength and mobility than animal hair, and moths won't touch it. Modern developments in plastics, and those to come, open the door still farther.

In the future of salmon flies we shall see a decline in preference for fancy patterns and in the use of rare and unnecessary feathers. Undoubtedly there will be more extensive use of offset and double-offset hooks. We probably shall see fewer hooks in the familiar black Japanned finish and more of them plated in chrome, nickel and gold. We expect that opaque feather-wing patterns will give way more and more to mobile and less destructible hair-wings, and we expect more of the hair-wings to be made of artificial materials. Undoubtedly we will see unanticipated innovations in floating lure design and in floating lure materials. We will see streamers, nymphs and dry flies in more startling designs enjoy more extensive worldwide uses. Probably a generation or two hence this book will be as outdated as Kelson's is today, but the person who wrote it hopes it will remain equally as interesting!

Several years ago while sitting on the beach of a salmon stream I admired the superb tackle owned by a distinguished old gentleman, and particularly his boxes of feather-winged flies most of which had been expensively dressed by the greatest experts in Scotland. As we talked he took from a box a new *Jock Scott* so beautifully made that I would have preserved it as a museum piece. He used a pin to separate the carefully married sections of the wing and he kept stroking the pin through the fly until every fiber was separated, thus making the wing look as if it had been made of hair. A gorgeous example of the fly-dressers' art had been ruined.

"It seems a shame to treat a beautiful fly that way," I ventured. "Why don't you use a hair-wing of similar pattern?"

The old man shook his head. "I've always used traditional patterns," he said, "and I guess I'll never change. Trouble with them is they don't have enough action, so I separate all the fibers to make them pulsate in the water. I catch more salmon that way."

Since then I've seen several anglers of the old school do the same thing. While clinging to the old methods they unconsciously bow to the new!

# X

# North American
# Feather-Wing Patterns

It is rather disconcerting for this author, who has profound appreciation for the beauty and artistry of classical feather-wing patterns, to
have to report that he was tempted to title this chapter "Requiem for
the Feather-Wings" insofar, at least, as their future popularity in
North America is concerned.

The cooperation of officials in the Ministère du Tourisme de la
Chasse et de la Pêche of the Province of Quebec made available
voluminous records for the years 1964 through 1969 of guides'
reports of catches of Atlantic salmon on typical Quebec rivers such
as the St. Jean, Matapedia and Little Cascapedia, detailing indicative
information regarding successful flies used there, together with dates,
locations, weather conditions, names of anglers, names of guides and
so forth.

The author took the time to tabulate all this material with the
hope of providing information of useful interest. He realizes that
what holds true for a few rivers may not establish a pattern for them

all, so he offers the results of the study for whatever they seem to be worth.

Four flies stand out, all the others enjoying less than twenty-five per cent of the popularity of these four. Of the top four, the *Rusty Rat* is twice as popular as any of the other three, these being in order of importance the *Green Highlander*, the *Silver Rat* and the *Black Dose*. Now of course the two *Rat* patterns are hair-wings. The other two are classic feather-wing patterns, but there was no information as to whether they were hair-winged adaptations. As far as the *Green Highlander* is concerned, the author suspects that the majority were hair-wings because this version enjoys top popularity on Quebec rivers. The *Black Doses* probably were feather-winged, but no doubt some were in the hair-wing or reduced variations.

The other popular classic patterns are *Silver Grey*, *Silver Doctor*, *Jock Scott*, *Blue Charm* (usually low-water), *Lady Amherst* and *Dusty Miller*, in that order. In tabulating salmon caught on these flies in 1964 and again in 1969 we find that the popularity of these flies has decreased by eighty per cent, although this may have been influenced in part by a fishery that declined about fifty per cent in volume during the six years.

Other popular hair-wings of the area include the *Black Rat*, *Cosseboom* (often fished dry), *Grey Rat*, *Royal Coachman* (often probably fished dry, as in the Wulff pattern), and the *Orange Blossom*.

Popular dry flies (in addition to the two above) are the *Grey Wulff*, *White Wulff* and *Rat-Faced MacDougall*. The reports didn't indicate increased use of dry flies over these years, but this is true in other areas.

The "also-rans" (omitting a few unknown ones) comprised about fifty patterns which took relatively few fish. These included several bucktails or streamers the most productive of which was the *Mickey Finn*.*

Anglers fishing in Nova Scotia and farther north in Labrador and Newfoundland will find that the classic patterns mentioned are among the favorites there and that they are more popular than in

---

* The MICKEY FINN is a bucktail with a silver tinsel body and a wing of yellow over red over yellow hair, each sparse and in equal parts.

(*A. Oglesby*)

Fig. X-1

BEACHING A SALMON

199

regions to the south. The dry flies mentioned also are popular in these areas, inclusive of a few bivisibles and spiders. Usual hook sizes are between No. 4 and No. 10. The popularity of hair-wings seems to be increasing year by year, and the ones mentioned should provide a good list.

Hair-wing patterns also are predominant in New Brunswick, probably more so than anywhere else, and will be discussed in the next chapter. Meanwhile, even if the popularity of the feather-winged flies of New Brunswick declines, they are very important in the history of salmon fishing in North America. Also, there are several which can be very handy at times.

Anglers who fish anywhere on the vast network of the Miramichi usually drive north through Doaktown, which is famous mainly because Wally Doak lives there. Wally is proprietor of a neat little tackle shop on the main street, and it is customary to drop in to learn about new styles in flies; to purchase tackle; to inquire how the river is; and to find out who's around and what is going on.

Late one evening Wally shooed out his last customer, locked the door, and we gossiped about flies in the back room.

"What are the best feather-wings nowadays?" I asked him, knowing that selling thousands of flies every year made him the regional oracle on the subject.

"Well, by far the biggest percentage of the flies I sell are hair-wings. Among the feather-wings the earliest ones included the *Abe Munn Killer*, *American Jock Scott*, *Dillinger*, *McGinty* and the *Nipisiguit Grey*. Nowadays it would be the *Black Fairy*, *Fiery Brown*, *Silver Grey*, *Black Dose*, *Oriole* and the *Reliable*. You know that the *Oriole* and the *Reliable* were originated by Ira Gruber. Hook sizes usually are between No. 4 and No. 10, depending on water conditions. Using single or double hooks is a matter of choice."

Wally and I discussed flies until we both became tired of it, which was long past his bedtime. On another evening this perennial discussion was renewed with Father Smith.

"Here are boxes containing all the important flies that Ira Gruber originated," Father Smith said. "Ira's son, Ed Gruber, thought you should have them. This is a complete set, and Ed thought you might like to include some of them in your book."

Fig. X-2

HAND-TAILING A SALMON

201

I accepted the offering gratefully and have included as many patterns as possible because Ira Gruber made a lasting mark on North American salmon fishing.

Ira Gruber owned a cotton-knitting mill in Spring City, Pennsylvania, and he retired to his beloved Miramichi River in 1915 to spend the rest of his life hunting and fishing. He hired Wilson ("Bing") Russell as a guide in 1930, and the affable Bing remained with him until Gruber's death. Ira was taught to tie flies by a local expert named Everett Price. Ira and Bing fished for salmon on every suitable day from summer to fall for many years. They began by using big flies (6 and 4 doubles) but, as Ira learned more about it, he often used ones as small as 12's.

Bing says that in the early years people stopped fishing when the water became low and clear because salmon were too hard to catch despite the fact that many could be seen. Ira showed them how to do it with small flies, and he became one of the most important (if not the most important) of the inventive anglers and fly-dressers in the development of the Miramichi salmon fishery. Most of his patterns were developed between 1935 and 1945. His *Black Spider* was one of the earliest and proves that hair-wings with colored butts are at least as old as 1935.

Ira, more than anyone else, was responsible for developing the general conformation of the Miramichi-type salmon fly with its short cigar-shaped body ribbed with fine, close-turned tinsel and with a wing which was short and hugged the body. Another feature of his style was the care with which throat hackle was tied in or wound on. The length of the hackles was shorter, and they were sparser than those on the average trout fly. Ira Gruber was among the first to use bronzed straight and offset hooks for salmon fishing. Almost all his flies were tied on Allcock Model Perfect hooks and, as the years went by, he seemed to prefer single hooks to doubles. Among his most famous patterns are the *Oriole* and the *Reliable*, still very popular as this is written. He passed away after a stroke about 1963, when he was in his early seventies, but his mark is left in the very effective and beautifully proportioned original flies described and illustrated here, and in the reproductions which grace the fly-boxes of anglers who know what patterns will catch salmon in the summer when they are hard to hook.

While Ira's small flies are very effective under difficult conditions, we have observed that 10's and 12's may not hold as well as larger irons. Low-water patterns (small flies on larger, light hooks) are an alternative for this reason. On the Miramichi, the *Logie* and *Blue Charm* are very effective, as well as some of the Gruber patterns tied that way, and of course the new techniques we have described help to make difficult fishing easier.

The patterns which follow in this chapter include (I hope) all the important North American feather-wings, plus several also included for historical or for fly-dressing interest. Prominent among them are three of Harry Darbee's "reduced" British classics (here because they are American variations). These are the reduced *Black Dose*, *Dusty Miller* and *Green Highlander*. Also included is John Atherton's *Bastard Dose*.

## ABE MUNN KILLER

*Head color:* Black
*Tag:* About six turns of fine oval gold tinsel, or gold wire
*Tail:* Two extremely narrow sections of an Oak Turkey wing feather, merging together and extending a little beyond the bend of the hook
*Body:* Buttercup-yellow wool, smooth
*Ribbing:* Fine oval gold tinsel
*Throat:* Two or three turns of a brown hackle, veiled (fronted) by an extremely small bunch of Oak Turkey fibers. The brown hackle is pulled down and tied slightly backward, the longest fibers extending no more than to the tip of the point of the hook. The Oak Turkey is somewhat shorter, and very sparse
*Wing:* Applied in four sections, two on each side of Oak Turkey wing sections extending very slightly beyond the bend of the hook to a point halfway of the tail. The wing is applied low—close to the body

Abe Munn (sometimes incorrectly called "Moon" or "Muhn" because that is the way he pronounced it) was a guide in the early days of fly-fishing for salmon in the vicinity of Boiestown, New Brunswick. Since he tied this fly about 1925, it seems to be the earliest named North American fly used on the Miramichi River. This dressing and the sample of the fly were provided by Wallace Doak, who copied it from Abe Munn's original pattern.

ORIOLE        STONE FLY        RELIABLE

The patterns above were originated and dressed by
Mr. Ira Gruber (A)


BASTARD DOSE        NIGHT HAWK        BLACKVILLE

Dressed by            Dressed by         Originated and
Mr. Robert Cavanagh (A)   The Orvis Company (P)   Dressed by
                                             Mr. Bert Miner (P)


SPATE FLY                    MITCHELL

Originated and              Originated by
Dressed by              Mr. Archibald Mitchell
Mr. Harry Darbee (P)        Dressed by The
                        Rev. Elmer J. Smith (A)


NIPISIGUIT GREY              CRIMSON GLORY

Dressed by                  Originated by
Mr. L. A. Lapointe (P)      Mr. Herbert Howard
                            Dressed by
                        Mr. Burt Carpenter (P)


DOCTOR HALE        CRAYFISH        COPPER MARCH BROWN

Originated by         Originated and        Dressed by
Mr. John McDonald      Dressed by        Mr. Keith Fulsher (A)
Dressed by          Mr. Don Brown (P)
Mr. Charles DeFeo (A)


ABE MUNN KILLER     BROWN MOTH    AMERICAN JOCK SCOTT

Originated by        The patterns above were dressed by
Mr. Abe Munn              Mr. Wallace Doak (P)
Dressed by
Mr. Wallace Doak (P)


PLATE IV

North American Feather-Wing Patterns
*(The "Crayfish", not a winged pattern, is included here for*
*convenience.)*

204

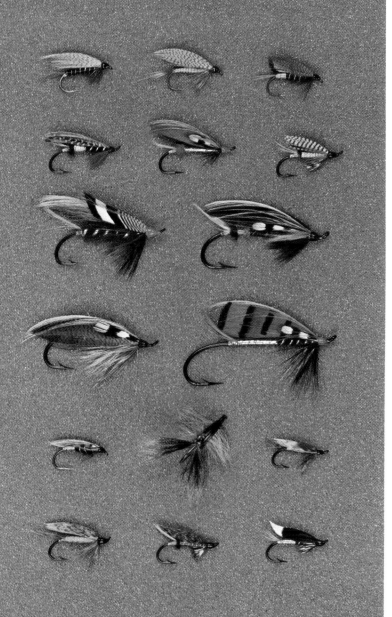

The fly was popularized in an article in *Fortune* (June 1948) wherein color illustrations of this fly and one called the *Abe Munn Upriver* evidently were transposed, with the latter incorrectly dressed. The *Abe Munn Upriver* is exactly the same as the *Abe Munn Killer* except that it was tied with Birch Partridge feathers instead of Oak Turkey. This seems to have been an expedient on Abe's part when he poled his canoe "upriver" where he didn't have any Oak Turkey but where he usually could kill a Partridge. The general opinion seems to be that the *Upriver* fly is an unnecessary variation which could be forgotten.

Ira Gruber used to like a fly he called the "Abe Mohn"; this may have been an attempt to imitate the *Killer* from memory. It is dressed in typical Gruber style, with a tail of red Golden Pheasant body fibers, smooth medium-yellow wool body, fine silver ribbing, brown hackle throat, and a 4-section wing of brown Mallard strips. In explanation of the "Mohn" spelling for Abe Munn (whose family was well-known by that name on the Miramichi), the always meticulous Ira Gruber packaged his flies in special cardboard boxes (3-3/4 ×2-1/4″×3/4″) finished in different colors, with a balsa-wood strip glued to the bottom into which the flies' barbs were stuck, and with his name and address printed on the covers. The flies' name, size and other identification were printed on box-end labels. He printed "Abe Mohn" on boxes for that pattern presumably because he didn't know the proper spelling. This adaptation came at least ten years after Abe first tied his well-known *Killer*.

## AMERICAN JOCK SCOTT

*Head color:*  Black
*Tag:*  Fine oval silver tinsel
*Tail:*  A Golden Pheasant crest feather
*Body:*  Rear half: medium yellow silk floss Front half: black silk floss
*Ribbing:*  Fine oval silver tinsel
*Throat:*  A small bunch of Guinea Hen fibers, quite short
*Wing:*  White tipped Blue Mallard, in four sections, two on each side

This is an American simplification, dated about 1930, of the popular British *Jock Scott*. A variation includes a black Ostrich herl butt and a wing (in four sections) of bronze Mallard side feathers.

Color may be added between the wing sections in red, yellow and blue. The fancy versions add a topping of a Golden Pheasant crest feather and include a black hackle throat veiled with Guinea Hen.

In Charles Phair's *Atlantic Salmon Fishing*, he says, "Lord Scott, who was a famous salmon fisherman, had a man who acted as his ghillie, and who came to him as a boy. All the name he had was Jock, and growing up as he did with Lord Scott, became known as Jock Scott. He became a very skillful fly dresser, a real genius with furs, feathers and silks. On a steamer once, going to Norway for some fishing, he dressed the fly which was named for him, and which has since become famous. It is a great fly in all sizes and all stages of water." Jock's British classic is much more complicated than this simple American version. (See also the hair-wing *Jock Scott*.)

## BASTARD DOSE (BASTARD BLACK DOSE)

*Head color:*  Black     Hook sizes: 2, 4, 6, 8
*Tag:*          Fine oval silver tinsel
*Tip:*          A few turns of yellow-orange or medium yellow silk floss
*Tail:*         A Golden Pheasant crest feather
*Butt:*         Black Ostrich herl
*Body:*         Rear quarter: light blue Seal's fur or wool   Forward part: black Seal's fur or wool
*Ribbing:*      Oval silver tinsel
*Throat:*       A small bunch of claret hackle fibers
*Wing:*         An underwing of a pair of Golden Pheasant tippets, back to back, over which, in four strips, two on each side, are sections of dark Teal not entirely covering the tippets
*Topping:*      A Golden Pheasant crest feather

This dressing is so-called because it is a simplified adaptation of the popular *Canadian Black Dose*. This pattern is as recommended by John Atherton in his book, *The Fly and the Fish*. He says, "In the larger sizes I usually cover the top or back of the wing with strips of bronze Mallard."

Usually, the *CANADIAN BLACK DOSE* is dressed with a black silk floss butt one-fifth of the body's length, and a body of black Seal's fur, with black hackle on body and throat. The wing is much more complicated than in this simplified version.

(See also the hair-wing *Black Dose*.) All dressings of this fly are very popular on many salmon rivers.

## BATS

*Head color:* Black    Hook sizes: No. 10 to 3/0; low-water
*Tag:*    Flat gold tinsel
*Tail:*    A Golden Pheasant crest feather, dyed orange
*Body:*    Green Seal's fur (*Green Highlander* green)
*Ribbing:*    Flat gold tinsel
*Throat:*    A few Guinea Fowl fibers, rather short
*Wing:*    A very few Red Fox guard hairs, over which are four or five green
Peacock sword fibers, over which are from two to six Golden Pheasant crest
feathers (one on top of the other) dyed orange. Each wing component is a bit
longer than the preceding one, with the toppings extending to the end of the
tail
*Cheeks:*    Jungle Cock

This is one of two patterns originated in 1921 by Dr. Elizabeth Brokaw, of Bound Brook, New Jersey. The fly is dressed in a wide range of sizes and has been effective on rivers throughout the world. It also is a good fly for sea-trout.

## BLACK DOSE (Reduced)

*Head color:* Black    Hook sizes: 12 to 2 (Dry fly)
*Tag:*    Oval silver tinsel
*Tail:*    A Golden Pheasant crest feather
*Body:*    Black silk floss
*Ribbing:*    Oval silver tinsel
*Throat:*    Two or three turns of a black hackle, applied as a collar and pulled
down
*Wing:*    Strips of black Crow (set to curve upward), extending to the tip
of the tail
*Cheeks:*    Jungle Cock, very small

This simplified adaptation of the famous *Black Dose* was originated about 1930 by Roy Steenrod, of Liberty, New York, a fishing companion of Theodore Gordon. The pattern was dressed for use on the Little Codroy River, in Newfoundland, and was given by Mr. Steenrod to Mr. Harry A. Darbee, who gave it to the author. This is a special dressing on a light-wire (Wilson dry fly) hook for use as a "riffling" fly (actively riffled, or skated, on the surface). It is used on most salmon rivers in Maine and in Canada and also is tied in regular and low-water dressings. (See also *Black Dose* and hair-wing *Black Dose*).

## BLACK HAWK

*Head color:*   Black      Hook size: #8, Model Perfect
*Tail:*          A few fibers of Summer Wood Duck
*Body:*          Light slate-grey silk floss (The original seems to have a pale yellow olive-grey color)
*Ribbing:*       Black tying thread
*Throat:*        A black hackle (off-black, with a mahogany hue) wound on as a collar and pulled down before the wing is applied. The hackle is tied in midway of the body and is palmered to the throat before winding the throat. It extends no longer than to the tip of the hook-point, and is quite sparse
*Wing:*          In four sections, two on each side, of slate-grey duck wing tapering to an off-white. The wing extends barely beyond the bend of the hook, is fairly full, and hugs the body closely

   This is one of the historic Ira Gruber patterns, tied primarily to be used in Big Hole Brook Pool, upriver from Doaktown, on the Miramichi River. This is a very large pool fed by spring water running down Big Hole Brook. When the water in the river rises to 70°F. or above, salmon, grilse and trout lie in this cooler water, sometimes in great numbers. For many years, Mr. Gruber leased the pool from Sherman Hoyt, who owned it at that time, about 1940. Mr. Gruber was one of the first men to learn that even in the hottest part of the summer salmon could be caught in the pool by using small wet or dry flies (even down to size #12) when they wouldn't take larger ones. This reminds us of a comment elsewhere in this book that some of the small flies used for trout occasionally are very effective for salmon.

## BLACKVILLE (OR BLACKVILLE SPECIAL)

*Head color:*   Black
*Tag:*           A very few turns of fine oval silver tinsel
*Tip:*           A few turns of medium yellow floss
*Tail:*          A Golden Pheasant crest feather, slightly longer than the bend of the hook
*Butt:*          Two or three turns of Peacock herl, quite sparse
*Body:*          Flat medium embossed silver tinsel
*Ribbing*        Fine oval silver tinsel
*Throat:*        One or two turns of a bright orange hackle, applied as a collar and tied back before the wing is put on. Forward of this (as a veil) is a very small bunch of Guinea Hen hackle, applied under the body, as a beard. Both collar and beard barbules are of equal length, extending about two-thirds of the way toward the point of the hook
*Wing:*          Four sections of grey Mallard flank feather; two sections on each side, extending nearly to the tip of the tail

This very important fly, used extensively on Canadian rivers, was originated by the famous fly-dresser and guide, Bert Miner, of Doaktown, New Brunswick, prior to 1950. Except for the simplified wing, the fly is very similar to the *Dusty Miller* and was adapted from this old British classic. The *Blackville* and the *Blackville Special* (as it sometimes is called) are the same fly. The *Blackville* has inspired several hair-wing descendants of which the earlier versions are from the bench of Bert Miner. Best known of these is the *Silver Down-Easter* (that is the correct name), which has a very similar body and a wing of black Squirrel tail hair, or Black Bear hair.

Since before 1960, Bert has been tying a fly which is exactly the same as the *Silver Down-Easter* except that it has a wing of natural *brown* Squirrel tail (instead of black). Bert named this version the *Cains River*, and it is very popular in that area. Other flies adapted from the original *Blackville* are the *Orange Blossom* (essentially a *Cains River*) and, more recently, the *Colonel Bates*, an adaptation of the streamer fly of the same name; this one, the hair-wing version.

A fly very similar to the *Blackville*, and unfortunately also called the *Blackville*, is described in John Atherton's book, *The Fly and the Fish*, and is one of his ten favorites. Evidently it is one of his several adaptations. It is the same as the above except that orange floss is used for the tag instead of yellow; the butt is black Ostrich herl (or black wool); there is no ribbing; the throat is bright orange, with no Guinea Hen; and each wing is of two sections of Widgeon or Pintail flank feathers. Both flies originated in Blackville, New Brunswick.

In some of these patterns the distinctive orange collar is wound on after the wing has been applied. Occasionally, other types of hair, such as Polar Bear, Fitch tail and brown bucktail are used. On modern flies, the tip (or butt, when it is not of a feather) is of a fluorescent material.

Ira Gruber tied a fly similar to the *Blackville* which he called the *Favorite*. It differs from the *Blackville* in that there is no tag or tip. The throat hackle (wound on as a collar and pulled down, as usual, before the wing is applied) is Plymouth Rock dyed orange. Very small Jungle Cock eyes extend half as long as the body, which extends no longer than the bend of the hook. This fly may have been referred to as the *Blackville Special*.

## BROWN MOTH

*Head color:* Black
*Tag:* Three or four turns of fine oval gold tinsel, or wire
*Tip:* Bright orange silk floss, quite sparse
*Tail:* A few yellow hackle fibers
*Butt:* About two turns of black Ostrich herl (Black chenille can be used on large sizes)
*Body:* Medium brown silk floss (not built up)
*Ribbing:* Fine oval gold tinsel
*Throat:* A small bunch of Guinea Hen fibers, tied on quite short
*Wing:* Four sections, two on each side, of speckled brown hen wing feathers, tied down low on hook (Bronze Turkey was used for the wing on the original pattern)

This is an old standard pattern, dating about 1929, and is one of the earliest flies used on the Miramichi River. It has been copied, perhaps with slight variations, and given new names, such as the *Brown Mystery* (which calls for a body of orange fluorescent floss), but the above pattern is the original.

## CHARLIE O

*Head color:* Red
*Tag:* Oval silver tinsel
*Tip:* Yellow silk floss
*Tail:* A Golden Pheasant crest feather
*Body:* Royal blue wool, not built up
*Ribbing:* Oval silver tinsel
*Throat:* A small bunch of Guinea Hen hackle, forward of which, wound on as a collar and pulled down, are two or three turns of hackle of Kingfisher-blue color
*Wing:* A tiny bunch of red bucktail, over which is a small bunch of brown bucktail twice the size of the red. Over this are about 8–10 strands of Peacock sword, all of same length
*Topping:* A Golden Pheasant crest feather (Optional)
*Cheeks:* Jungle Cock

This is one of the patterns tied in 1914 by Herbert Howard and Roy A. Thomson for Colonel Ambrose Monell and Dr. Orrin Summers, with the idea of using classic British feather-wing bodies with hair-wings in interesting combinations. This one has a body somewhat similar to the *Blue Doctor*. The fly was named for a guide.

## CRAYFISH

*Head color:* Black        Hook sizes: 1/0 to 12; Mustad #36890
*Claws:* Red Squirrel tail (as soft as possible)
*Body:* Dark brown yarn (formerly chenille)

*Legs:*          A brown saddle hackle tied palmer the length of the body
*Shell:*        A strip of dark brown Goose quill as wide as the body diameter
     tied in between claws, folded over body, and tied off at head

Although this is a crayfish imitation, it has been very successful for salmon due, probably, to the high degree of mobility of the claws and legs. It can be fished floating (when it seems to be most successful) until it sinks, then being fished wet, with very slight bucktailing action. It is effective on the surface and at all levels. The *Crayfish* originally was developed for fresh water bass (use Mustad #9671 hook for fresh water) but was tried for salmon in 1969 with considerable success. The pattern also is effective in hot-orange.

The method of tying is: 1) Wrap thread around hook-shank from eye toward bend, stopping just above the point of the hook. 2) Place a bunch of soft Red Squirrel tail hairs over the hook-shank and wrap firmly to shank. The hair should extend beyond the hook bend by an amount equal to the length of the hook. 3) Divide the hair into equal amounts and separate it by wrapping a few turns in Figure 8 fashion. The claws should be as nearly as possible at right angles to the hook-shank and divided above the point of the hook. 4) Tie in a strip of dark brown Goose quill with the glossy side facing down. (Later when the quill is folded over, the glossy side will face out.) 5) Tie in one brown saddle hackle. 6) Tie in dark brown yarn or chenille for body, wrap and tie off. (Note: On hook sizes #6 and smaller, tie in the body material at the claws, wrap to the hook eye and tie off. On hook sizes #4 and larger, it is best to build up the body with two or three wrappings of chenille or yarn.) 7) Wrap hackle palmer-style toward hook eye and tie off. Using thumb and index finger, fold hackle down. 8) Fold brown Goose quill over and tie off at eye of hook. 9) Apply two or three coats of polyurethene varnish to Goose quill and all windings.

## CRIMSON GLORY

*Head color:*    Red      Hook sizes: 8 to 5/0
*Tag:*             Oval gold tinsel
*Tail:*            A Golden Pheasant crest feather, dyed orange
*Body:*         Rear half: Flat silver tinsel    Front half: Peacock herl
*Ribbing:*     Oval gold tinsel
*Throat:*      A few turns of a black hackle, applied as a collar and pulled down

*Wing:*        Of Golden Pheasant tippets, dyed crimson; one pair extending nearly to tip of tail; another shorter pair fitted with outer black bar superimposed on second black bar of inner tippets
*Topping:*   A Golden Pheasant crest feather, dyed orange
*Cheeks:*    Jungle Cock

This colorful fly was originated by Herbert L. Howard in 1925 and the example shown was tied for him by Burt D. Carpenter, of Elmsford, New York, and given to the author by Mr. Howard. It has been used successfully in Norway, Newfoundland and on Quebec and New Brunswick rivers.

## DILLINGER

*Head color:*  Black
*Tag:*          Fine oval silver tinsel
*Tail:*         A Golden Pheasant crest feather
*Butt:*         Black chenille
*Body:*         Flat silver tinsel
*Ribbing:*      Fine oval silver tinsel
*Throat:*       Two or three turns of a medium blue hackle tied on as a collar and pulled down
*Wing:*         Four sections, two on each side, of speckled hen or bronze Turkey. The wing is applied close to the body, curving upward.

This is one of the early Miramichi River flies, dated about 1930. Since so many flies had been named with the word *killer* (*Abe Munn Killer*, etc.) at that time, this one was named for a notorious killer and bandit of the period.

## DR. HALE (OR DR. HILL)

*Head color:*  Black
*Tag:*          Three turns of fine gold wire or oval tinsel
*Tail:*         A Golden Pheasant crest feather
*Body:*         Rear quarter: Pale yellow silk or wool   Remainder: Black silk or wool
*Ribbing:*      Fine oval gold tinsel
*Throat:*       About two turns of a natural black hackle applied as a collar and pulled down (Blue dun sometimes is used)
*Wing:*         Strips of brown mottled hen Turkey tail
*Topping*       A Golden Pheasant crest feather
*Cheeks:*       Jungle Cock (the very smallest, tied in very short)

This fly was originated by John McDonnald, an accomplished angler and fly-dresser of Cambridge, Massachusetts. He named it for his doctor, Dr. Hill, but anglers mispronounced the name and the fly became known as the *Dr. Hale*. This was John McDonnald's favorite fly. He rarely used anything else and usually stopped fishing if salmon wouldn't take it. The black part of the body should be fat. The wings should lie close to the body and should extend only slightly beyond the bend of the hook (Mr. McDonnald used bronzed ones). Thus, the style of the fly is identical with some of the Ira Gruber patterns.

Another fly, perhaps associated with this one, is called the

## HALE SPECIAL:

| | |
|---|---|
| *Head color:* | Black |
| *Tag:* | Oval silver tinsel |
| *Tip:* | Gold silk floss |
| *Tail:* | A Golden Pheasant crest feather |
| *Body:* | Rear half: Lemon silk floss    Front half: Black silk floss |
| *Ribbing:* | Coarse oval silver tinsel |
| *Throat:* | About two turns of a black hackle applied as a collar and pulled down |
| *Wing:* | Strips of dark brown mottled Turkey tail, over which are strips of brown Mallard |
| *Topping:* | A Golden Pheasant crest feather |
| *Cheeks:* | Jungle Cock |

## DUSTY MILLER (Reduced)

| | |
|---|---|
| *Head color:* | Black    Hook sizes: 12 to 2 (Dry fly) |
| *Tag:* | Fine embossed silver tinsel |
| *Tail:* | A Golden Pheasant crest feather |
| *Body:* | Rear two-thirds: Embossed silver tinsel    Front third: Pink silk floss |
| *Ribbing:* | Fine oval silver tinsel |
| *Throat:* | A very small and short bunch of grey Guinea Hen fibers, tied under the hook |
| *Wing:* | Fairly narrow strips of bronze Mallard, extending to the end of the tail |
| *Cheeks:* | Jungle Cock, very small |

This adaptation is the work of the famous angler and fly-dresser, Harry A. Darbee, of Livingston Manor, New York. It was developed in 1950 and since then has been used on rivers in Nova Scotia, Labrador, Newfoundland and elsewhere. This is a sparse dressing on a light-wire (Wilson dry fly) hook, but the pattern also is dressed in regular and low-water styles. It has been very successful also on 1/0 hooks, and larger.

## GOBLIN

*Head color:* Red    Hook sizes: 10 to 2; low-water
*Tag:* Two or three turns of flat silver tinsel
*Tail:* A Golden Pheasant crest feather
*Body:* There is no body material. The ribbing is put on as usual and is lacquered.
*Ribbing:* Flat silver tinsel
*Throat:* A very small bunch of iridescent blue-green Peacock breast feather fibers, fairly short
*Wing:* A very small bunch of black bucktail, over which are a very few Peacock breast fibers about half the length of the bucktail
*Topping:* A Golden Pheasant crest feather
*Cheeks:* Jungle Cock, very small and short

This fly originated in Newfoundland before 1910. There are several patterns in this series, all having no body material other than the ribbing on a bare black hook. Various Scotch, English and Irish tyers did bodies this way, usually lacquering the hooks in various colors.

## GREEN DRAKE

*Head color:* Black
*Tag:* Oval gold tinsel
*Tip:* Yellow silk floss
*Tail:* A Golden Pheasant crest feather, over which are a very few shorter Golden Pheasant tippet fibers
*Butt:* Peacock herl, very small
*Body:* Pale honey-yellow silk floss
*Ribbing:* Flat gold tinsel, followed by a black thread
*Hackle:* A honey-colored hackle palmered from second turn of tinsel
*Throat:* About two turns of a Partridge hackle, pulled down and tied backward
*Wing:* Four strips, two on each side, of grey Mallard flank feather, dyed olive-green. The strips meet at the top, flaring out slightly below.

This May-fly imitation in simpler form is well known as a trout pattern. It is dressed with many variations, depending on the region where it is tied. This is the pattern of the LaPointes, who were famous salmon fly-dressers in the Matapedia area. The fly has been an old-time favorite in Canada but we haven't observed its use in recent years, perhaps because other patterns such as the green *Cosseboom* are preferred. Charles Phair, in his famous *Atlantic Salmon Fishing*, says that the *Green Drake* and the *Abe Munn Killer* were considered the two best flies (about 1935) on the Miramichi, and that the former also is good on the Matapedia, Restigouche and St. John Rivers.

A *Green Drake* which is popular on the Miramichi River is an adaptation of Ira Gruber. Its dressing is as follows, and it contains no tinsel of any kind.

*Head color:*    Black
*Tail:*          A few fibers from a red body feather of Golden Pheasant
*Body:*          Light green floss
*Ribbing:*       Black thread
*Throat*         A natural red hackle (i.e. brown), two or three turns of which are wound on as a collar and pulled down before the wing is applied
*Wing:*          An underwing of a few fibers of a brown-red Golden Pheasant body feather, on each side of which are two sections of grey Mallard dyed green drake (yellow-green) color (see note under *Oriole*).

## GREEN HIGHLANDER (Reduced)

*Head color:*    Black        Hook sizes: 12 to 2 (Dry fly)
*Tag:*           Very fine oval silver tinsel or silver wire
*Tail:*          A Golden Pheasant crest feather
*Body:*          Rear half: golden yellow silk floss:    Front half: bright green spun fur, all thinly dressed
*Ribbing:*       Very fine oval silver tinsel or silver wire
*Throat:*        About two turns of a bright yellow hackle, applied as a collar and pulled down, the longest fibers extending nearly to the point of the barb
*Wing:*          Strips of brown speckled Turkey wing, of moderate width, extending to the tip of the tail
*Shoulders:*     Jungle Cock, medium size and length

This simplified adaptation of the classic pattern is by Harry A. Darbee, of Livingston Manor, New York. It is a special dressing on a light wire (Wilson dry fly) hook and is used as a "riffling" fly. It is also tied in regular and low-water dressings (see also *Green Highlander* and hair-wing *Green Highlander*).

## HERMIT

*Head color:*    Black
*Tail:*          A few fibers of a red body feather of Golden Pheasant
*Body:*          Rear third: Bright yellow silk floss Forward two-thirds: Black silk floss (the body is slightly cigar-shaped, tapering to the rear)
*Ribbing:*       Narrow flat silver tinsel, over whole body
*Throat:*        Two or three turns of a brown hackle, wound on as a collar and pulled down before the wing is applied, after being palmered from the front half of the body
*Wing:*          Underwing: Several fibers of a red body feather of a Golden Pheasant

                 Overwing: A double wing, two sections on each side, of Grey Mallard dyed green drake color (as on all Gruber flies, the wing is tied low, hugging the body)

This is another of the several Gruber originals, dated about 1939. Mr. Gruber often used the *Hermit* and the *Oriole* alternately, in all levels of water. He dressed some of them heavily and in large (No. 6 and No. 4) sizes for high water, and others lightly dressed in smaller sizes for low water.

## HORNBERG

*Head color:*   Black      Hook size: 6 or 8, usually
*Body:*          Flat silver tinsel
*Wing:*         Two barred grey Mallard breast feathers one and one-half inches long, between which are the very narrow tips of two yellow neck hackles as long as the Mallard and nearly concealed by it. These cover the shank of the hook, and are stroked to a point at their ends by applying a small amount of lacquer, rubbed between thumb and forefinger. The width of the feathers (for a size 6 hook) is at least a quarter of an inch, with the yellow hackles narrower. (An easy way to apply the Mallard is to strip the lower sides of the feathers from the quills.)
*Cheeks:*      Jungle Cock, fairly long
*Hackle:*     Four or five turns of a grizzly hen neck hackle wound on as a collar after wing and cheeks have been applied. (The hackling should be fairly wide and heavy. The wing should not be applied too far forward, to accommodate it.)

This is a trout fly which has been very successful for salmon. The technique is to fish it dry until it sinks, then to finish the cast by fishing it wet. The pattern was developed by retired Conservation Warden Frank Hornberg, of Wisconsin. In the eastern United States many anglers do not apply lacquer to the wing-tips. Some variations use yellow hair instead of the yellow hackles, and Teal instead of the Mallard.

## LITTLE JOE

*Head color:*   Black      Hook size: #6, Model Perfect
*Tail:*          A few fibers of a barred black and white Wood Duck feather
*Body:*          Black nylon wool, tapered at both ends and built-up in the middle
*Ribbing:*     A fairly heavy brownish copper-colored thread
*Throat:*      About two turns of a very light dun hackle, wound on as a collar and pulled down before the wing is applied. The hackle extends no longer than to the point of the hook.
*Wing:*         In four strips, two on each side, of sections of brown Mallard. The wing is fairly full, extending no longer than the bend of the hook, and is applied low against the body.

This is one of Ira Gruber's originals which he used chiefly in the fall of the year at the mouth of the Dungarvon River, in New Brunswick. It dates from about 1940.

## MARCH BROWN, COPPER

*Head color:* Black
*Tail:* Two tiny sections of speckled brown Partridge wing, back to back
*Body:* Round copper wire, or oval copper tinsel, or flat copper tinsel ribbed with fine oval copper tinsel
*Throat:* A darkish-brown Partridge back feather, wound on as a collar and tied down (a Partridge rump feather is used in larger sizes)
*Wing:* Four sections, two on each side, of strips of hen Pheasant wing, tied low on the body (hen Pheasant tail strips also are used)

The *March Brown* is well known both as a wet and as a dry fly for trout. This copper-bodied version is popular on North American salmon rivers. John Veniard's *Fly Dressers' Guide* (Third Edition) lists a British salmon pattern more like the historic wet fly for trout. It has a tag of fine round (or oval) silver tinsel, a tail of a Golden Pheasant crest feather, and a spun-on body of fur from a hare's face (well picked out) and ribbed with silver tinsel. The throat and wing are as above.

Veniard also lists a pair of British "lake flies" which should be good salmon patterns. The *Gold March Brown* is dressed the same as the *Copper March Brown* except that the body is of gold tinsel. The *Silver March Brown* is the same, except with silver tinsel. Using either Partridge or Golden Pheasant for the tail could be a matter of choice. The original English trout pattern probably dates from between 1840 and 1850. The *Copper March Brown* evidently inspired the American *Copper Killer*, which is better known on North American salmon rivers.

## MATANE TERROR

*Head color:* Red    Hook size: No. 10 to 3/0; low-water
*Tag:* Flat gold tinsel
*Tail:* A Golden Pheasant crest feather, dyed red
*Body:* Red wool, fairly slim
*Ribbing:* Flat gold tinsel
*Throat:* About two turns of a fairly wide brown hackle, tied back slightly but not pulled down
*Wing:* Between two and four (depending on hook size) Golden Pheasant crest feathers, dyed red, one over the other, extending to tip of tail
*Cheeks:* Jungle Cock, quite short

This fly, sometimes called the *Matane Killer*, was originated in 1921 by Dr. Elizabeth Brokaw, of Bound Brook, New Jersey. It has been effective on many Canadian rivers, especially for fall fishing. It is long and slim, nearly a streamer type.

## McGINTY (OR BUMBLEBEE)

*Head color:*  Black     Hook sizes: 4, 6, 8, 10
*Tail:*     A few fibers of grey Mallard over which are a few fibers of a red hackle
*Body:*     In four sections, alternating from the tail yellow, black, yellow and black, of chenille in size proportionate to the size of the hook to provide a fairly fat body
*Throat:*     A few turns of a brown hackle tied on as a collar and pulled down; the hackle should be quite short and sparse
*Wing:*     In four sections, two on each side, of white-tipped Blue Mallard, tied close to the body and curving upward

The *McGinty* has for many years been well known as a trout fly and often has been found to be deadly on salmon rivers, especially during the bee season in the summer. A very similar pattern, called the *Bumblebee*, has the same dressing except for a slate-grey wing. This body is also excellent when dressed as a hair-wing, using bucktail, squirrel or any other hair of suitable texture and color. It is very effective when used as a dry fly until it sinks, then as a wet fly. When salmon can be located, skittering it on the surface in front of them often brings action.

## MITCHELL

*Head color:*  Black, with rear band of bright red lacquer     Hook sizes: 2 to 8
*Tag:*     Three turns of oval silver tinsel
*Tip:*     Two turns of golden yellow floss (very small)
*Tail:*     A Golden Pheasant crest feather, over which is sparse Blue Chatterer (or Kingfisher) half as long
*Butt:*     Black Ostrich herl
*Body:*     Two or three turns of golden yellow floss, forward of which is a second butt of bright red Ostrich herl, with the remainder of the body black floss. The black floss occupies about four-fifths of the body.
*Ribbing:*     Fine oval silver tinsel, over black floss only
*Throat:*     A sparse bunch of yellow hackle tied on as a beard, forward of which are three turns of a black hackle applied as a collar, pulled down and tied back
*Wing:*     Two sections of black Crow, Swan, Goose or Duck wing feathers
*Topping:*     A Golden Pheasant crest feather
*Cheeks:*     Jungle Cock, fairly long, veiled by Blue Chatterer (or Kingfisher)

This fly was originated by Archibald Mitchell, of Norwich, Connecticut, in 1887. There is a variation with a silver body which is very similar to the *Night Hawk*. In *Favorite Flies*, Mr. Mitchell said, "I conceived the idea that a very dark fly would be a success on the Penobscot River (Maine) for salmon, and tied a few of them for the first time during the winter 1887-88. It is my own invention and was not copied from any other fly." In Mr. Mitchell's original pattern there is no gold floss at the rear of the body, the red butt (evidently floss) being immediately forward of the tail. The *Mitchell* is a favorite fly in Newfoundland and other areas. It is dressed with many slight variations, usually in 6's and 8's.

## MOOSE FLY

*Head color:* Black    Hook size: #8, Model Perfect
*Tail:* A few fibers of Summer Wood Duck
*Body:* Wound with a Moose hair which is cream color, with black edges. The body is fairly fat forward, tapering very fine to the rear, nymph-style. It is clear-lacquered to give a smooth and shiny appearance.
*Throat:* About two turns of a small light dun hackle, wound on as a collar and pulled down before the wing is applied. The hackle is quite sparse and extends no longer than to the tip of the hook-point.
*Wing:* In four sections, two on each side, of very light slate-grey duck wing. The wing is very short, extending only two-thirds of the length of the body. It is fairly full, and tied low to the hook.

This is one of Ira Gruber's patterns, used under low-water summer conditions. Evidently it is not one of his best-known ones, but the dressing is unusual.

## NIGHT HAWK

*Head color:* Red
*Tag:* Oval silver tinsel
*Tip:* Yellow silk floss
*Tail:* A Golden Pheasant crest feather, over which is a very small strand or two of blue Kingfisher, half as long as the crest feather
*Butt:* Two or three turns of red wool
*Body:* Flat silver tinsel
*Ribbing:* Oval silver tinsel
*Wing:* Two sections of black Turkey feather, extending to the tip of the tail
*Throat:* A small bunch of black hackle fibers, rather short
*Shoulders:* Jungle Cock, half as long as the wing

*Cheeks:*      Sections of a blue Kingfisher feather, set outside and over the
   Jungle Cock, nearly as long as the Jungle Cock but narrow enough so as not
   to conceal it

*Topping:*     A Golden Pheasant crest feather, curving to the end of the tail

This is a popular Canadian pattern which has gained prominence in the British Isles and other countries.

The hair-wing version is as above except that it has no tip, cheeks or topping. The Jungle Cock eye is short, and the wing is black Squirrel.

## NIPISIGUIT GREY

*Head color:*   Black
*Tag:*          Fine oval silver tinsel, or round silver wire
*Tip:*          Bright yellow silk floss
*Tail:*         A Golden Pheasant crest feather
*Butt:*         Two or three turns of Peacock herl or black wool
*Body:*         Medium-grey wool, not built up
*Ribbing:*      Fine oval silver tinsel
*Throat:*       A few turns of a Barred-Rock hackle feather tied on as a collar
   and pulled down
*Wing*          In four sections, two on each side, of bronze Mallard

This is an old-time pattern, first tied near Pabineau Falls on New Brunswick's Nipisiguit River about 1927. It was the best fly on the river for many years. In his classic *Atlantic Salmon Fishing*, Charles Phair says about it, "I often have thought that perhaps there was something to Kelson's idea that there were 'grey rivers' and red ones, and rivers of other colors, that is, that the fish in certain rivers were most susceptible to a fly of a certain color. Flies of a very pronounced color, such as *Capsapscal* and *Green Drake*, which will kill on the Matapedia, Restigouche, Miramichi and St. John, positively will not take fish on the Tobique; and the *Nipisiguit Grey*, which is famous on that river and will occasionally take a fish on the Tobique, is of no account anywhere else I know of."

In the larger sizes the wing is more ornate: an inner wing of Oak Turkey over which are married strips of blue, red and yellow Swan, with an outer wing of bronzed Mallard. The ornate pattern also calls for Jungle Cock eyes and a topping of a Golden Pheasant crest feather. Probably the fly was originated by D. A. Lapointe, of Atholville, New Brunswick. The Nipisiguit is no longer a good salmon river due to netting near its mouth. It is near Bathurst, New Brunswick.

Although Mr. Phair passed away many years *after* hair-wing flies were being developed on the Miramichi, evidently he either ignored them or was unfamiliar with them. The feather-wing *Nipisiguit Grey* is so similar to the hair-wing *Grey Rat* that when either swims by a salmon it is doubtful that he could detect the difference. Mr. Phair indicates that the *Nip* is of "no account" on the Matapedia and the Restigouche, for example. The *Rat* series (especially the *Rusty Rat*) currently are killers there. The salmon's taste in flies may have changed, but there seems to be no reason why the *Nip* shouldn't do well elsewhere than on the river where it was born. However, the pulsating action of hair-wing patterns probably makes a difference. In the hair-wing version brown bucktail replaces the bronze Mallard. Grey Fox hair also is used.

## ORIOLE

*Head color:*   Black
*Tail:*   A few fibers from a red body feather of Golden Pheasant
*Body:*   Black nylon wool, cigar-shaped
*Ribbing:*   Fine oval silver tinsel, with two turns taken under the tail, as a tag
*Throat:*   A brown hackle, two or three turns of which are wound on as a collar and pulled down before the wing is applied. The fibers extend two-thirds of the way to the point of the hook.
*Wing:*   Underwing: Several fibers of the brown-red body feather of a Golden Pheasant
   Overwing: In four sections, two on each side, of grey Mallard dyed green drake color*. (As in all Gruber patterns, the wing is applied low, to hug the body).

The *Oriole* is usually considered the most important of the Gruber originals and is used extensively not only on its native Miramichi River, but on many rivers internationally. Note other comments under the "*Hermit*" pattern. It is frequently referred to as *Gruber's Oriole*.

## PARR

*Head color:*   Black    Hook sizes: 2 to 8
*Tag:*   Silver thread or fine oval silver tinsel
*Tip:*   Golden-yellow silk floss

* The grey Mallard dyed green drake color which is called for in some of the Gruber patterns can be obtained from E. Veniard (Retail) Ltd., Thornton Heath, Surrey CR4 8YG, England.

*Tail:*          A Golden Pheasant crest feather
*Butt:*         Scarlet Berlin wool
*Body:*        Flat silver tinsel
*Ribbing:*     Fine oval silver tinsel
*Throat:*     A turn or two of a pale blue hackle, tied on as a collar and pulled downward, forward of which is a very small bunch of Widgeon fibers, all fairly short and quite sparse
*Wing:*      Red, blue and yellow strands of fluorescent floss covered with strips of barred black and white Teal or Wood Duck
*Topping:*    A Golden Pheasant crest feather
*Cheeks:*    Jungle Cock eyes

This adaptation is attributed to Charles De Feo, who considered that it resembles the coloration of salmon parr, which salmon and grilse are known to strike at occasionally. This fly actually is a *Reduced Silver Doctor*. All components are the *Silver Doctor* dressing except for the wing, which is a simplified version of the same pattern.

## PEACOCK

*Head color:*  Black
*Tail:*          A Golden Pheasant crest feather
*Body:*        Rear third: Bright yellow silk floss, ribbed with fine bright green silk thread
                 Forward two-thirds: Peacock herl (The bodies on all Gruber flies are cigar-shaped; tapering to the rear.)
*Throat:*     About two turns of an olive-green hackle, tied on as a collar and pulled down before the wing is applied. The hackle is sparse and short.
*Wing:*      A double wing of two right and two left sections of bronze Mallard, extending to the end of the tail, or very slightly beyond the bend of the hook

Although not as well known as Gruber's *Reliable* and *Oriole*, this is one of his valuable contributions to the early art of fly fishing on the Miramichi River. The fly was originated about 1936 and, while Ira Gruber used it mainly as a fall fly, it is good all during the season.

## PORTLAND COLONEL

*Head color:*  Black
*Tag:*          Flat silver tinsel
*Tail:*          A Golden Pheasant crest feather
*Butt:*         Peacock herl (green)
*Body:*        Flat silver tinsel
*Ribbing*     Fine oval silver tinsel
*Throat:*     A small bunch of medium-blue hackle fibers
*Wing:*      Strips of barred black and white Wood Duck or Teal
*Topping:*    A Golden Pheasant crest feather
*Cheeks:*    Jungle Cock (short)

## PRICE'S DOSE

*Head color:*   Black     Hook sizes: 8 to 12, double
*Tag:*          Fine oval silver tinsel
*Tip:*          Bright yellow silk floss (small)
*Body:*         Black wool, fairly slim
*Ribbing:*      Fine oval silver tinsel
*Wing:*         A few Golden Pheasant tippet fibers, over which are a few red
hackle fibers. Veiling these on both sides and meeting at the top are sections
of grey Mallard flank feather. The wing is set low, nymph-style.
*Throat:*       A few black hackle fibers, very sparse
*Cheeks:*       Jungle Cock, extending to end of body

This dressing is taken from an original pattern by Everett Price,
a member of a prominent angling family which lived in Lower Blackville, New Brunswick. The original was dressed on a No. 10 double
hook and had been retired after catching many salmon. Evidently
Mr. Price made some of his double hooks by using two singles;
cutting off the eye of one; honing them to match; and binding them
together. This fly is somewhat similar to a reduced *Black Dose* or to
Ira Gruber's *Reliable*. It is fairly typical of the popular and productive feather-wings in the Miramichi area. (Everett Price taught Ira
Gruber how to tie flies.)

## PROFESSOR

*Head color:*   Black     Hook sizes: 6 to 10; regular or low-water
*Tag:*          Flat gold tinsel
*Tail:*         A Golden Pheasant crest feather
*Butt:*         Black Ostrich herl
*Body:*         Yellow silk floss
*Ribbing:*      Oval gold tinsel
*Throat:*       Two or three turns of a brown hackle, pulled down and tied back
slightly
*Wing:*         Four narrow strips of grey Mallard breast feather, applied as two
pairs, tied low against hook
*Cheeks:*       Jungle Cock (optional)

We have seen that many early American salmon flies were adaptations of trout patterns, of which this is one. A tail of two thin
sections of a red feather, such as Swan or Goose, often is used instead
of the Golden Pheasant. While not as popular as formerly, this fly
is used on North American salmon rivers.

## RELIABLE

*Head color:*    Black        Hook size: #6, Model Perfect
*Tail:*          A few fibers of the red body feather of a Golden Pheasant
*Butt:*          Bright yellow silk floss, occupying about one-third of the body
*Body:*          Black silk floss (forward two-thirds). The body is dressed fairly
full, tapering to the tail.
*Ribbing:*       Fine silver oval tinsel, of which two turns are made under the tail.
Use finest tinsel, or wire.
*Throat:*        About two turns of a black hackle, wound on as a collar and
pulled down, extending no longer than to the tip of the hook-point
*Wing:*          Underwing: Two matched sections of orange and black Golden
Pheasant tippet
Overwing: Sections of brown Mallard, as a veil; one section only
on each side. As usual on Gruber patterns, the wing extends no longer than
to the bend of the hook and it is tied low to hug the body.

This is another of Ira Gruber's famous originals. He called it the
*Reliable* because he considered it a good fly any time of the year.
Essentially, it is one of the black-bodied yellow butt flies with a
feathered wing. Fred Grant, a guide and fly-dresser of Juniper,
New Brunswick, tied a variation of this fly in the 1950's which he
called the *Grant Special.* It is the same except that the tail is a
section of a dyed red wing feather; the throat is a brown hackle tied
full under the wing; and sections of grey Mallard are used instead of
brown Mallard.

## SHERMAN

*Head color:*    Black        Hook size: #8, Model Perfect
*Tail:*          A few fibers of a Summer Wood Duck feather
*Body:*          Black silk floss, tapered to the rear and front
*Ribbing:*       Very fine silver oval tinsel
*Throat:*        A light brown hackle, tied on as a collar and pulled down, before
the wing is applied. The throat is quite sparse and the hackle extends no longer
than to the point of the hook.
*Wing:*          In four sections, two on each side, of dark grey duck wing feathers
tied low on the hook-shank and extending no longer than to the bend of the
hook

This is one of Ira Gruber's originals, named for Sherman Hoyt,
who owned the Big Hole Brook Pool which Mr. Gruber leased for
many years. This pool is on the Miramichi River, near Doaktown,
New Brunswick. The fly dates from about 1939 and is an early example
of the silver-ribbed, black-bodied types later so popular as hair-wing
patterns.

## SPATE FLY

*Head color:* Red
*Tag:* Oval gold tinsel
*Tail:* A Golden Pheasant crest feather
*Body:* Dark brown Seal's fur or Polar Bear fur, spun on and slightly picked out
*Ribbing:* Medium size oval gold tinsel
*Throat:* Several turns of a black hackle, tied on as a collar and pulled down, the longest fibers reaching nearly to the point of the hook
*Wing:* A bunch of brown bucktail, reaching to the point of the tail
*Shoulders:* Fairly wide strips of black and white Wood Duck, set on both sides of the bucktail and two-thirds as long

This attractive and unusual fly was originated in 1946 by Harry A. Darbee, of Livingston Manor, New York. It is dressed in sizes to suit water conditions (usually about 1/0) and is used when rivers are in "spate," that is, high and discolored. Originally it was dressed on the Margaree River, Cape Breton, Nova Scotia, and it has accounted for many large fish under such conditions.

## STONE FLY

*Head color:* Black      Hook size: #6, Model Perfect
*Tail:* A few fibers of a Plymouth Rock hackle, dyed yellow
*Body:* Bright yellow silk floss, moderately built-up and tapering at both ends
*Ribbing:* Very dark green thread
*Throat:* Two or three turns of a Plymouth Rock hackle, dyed yellow, applied as a collar and pulled down before the wing is put on. The hackle extends no longer than to the point of the hook.
*Wing:* In four sections, two on each side, of grey Mallard dyed a green drake color. The wing is fairly full and extends slightly beyond the bend of the hook

This is another Ira Gruber original in which he used as a wing the *Oriole* feather of his fly by that name, which is a grey Mallard breast feather specially dyed a green drake color by Mr. Gruber. The exact color that he used is available from E. Veniard (Retail) Ltd., Thornton Heath, Surrey, England.

## U-NO

*Head color:* Black      Hook size: #6, Model Perfect
*Tip:* Dull gold silk floss
*Tail:* A Golden Pheasant crest feather

*Body:*        Rear half: A few turns of light grey silk floss, forward of which and blending in are a few turns of medium brown silk floss
                Front half: Black silk floss (The body is dressed to blend in the three colors, from grey to brown to black.)

*Ribbing:*     Very fine oval silver tinsel

*Throat:*      Two or three turns of a slate-colored hackle, wound on as a collar and pulled down, extending no longer than to the point of the barb

*Wing:*        In four sections, two on each side, of slate duck wing, extending no longer than to the bend of the hook, and dressed low to hug the body

*Cheeks:*      Jungle Cock; very small feathers, laid in the middle of the wing and about two-thirds its length

This is one of Ira Gruber's favorite originals, and is a fly to which he never gave a name. When he wanted one, he would call to his guide and companion, "Bing" Russell, and say, "Bring me that fly—you know the one." This happened so often that Bing called it the *You Know*, and it has been the *U-NO* ever since. Ira Gruber used it, usually in size #6, for many years on the Miramichi River, beginning about 1938.

# X I
# North American
# Hair-Wing Patterns

The sports at Jack Russell's camp at Ludlow on the Miramichi happily were catching salmon on classic British feather-wing flies back in 1930 and they were using little, if anything, else. In his book, *Jill and I and the Salmon* (Little, Brown & Co., Boston, 1950) Jack complacently said, "There has been little change in the basic patterns of flies from the beginning of salmon angling on this continent. I do not mean to imply that there have not been changes, yet the standard patterns such as *Jock Scott, Black Dose, Silver Gray, Dusty Miller, Silver Doctor, Durham Ranger* and *Mar Lodge* hold good year after year."

Of course, Jack and his wealthy guests must have known about hair-wings, but perhaps they thought they were too vulgar to be associated with their fine split-bamboo rods made by experts such as Leonard, Payne, Hardy, Orvis and Thomas. Anyway, if the sports at Jack's camp and many others up and down the river and on its many tributaries knew about them, they seemed to ignore them with quiet disdain.

Meanwhile, down the river a few miles, inquiring anglers like Everett Price, Bert Miner, Fred Merseau, Sandy Munn, Everett Lyons, Van Storey, Ira Gruber and others were experimenting with simplified American hair-wings and feather-wings and evidently were catching as many salmon with them—or more—as were others using fancy imported creations costing several times as much.

These men were the pioneers in hair-wing development back in the 1930's and 1940's. They developed a permanent, highly effective style (discussed in the previous chapter) consisting of a short, cigar-shaped body ribbed with fine, close-turned tinsel, with a short and sparse wing which hugged the body and with short, sparse hackles. One of the earliest named patterns was the *Gorilla*, originated by Ira Gruber. Hair-wing patterns at about this time also were being developed in other areas, notably by Harry Smith and his cronies in Cherryfield, Maine (see *Black Bear* hair-wing), but the now-classic hair-wing style which proved most successful evidently originated on the Miramichi.

Trial and error developed numerous patterns, some with so many variations that they are known only by descriptive names. Early in the game anglers found that adding a colored butt was productive. When fluorescent yarns and floss became available, butts of these materials were found to be even better because they added a "glow of life" to the fly, making it more visible, and tempting salmon with something new. Bodies of various colors were tried, but fishermen usually settled on black because of its greater visibility when viewed from below. Brown bodies took second place, but were a very poor second. In using these descriptive names it became obvious to anybody who knew anything about it that a *Bear Hair, Green Butt* is a fly with a tinsel-ribbed black body, a black wing and throat, and a green butt, probably of a fluorescent material. Tails and Jungle Cock and all such frivolities were considered unnecessary, and whether the ribbing was silver or gold didn't seem to make any difference.

These flies were tied on salmon hooks or on bronzed straight or offset hooks usually ranging between numbers 4 and 10. Whether they were singles or doubles was a matter of choice but the choice of doubles seemed to have an edge in fast water.

The hair used also varied widely and included not only bucktail and the various species of bear and squirrel, but also woodchuck, skunk, beaver (hair from the ankles of the front legs only), calf or what have you. The degree of straightness and softness of the hair became a matter of debate. Some fly-dressers considered Black Bear too curly, squirrel-tail too soft, and Monga (Ring-tail) just about right. Butts were tried in all the bright colors, and the choice among red, green, yellow and orange never seems to have been decided.

Flies of this sort enjoy major popularity as this is written, principally on the Miramichi but also, to an extent, everywhere else. Anglers who look in this book for named flies in this category won't find them because no one person originated them, and the descriptive names such as *Squirrel-tail, Orange Butt* are as good as any. One enterprising individual named Charles ("Chuck") Conrad did succeed in having some flies marketed under the name *Conrad*, but they are merely the basic idea of black body, wing and throat with oval silver ribbing and a fluorescent butt of whatever color desired. Conrad did add a tinsel tag, so perhaps he considered that he had originated something! He didn't seem to realize that Ira Gruber developed the *Black Spider*, which is almost identical, way back in 1935!

On the Miramichi many of the original old flies remain very popular. Instead of a colorful butt, the original *Squirrel Tail* had a tail of red hackle fibers or red hair. The body was black, ribbed with fine silver tinsel. Usually there was a sparse and short black throat (sometimes brown), and the wing was native Canadian Red Squirrel (not Fox Squirrel). Later on clipped red floss or yarn was used for the tail. This gave way to the tailless fly with a floss or wool butt, which finally became fluorescent.

Another favorite still is the *All Black*, a Miramichi basic. Probably it is a development of the *Black Bear*: no tail; a black body ribbed with fine oval gold tinsel; a sparse black throat; and a wing of Black Bear or squirrel. No Jungle Cock is used on these patterns.

As this was written, many anglers dress these patterns with Peacock herl bodies instead of black silk or wool because they think the sheen of the Peacock is more effective. A few herls are twisted only three or four times around the black thread because, when this is wound on the body, the winding produces added twisting.

Anglers who visit salmon rivers in widely separated regions often wonder why flies which are very popular in one area are not used very much in others. On many Quebec rivers, for example, we have seen that the *Rusty Rat* and the *Green Highlander* (hair wing) are top favorites, and if the *Cosseboom* is used at all it usually is the dry fly variation. Down on the Miramichi (as this was written) the *Rats* and the *Green Highlander* rarely are used, and the *Cosseboom* is a prime favorite fished either dry or wet. The *Butt* patterns, so popular in New Brunswick, are virtually ignored in Quebec. The *Ingalls' Butterfly*, an unusual pattern which can be fished either on top or down under, is one of the very best on the Miramichi but is rarely used elsewhere.

The average angler who can afford only a week or two annually for salmon fishing isn't going to risk failure by using flies which are not popular in the area he is visiting. He uses patterns indigenous to the area. He might do better by showing the salmon something new! Without doubt the *Butt* flies and Maurice Ingalls' pattern would do well in Quebec, and New Brunswick should see more of the *Rats*.

The following North American hair-wing patterns contain a few innovations. Presumably this is the first book to describe the ultra-important *Rat* series correctly, and to show in color one of them dressed by Roy Angus Thomson himself. The success of the *Cosseboom* series led to the development of at least thirty-one patterns, but only those of primary interest are included and, in the author's judgement, only the *Cosseboom Special*, or the *Cosseboom*, as it usually is called, is of major importance. The color plates illustrate one of the few remaining patterns of it dressed by the originator. As before, some of the patterns of other flies are included for historic value, others because they are of regional interest, and many because they are the most productive hair-wing flies known to North American anglers.

## BLACK BEAR

| | |
|---|---|
| *Head color:* | Black |
| *Tail:* | Two thin sections of a black feather, such as dyed Swan or Goose |
| *Body:* | Black wool |
| *Throat:* | A small bunch of Black Bear hair, extending to end of hook |
| *Wing:* | A small bunch of Black Bear hair, extending to end of tail |

This is the original dressing of Harry Smith, a pioneer in hair-wing salmon fly development of Cherryfield, Maine. It is one of the earliest hair-wing patterns, probably dating to the 1920's. Many patterns evolved from it. One, with the same wing and throat, has a tail of Black Bear hair and a body of flat gold tinsel ribbed with oval gold tinsel.

Another, called the *Belfast Killer* was sent to the author by Arthur H. Grove, of Belfast, Maine. This has a tag of gold wire, a clipped tail of red Amherst Pheasant crest, and a black silk body ribbed with gold wire. The wing is Black Bear hair and the black hackle is applied as a collar, Cosseboom-style. Some anglers on Maine's salmon rivers, where this fly is very popular, dispense with the hackle altogether, or tie in a very small and short hair throat under the hook. Since the wing should lie close to the body, the fly can be fished as a nymph. Standard and fluorescent butts often are added in orange, red or green, the favorite being a burnt-orange color.

No one can be sure where these popular *Butt* patterns originated, but several old-time anglers think that Harry Smith should be given credit for them. Others think they were developed independently in various areas, most probably on the Miramichi. Wings often are made of Woodchuck tail, or in a mixture of red and yellow, or red, yellow and blue, similar to a hair-wing *Black Dose*.

## BLACK BOMBER

| | |
|---|---|
| *Head color:* | Black |
| *Tag:* | Silver wire |
| *Tip:* | Yellow floss |
| *Tail:* | A Golden Pheasant crest feather |
| *Body:* | Black wool |
| *Ribbing:* | Oval silver tinsel |
| *Throat:* | A black hackle wound on as a collar, pulled down, and tied back slightly |
| *Wing:* | A small bunch of black squirrel tail hairs |
| *Topping:* | A Golden Pheasant crest feather |
| *Cheeks:* | Jungle Cock |

The *Black Bomber* and the *Brown Bomber*, and presumably the *Silver Bomber*, were originated before 1929 by Joe Aucoin, the well-known fly-dresser of Waterford, Nova Scotia. They first were used on the Margaree River and are important all over North America, particularly in Nova Scotia. The British *Black Bomber* is a later fly and probably an adaptation. The *Brown Bomber* has the same tag, tip, tail, ribbing, cheeks and topping as the *Black Bomber*. It has a butt of black chenille, a body of brown wool, a brown throat and a wing of Fox Squirrel tail. The *Silver Bomber* has the same tag, tip and tail as the *Black Bomber*. It has the same topping and cheeks, but they are optional. It has a butt of black chenille, a body of flat silver tinsel, oval silver ribbed, a throat of speckled Guinea and a wing of brown bucktail with a little white bucktail mixed in.

## BLACK JACK

*Head color:*    Black      Hook sizes: 5 to 9; low-water
*Tag:*          Three or four turns of fine round silver wire
*Tail:*         Five of six fibers of a Golden Pheasant tippet, tied in just below
the second black band
*Body:*       Black silk floss, very slim, without taper (The body occupies not
more than two-thirds of the length of the long-shanked hook.)
*Ribbing:*     Very fine oval silver tinsel or silver wire
*Hackle:*      Two black hackles, tied on together as a collar, dressed fairly
thickly because this fly has no wing. The longest fibers are no longer than the
length of the body.

The *Black Jack* is one of the most popular of the low-water patterns in North America, and is especially effective on Quebec's Restigouche and Matapedia Rivers.

## BLACK SPIDER

*Head color:*    Black      Hook size: #6, Model Perfect
*Tail:*         A few hairs of black Squirrel tail
*Butt:*        Burnt-orange silk floss narrow and small
*Body:*       Black wool, not built-up
*Ribbing:*     Fine oval silver tinsel. Two or three turns of the tinsel are taken
under the tail, as a tag. The butt is wound over the tinsel before it is used as
ribbing
*Throat:*      Two or three turns of a black hackle, applied as a collar and pulled
down, before the wing is applied. The hackle is quite short and sparse.
*Wing:*       A small bunch of black Squirrel tail hairs, extending to the bend
of the hook and tied low against the body

This one of Ira Gruber's patterns was originated about 1935 and is important mainly because it indicates that the colored butt, black-bodied hair-wing patterns which many years later became so popular on the Miramichi River system were originated long before they became known as *Butt* flies. Presumably, this is the earliest authenticated pattern of this type. Currently it would be known as the *Black Squirrel, Orange Butt*. The type may have been originated by Ira Gruber, or possibly by Everett Price, who taught Mr. Gruber to dress salmon flies about 1935.

## BUTTERFLY

(Also called INGALLS' BUTTERFLY and INGALLS' SPLAY-WING COACHMAN)

*Head color:*  Black     Hook sizes: 6 to 10, 2x or 3x long
*Tail:*        A dozen or so fibers of a bright red hackle, fairly long
*Body:*        Wound with rusty Peacock herl (Some instructions say that one turn of herl is added in front of the wing, but the original pattern does not show this. The body originally was tied with black wool, but Mr. Ingalls later preferred the Peacock.)
*Wing:*        A divided wing of white goat hair, slightly longer than the body and set a bit above the body, slanted backward at an angle of about 45°. The wings are very sparse and the hair should be from a small goat, as the hair from large goats is too brittle and too stiff.
*Hackle:*      Two turns of a brown hackle wound on as a collar, one turn behind the wings and one in front. The hackle is about half as long as the wing hair, is applied dry-fly style, and should be very sparse.

This wet fly was originated by Maurice Ingalls, of Fort Lauderdale, Florida, in 1956, when he was in Blackville, New Brunswick. Wallace Doak, fly-dresser and tackle dealer of Doaktown, New Brunswick (Canada) says, "For three years now the *Ingalls Butterfly* has outsold and outcaught all other wet fly patterns. It has been tied in many different styles, but none have ever come up to the original fly."

Mr. Ingalls says, "The *Butterfly*, if tied with *goat* hair, is probably the best fly ever used on the Miramichi River. Due to its unusual appearance, it took time for it to gain popularity, but it seemed as though every time I dropped it in where salmon were, I'd get a strike! I have caught my limit a good many times in from four to six casts. My wife and I put it on every season and never exchange it except for another *Butterfly*."

This is a breather-type fly tied in the color scheme of a *Coachman* which can be cast and fished as a dry fly and then allowed to sink. When sunk, it is given slight action with the rod-tip to make it pulsate, or "breathe." The design has been tried (not as successfully) in different color schemes such as the *Cosseboom*, *Silver Rat* and black-bodied flies with various colored butts. Successful variations include adding a gold tag and ribbing and a red wool butt.

One variation attributed to Mr. Ingalls, but not claimed by him, is no longer popular but is included as a matter of record. This is tied in the manner of a *Royal Coachman*, and is called :

## WHIRLYBIRD

*Head color:*    Black      Hook sizes: 6 to 10, 2x or 3x long
*Tail:*          A few fibers of an orange and black barred Golden Pheasant
   tippet
*Body:*        In three sections; Peacock herl, red silk floss, Peacock herl (as in
   a *Royal Coachman*)
*Wing:*       Divided, of white goat hair, as with the *Butterfly*
*Hackle:*     Two turns of a brown hackle, the same as the *Butterfly*

## COPPER KILLER

*Head color:*    Red
*Tag:*          About three turns of fine copper wire
*Tip:*           Pale green floss, very small
*Tail:*          A very small bunch of rusty-red Partridge hackle fibers, extending
   slightly beyond bend of hook
*Butt:*         Bright red floss, quite small
*Body:*        Flat copper tinsel
*Ribbing:*    Round copper wire, or very fine oval copper tinsel
*Hackle:*     About two turns of a bright orange hackle, applied as a collar
   before the wing is applied. The hackle should be no longer than the copper
   part of the body, extending no longer than the tip of the point of the hook.
   The hackle is tied backward so the lower barbules point to the point of the
   hook
*Wing:*       A small bunch of Fox Squirrel tail hairs, extending no longer than
   the end of the tail

This fly is an old favorite, especially in the Cains River area of New Brunswick's Miramichi River. The above dressing and the fly were given to the author by Bert Miner, of Doaktown, New Brunswick, who has dressed and fished flies on the river almost since the inception of fly-fishing there. He states that this dressing is the correct one and an exact duplicate of the original pattern.

Later variations include the use of a tiny bunch of Fox Squirrel hairs for the tail, presumably because the red Partridge is not always obtainable. (Bert may have made an error in calling this Partridge because the tail fibers look like the rusty-red ones of the

Ring-necked Pheasant.) Sometimes an orange butt is used instead of the green tip and red butt as above. In modern dressings, the green tip is fluorescent.

## THE "COSSEBOOM" SERIES

John C. Cosseboom was a fascinating character endowed with an unusual name and pronounced ability not only as a poet and newspaper writer but also as a champion fly-caster and as an angler for Atlantic salmon. He was very profitably established in the insurance business in Woonsocket, Rhode Island, and lived approximately between 1885 and 1935. While it was not my pleasure to have known him, he fished for salmon very often with my old friend, Herbert L. Howard, of Mamaroneck, New York, who provided the following notes about the *Cosseboom* flies, with which he was intimately involved.

John Cosseboom, in common with Roy Thomson (originator of the *Rat* series) and a few other anglers, tied his flies (or had them tied) only with red tying thread. (The only exception is the *Orange Cosseboom* which, for one reason or another, was dressed with a black head.) He was very emphatic about the red head. While it may have been a whim, it may also be because he thought the red head looked "bloody." Once he bet Jack Russell* one hundred dollars that he could take more fish on a red-headed fly than on a black-headed one. John took six salmon to Jack's one. When they exchanged flies, Jack Russell caught five with the red head while John took only one with the black—or so the story goes.

The success of the Cosseboom patterns led to considerable experimentation during which over thirty variations were tried. Of these we give seven of the most popular, but the *Cosseboom Special*, or *Cosseboom* as it usually is called, is by far the best one. It is the one referred to when the name is mentioned, and it is good all over the world. A tail of silk floss is called for on most of the patterns. This should not extend beyond the bend of the hook, to help prevent short strikes.

* Jack Russell, author of *Jill and I and the Salmon*, owned a fishing camp near Ludlow, on New Brunswick's Miramichi River in the 1930's.

| BLACK BEAR | BLACK SPIDER (c.1935) | RED BUTT |
|:---:|:---:|:---:|
| Originated and | Originated and | (or BLACK BEAR, RED BUTT) |
| Dressed by | Dressed by | Dressed by |
| Mr. Harry Smith (A) | Mr. Ira Gruber (A) | Mr. Keith Fulsher (A) |

| HALF-STONE | ORANGE BLOSSOM | THE PRIEST |
|:---:|:---:|:---:|
| (LOW-WATER DRESSING) | Dressed by | Originated and |
| Dressed by | Mrs. Carmelle Bigaouette (P) | Dressed by The |
| Mr. Robert Cavanagh (A) | | Rev. Elmer J. Smith (A) |

| COPPER KILLER | COSSEBOOM | BUTTERFLY |
|:---:|:---:|:---:|
| Dressed by | Originated and | Originated and |
| Mr. Bert Miner (P) | Dressed by | Dressed by |
| | Mr. John Cosseboom (A) | Mr. Maurice Ingalls (A) |

| SHRIMP | RED ABBEY |
|:---:|:---:|
| Originated and | Dressed by |
| Dressed by | Mr. Burt Carpenter (P) |
| Mr. L. A. Lapointe (P) | |

| HERB JOHNSON SPECIAL | MUDDLER MINNOW |
|:---:|:---:|
| (*A Bucktail Pattern*) | Originated by |
| Originated and | Mr. Don Gapen. Dressed by |
| Dressed by | Mr. Philip Foster (P) |
| Mr. Herbert Johnson (A) | |

| RUSTY RAT | GREY RAT | SILVER RAT |
|:---:|:---:|:---:|
| Dressed by | Originated and | Dressed by |
| Mr. Herbert Howard (P) | Dressed by | Mr. Herbert Howard (P) |
| | Mr. Roy A. Thompson (A) | |

PLATE V

North American Hair-Wing Patterns

236

The original *Cosseboom* was a streamer fly or bucktail which first was tied on the Margaree River about 1922. As noted below, it contained Peacock herl in the wing until it was discovered that the fly worked equally well without it. The fly was dressed on a long-shank hook as follows:

*Head color:*   Red
*Tag:*   Silver tinsel
*Tail:*   A small Golden Pheasant crest feather
*Body:*   Orange silk floss
*Ribbing:*   Flat silver tinsel
*Wing:*   Extremely small bunches of four items: Bronze Peacock herl over which is Grey Squirrel over which is green Peacock herl over which is Fox Squirrel. All four are repeated over this to make eight tiny bunches, one on top of the other
*Hackle:*   A black and white Teal feather, wound on as a collar
*Cheeks:*   Very small Teal body feathers, one on each side, over which are short Jungle Cock eyes, if available

This rather complicated pattern is included not only because of its historic interest but also to indicate an early use for streamers and bucktails in salmon fishing—a method which has grown more popular in recent years. The classic *Cosseboom* salmon fly is

COSSEBOOM SPECIAL (usually called the *Cosseboom*)

*Head color:*   Red       Hook sizes: 10 to 6/0
*Tag:*   Embossed silver tinsel
*Tail:*   Olive-green silk floss, cut off short
*Body:*   Olive-green silk floss, moderately dressed (Pearsall's shade #82)
*Ribbing:*   Embossed silver tinsel
*Wing:*   A small bunch of Grey Squirrel tail hairs extending to the end of the tail
*Hackle:*   A lemon-yellow hackle tied on as a collar after the wing is applied and slanted backward to merge with the top of the wing
*Cheeks:*   Jungle Cock (optional)

This dressing is from one of the few original *Cossebooms* in existence. The original, dressed personally by John Cosseboom, is illustrated in Plate V. (Note size and position of the tag and tail, which should be the same on all patterns calling for floss tails.) The author notes that in most commercial dressings of this fly the green color is darker than the olive-green in the original. The fly was first used on the Margaree River in 1923 and is one of the most famous American salmon fly patterns. It is dressed both as a standard and a

low-water fly and is very successful for trout. In Norway, sizes 5/0
and 6/0 are popular, and 5/0's often are used on large Canadian
rivers. Six other notable patterns are:

## BLACK COSSEBOOM

*Head color:*  Red
*Tag:*  Embossed silver tinsel
*Tail:*  Black silk floss or wool, cut off short
*Body:*  Black silk floss or wool, moderately dressed
*Ribbing:*  Embossed silver tinsel
*Wing:*  A small bunch of Grey Squirrel tail hairs, extending to the end of
the tail, or shorter
*Hackle:*  A black hackle wound on as a collar after the wing is applied and
tilted backward slightly to merge with the wing
*Cheeks:*  Jungle Cock (optional)

## ORANGE COSSEBOOM

*Head color:*  Black (This is the only one with a black head.)
*Tag:*  Flat gold tinsel
*Tail:*  Orange silk floss or wool, cut off short
*Body:*  Orange silk floss or wool, moderately dressed
*Ribbing:*  Flat gold tinsel
*Wing:*  A small bunch of Grey Squirrel tail hairs, over which are about
four Peacock sword fibers, both extending to the end of the tail, or shorter
*Hackle:*  A black hackle wound on as a collar after the wing is applied and
tilted backward slightly to merge with the wing
*Cheeks:*  Jungle Cock (optional)

## YELLOW COSSEBOOM

*Head color:*  Red
*Tag:*  Embossed silver tinsel
*Tail:*  Yellow silk floss or wool, cut off short
*Body:*  Yellow silk floss or wool, moderately dressed
*Ribbing:*  Embossed silver tinsel
*Wing:*  A small bunch of Grey Squirrel tail hairs, extending to the end
of the tail, or shorter
*Hackle:*  A grizzly hackle wound on as a collar after the wing is applied and
tilted backward slightly to merge with the wing
*Cheeks:*  Jungle Cock (optional)

## RED COSSEBOOM

*Head color:*  Red
*Tag:*  Embossed gold tinsel
*Tail:*  Red silk floss or wool, cut off short
*Body:*  Red silk floss or wool, moderately dressed
*Ribbing:*  Embossed gold tinsel

*Wing:*          A small bunch of Grey Squirrel tail hairs, extending to the end of the tail, or shorter
*Hackle:*          A black hackle wound on as a collar after the wing is applied and tilted backward slightly to merge with the wing
*Cheeks:*          Jungle Cock (optional)

## PEACOCK COSSEBOOM

*Head color:*          Red
*Tag:*          Embossed silver tinsel
*Tail:*          A small bunch of Peacock sword fibers, very short
*Body:*          Rear half: Embossed gold tinsel Front half: Peacock herl
*Ribbing:*          Oval silver tinsel over whole of body
*Wing:*          A small bunch of Grey Squirrel tail hairs, over which is a small bunch of Peacock sword fibers of same length as the throat
*Throat:*          A small bunch of Peacock sword fibers, about half as long as the body
*Cheeks:*          Jungle Cock (optional)

## GOLD COSSEBOOM

*Head color:*          Red
*Tag:*          Embossed silver tinsel
*Tail:*          A Golden Pheasant crest feather
*Body:*          Embossed gold tinsel
*Ribbing:*          Oval silver tinsel
*Wing:*          A small bunch of Grey Squirrel tail hairs, over which are about four Peacock sword fibers, both extending to the end of the tail, or shorter
*Hackle:*          A light-blue hackle wound on as a collar after the wing is applied and tilted backward slightly to merge with the wing

The *Gold Cosseboom* was originated on the Margaree River in 1923 and was later used that year on Anticosti Island, in Canada's St. Lawrence River estuary by Mr. Howard and Mr. Cosseboom. It is especially effective in clear water. The flies in this series are popular as dry-fly patterns when dressed in the style of the *Wulff* series.

## FRAZER SPECIAL

*Head color:*          Red          Hook sizes: 4 to 5/0
*Tag:*          Oval silver tinsel
*Tail:*          A short section of yellow wool
*Body:*          Rear third: Yellow wool. Middle third: Dark green wool. Front third: Black wool
*Ribbing:*          Oval silver tinsel
*Wing:*          A tiny bunch of green bucktail, over which is a tiny bunch of Fox Squirrel tail hair, over which is a small bunch of Grey Squirrel tail hair in proportions of 1/4, 1/4 and 1/2
*Hackle:*          Several turns of a black hackle, wound on after the wing has been applied
*Cheeks:*          Jungle Cock

This pattern was originated about 1928 by Andrew A. Fraser who owned the Cold Spring Camp on the Matapedia. It is a pretty fly, but not of major importance. The green should be *Green Highlander* green.

## GORILLA

*Head color:*   Black
*Tail:*         A few fibers of a black hackle
*Body:*         Black silk floss, slightly cigar-shaped
*Ribbing:*      Very fine oval silver tinsel, wound on fairly closely
*Throat:*       About two turns of a black hackle, wound on as a collar and pulled down, before the wing is applied. The hackle extends to the barb of the hook.
*Wing:*         A very small bunch of darkest Woodchuck hair, tied down to hug the shank of the hook

This is one of Ira Gruber's original patterns, dated about 1935. It is important because it is one of the earliest hair-wings used on New Brunswick's Miramichi River.

## GREY BUCK

*Head color:*   Black        Hook size: #6, Model Perfect
*Tag:*          Fine oval silver tinsel
*Tail:*         A few fibers of a very light blue dun hackle
*Body:*         Very soft and very light green wool, built-up slightly in the middle and tapered at both ends
*Ribbing:*      Fine oval silver tinsel
*Throat:*       About two turns of a very light dun hackle, applied as a collar and pulled down. The fibers are quite short
*Wing:*         A small bunch of Badger hair, extending to the end of the tail, and tied low against the body

This is an original Ira Gruber pattern which he used often at the mouth of the Dungarvon River, in New Brunswick. For Gruber patterns, the wing is unusually long, extending well beyond the bend of the hook. Since he used the word "Buck" in the name, it may be the only fly he dressed as a bucktail, and may be one of the earliest uses of the bucktail-type fly on the Miramichi River system. Its date is about 1940.

## GRIZZLY KING

*Head color:*   Black
*Tag:*          Silver tinsel
*Tail:*         A section of a red Ibis or red Swan or Goose feather, or a few red hackle fibers

*Body:*     Green silk floss
*Ribbing:*    Oval silver tinsel
*Wing:*     Mixed brown and white bucktail, or Grey Squirrel
*Hackle:*    A grizzly hackle, wound on collar-style, after the wing has been applied

This is a popular salmon pattern, especially in the Restigouche area of Canada. It should not be confused with the trout wet fly pattern of the same name, which usually is dressed with a tail of red or scarlet hackle fibers, a green floss or dubbing body, gold ribbing and tag, grizzly hackle throat and a wing of grey Mallard.

## HALF-STONE

*Head color:*   Black     Hook sizes: 10, 8, 6, 4; low-water
*Tag:*     Fine oval silver tinsel
*Tail:*     A Golden Pheasant crest feather (or a few strands of some speckled feather, such as Wood Duck)
*Body:*     Rear one-third: Yellow Seals' fur, dressed thin. Forward two-thirds: Black Seal's fur, dressed thin
*Ribbing:*   Fine oval gold tinsel
*Wing:*     A very small bunch of the speckled hairs from the base of a Fox Squirrel tail, dressed very thin and short
*Throat:*    A very small bunch of black or dark furnace hackle fibers, tied underneath, very thin and short

This low-water pattern is taken from John Atherton's book, *The Fly and the Fish,* in which he says it is his own adaptation, and evidently was one of his favorites. It seems to bear little or no resemblance to the British (Devonshire) *Half Stone,* which is discussed in several variations in angling classics, including the works of Halford, Taverner and Veniard. The British fly was tied to represent a hatching nymph. In this low-water pattern a light-wire hook is used and the dressing is very sparse, occupying only the forward half of the hook-shank. John Atherton, who lived in Shaftsbury, Vermont, was an outstanding artist, particularly of angling subjects, as well as an accomplished angler and fly-dresser. Evidently none of his patterns exists in an unused state.

## HATHAWAY'S HORROR

*Head color:*   Black     Hook size: 6-4XL, light wire
*Tail:*     Brown bucktail
*Body:*     Brown bucktail
*Ribbing:*   Black silk
*Wing:*     Tan deer body hair

This is a nymph-type fly somewhat similar to the *Muddler*. After winding the thread to a point over the tip of the barb and half-hitching it, the bucktail is laid over the hook-shank so the tip ends protrude well beyond the bend of the hook. After making about three tight turns of thread (thus flaring the tail slightly) the thread is half-hitched and then wound tightly as a ribbing with the hair completely surrounding and concealing the hook-shank. After securing the thread at a point about 1/4 inch behind the eye of the hook a small bunch of tan deer body hair is applied as a wing, the longest hairs extending to the mid-section of the tail. This is tightly half-hitched down so all the hair ends are flared. The hair-ends are pulled back and the dressing is finished with a small head. Then the hair ends are trimmed to within about 1/4 inch of where they were secured to form a collar, as on the *Muddler*.

This pattern was originated in 1964 by Norman Hathaway, of Brewer, Maine, after ten years of experimentation. He says it is especially effective in Labrador for Atlantic salmon and Brook Trout, letting it drift dry downstream and pulling it under when it starts to swing, thereafter retrieving it just under the surface to make a wake—a jerky retrieve for trout, a steady one for salmon. Mr. Hathaway recommends using natural unwashed hair as he has noticed that when fish mouth the fly they will take it in more readily than hair which has been washed or dyed.

## HATHAWAY SPECIAL

*Head color:*  Black     Hook size: 6-XL
*Body:*         Wound with yellow wool
*Ribbing*       Peacock herl, beside which is a stripped brown palmer hackle
*Wing:*         Brown Fox Squirrel tail, extending very slightly beyond bend of
hook

This fly was originated on the Narraguagus River in Maine in 1951 by Norman Hathaway, of Brewer, Maine, as a "combination of several good combinations." It has been successful in Labrador, New Brunswick, and in the salmon rivers of Maine. Mr. Hathaway says that it seems to work best at mid-day during normal dry-fly conditions, and has been effective year after year. The fly is unusual and is an interesting pattern.

## LADY ATHERTON

| | |
|---|---|
| *Head color:* | Black |
| *Tag:* | Silver wire or oval tinsel |
| *Tip (or Butt):* | Radiant orange floss |
| *Body* | Black Bear dubbing (thin) |
| *Ribbing:* | Oval silver tinsel |
| *Horns:* | Two long Black Bear hairs, half again as long as the hook |
| *Wing:* | Black Bear hair, fairly short, on top of the horns |
| *Cheeks:* | Jungle Cock, very small and short |
| *Hackle:* | One turn of a natural black hackle, pulled down and tied back slightly |

This pattern, by Charles De Feo, of New York City, was named by him for Mrs. Maxine Atherton Wyckoff, who caught and released thirty-six salmon with it the first season it was used. It is an interesting adaptation of the *Butt* patterns so popular on the Miramichi River.

## LEMAC

| | |
|---|---|
| *Head color:* | Black       Hook size: #6, Model Perfect |
| *Tail:* | A few Woodchuck body hairs |
| *Body:* | Black nylon wool, fairly fat and tapered at both ends |
| *Ribbing:* | Fine oval silver tinsel |
| *Throat:* | About two turns of a Plymouth Rock hackle, tied on as a collar and pulled down before the wing is applied. The hackle is quite short and sparse |
| *Wing:* | A small bunch of Woodchuck body hairs extending about to the bend of the hook. Over these is a very small bunch of cream-colored Polar Bear underhairs, extremely sparse and tied on about two-thirds the length of the Woodchuck hair |

This is one of Ira Gruber's originals, dating about 1940, which he used in very rapid water. It is one of the forerunners of the popular New Brunswick hair-wing patterns.

## LIGHTNING BUG

| | |
|---|---|
| *Head color:* | Black |
| *Tag:* | Fine oval gold tinsel |
| *Tail:* | Red fluorescent nylon wool, cut off short |
| *Body:* | Rear third: Green fluorescent nylon wool. Forward two-thirds: Peacock herl |
| *Ribbing:* | Fine oval gold tinsel, on forward part only |
| *Wing:* | Black Bear hair or black Squirrel tail hair, sparse, short and close to the body |
| *Throat:* | Black hackle, sparse and short |

This is a simple green-butt pattern with a red tail added, especially popular in the area of Arbeautown, near the mouth of the Cains River, on New Brunswick's Miramichi River. The green fluorescent nylon wool provides a translucent and very "buggy" appearance which excellently represents the fluorescent rear section of the Lightning Bug.

## MUDDLER MINNOW

*Head color:*   Black (use 4/0 thread)       Hook sizes: 4 to 6, XL (usually) 4XL if 8 or 10

*Tail:*         Two narrow sections of natural (light mottled) Turkey wing quill, of moderate length

*Body:*         Flat gold tinsel: tied in about a quarter inch behind hook eye; wound to tail, and back to starting point

*Rest of*
*dressing:*     1) Apply a small bunch of Grey Squirrel hairs as a wing, tied on about a quarter inch behind hook eye, extending two-thirds length of hook-shank. 2) On each side of the hair tie in a section of dark mottled Turkey wing about a quarter-inch wide, extending to tail (sections from a right and a left quill feather). 3) Apply over this a bunch of about 75–100 deer body hairs (as much as half the thickness of a lead pencil), leaving about a quarter-inch of the hair in front of the thread. Take 3 or 4 turns to secure and pull tight until hairs start to flare out and spread slightly around the bend of the hook. 4) Cut another bunch of deer hair and, after securing as above, cut off rear part so about a quarter inch is in front and in back of the thread. Pull tight to make the hair flare out, as in step #3. 5) Clip the flared short hair to desired shape, usually in cone-shape toward eye of hook. Also clip off and trim to the desired shape about half of the bunch of hairs applied in step #3, leaving enough to complete the desired dressing of the wing (the remainder of clipped hair adding to the dressing of the collar).

In doing this, more time will be spent trimming around the head than tying the rest of the fly. Enough cement should be used to insure that the winging and collar will not slip.

This popular pattern, originated on the Nipigon River in northern Ontario, by Don Gapen, of Anoka, Minnesota, is intended to represent the Cockatush minnow, sometimes called *Muddlers*. While it was originated for bass and other fresh-water species, it has been found to be an excellent salmon fly. It can be dressed either on standard or on light-wire hooks and, by sparse or heavier dressing and trimming, can be made to float (and be used as a skittering fly); can be made to float and then be pulled under; or can be made for fishing deep on a sinking line. Considered one of the most successful flies of modern times, it is dressed in many sizes and color combinations. One, recommended for salmon, is the *White Muddler* (or *Missoulian Spook*). This is tied with white or greyish-white materials, with a silver ribbed body of white wool. White calf hair usually is used in this dressing.

## ORANGE BLOSSOM

*Head color:* Black

*Tag:* Oval silver tinsel or round silver wire

*Tip:* Orange silk floss (yellow floss sometimes is used, but orange seems more in keeping with the design).

*Tail:* A Golden Pheasant crest feather, over which is an Indian Crow feather of about half the length (a few red hackle fibers are often substituted).

*Butt:* Black Ostrich herl

*Body:* Embossed silver tinsel which is palmered with a yellow hackle (the hackle often is eliminated on small sizes). An alternate dressing calls for the rear half of the body to be dressed with embossed silver tinsel, and the front half with bright yellow silk floss or Seal's fur. In this case, only the front half is palmered.

*Ribbing:* Oval silver tinsel, wound over the hackle, if it is used

*Wing:* A small bunch of pale brown bucktail, extending to the end of the tail. The wing should be very pale. Sometimes this is accomplished by mixing light brown bucktail with white bucktail. The wing is tied low, close to the hook.

*Hackle:* Two bright orange hackles tied on at the same time as a collar, after the wing has been put on. About three turns of both hackles should be made to make the collar fairly full. The longest fibers extend to the point of the hook, and all are tied back slightly.

This is the authentic dressing, from Mrs. Carmelle Bigaouette, the expert fly dresser whose shop is next to the Restigouche Hotel in Matapedia, Quebec. Sometimes Jungle Cock eyes are added for cheeks, but they are not considered necessary. This bright fly is especially productive in early spring when rivers are high and dirty around the end of June. Patterns as large as No. 1 are used under such conditions, often on double hooks. A fly called the *Orange Blossom Special* is an unimportant variation.

## THE PRIEST (*or* CHURCH OF ENGLAND *Fly*)

*Head color:* White      Hook size 6 or 8

*Tag:* Three turns of oval silver tinsel

*Tail:* A few light blue dun hackle fibers (sparse)

*Body:* White fluorescent wool (which has a decided purplish hue when in the water)

*Ribbing:*      Oval silver tinsel
*Throat:*       Light blue dun hackle applied as a collar and tied back slightly
(sparse)
*Wing:*         A very small bunch of white calf's tail hairs, sparse, tied low on
hook, extending to bend of hook only

This fly was originated by the Reverend Elmer J. Smith, of Doaktown, New Brunswick, one of North America's greatest experts on Atlantic salmon angling. He says, "On a day when no fish were being taken I took four on this fly. It is rather bizarre but it is killing in cold water pools, also effective in slow water if movement is imparted. It is a proven killer also in the fall. The pattern was given to several anglers, who did well with it. They went to Wally Doak for more and now it is a standard pattern with him as well as with L. L. Bean, Inc., Stoddard's of Boston, and other tackle stores." A fly called the *White Miller*, often used on the Miramichi, is very similar except that it does not have fluorescent body material and has a red hackle tail and white hackle throat.

## THE "RAT" SERIES

This series comprises nine patterns, all of which should have wings of the guard hairs (outer-fur) of a Grey Fox (of as nearly equal length as possible) and all of which should have throat hackling of two or three turns of a grizzly hackle added after tying in the wing and wound on like a collar. The hackle should be tied backward slightly to give better appearance and to facilitate sinking. In dressing the wing it is preferable to tie it on tightly in two very small bunches, one over the other, with the butt ends tapered and well cemented to provide a small head. The heads on *all* these flies are of *red* tying thread. The wing extends no longer than to the bend of the hook. The hackle's width extends more than halfway to the tip of the barb of the hook. Roy Thomson used short Jungle Cock eyes for cheeks in the original patterns; now it is considered optional. Dress the flies rather sparsely.

In the Restigouche-Matapedia area of Quebec (among others) double hooks are preferred. Hook sizes ordinarily are No. 4 with No. 2 or larger in high water and No. 6 or smaller in low water. In this area (as this is written) the favorite is the *Rusty Rat*, with the *Silver*

*Rat* a close second particularly during periods of discolored water. The *Rat* patterns are of major importance in salmon fishing but, of course, all of them are not essential.

The first of the series of *Rat* flies were originated by *Roy Angus Thomson* (R. A. T.) in New Brunswick, Canada, in the fall of 1911, according to my old friend, Herbert L. Howard, of Mamaroneck, New York. Mr. Thomson was a cousin of Colonel Ambrose Monell, inventor of Monel metal while with the International Nickel Company. Colonel Monell was a frequent fishing companion of George M. L. La Branche and other noted anglers of the time. It was his habit to purchase flies frequently in lots of many dozens and to give them to his friends, a fact which may help to account for their popularity.

Mr. Howard was instrumental in the development of the series and relates its history as follows:

In the spring of 1911 Mr. Howard was tying flies for Colonel Monell and was experimenting with dressing some of the classic Scotch and English feather-wing patterns more simply with wings of hair. When Colonel Monell brought Mr. Thomson to visit Mr. Howard, Mr. Howard showed them the skin of a Grey Fox he had shot and, since Colonel Monell considered the outer-fur ideal for salmon flies, Mr. Howard gave him half a pelt.

That fall Colonel Monell and Mr. Thomson went fishing at Monell's guide's lodge near a stream in New Brunswick containing big Brook Trout. When the guide said the best fly for these trout was a grey or brown one, Mr. Thomson tied one which later was named for his initials and was called:

## GREY RAT

*Tag:* A few turns of flat gold tinsel (use oval gold tinsel on double hooks).
*Tail:* A very small Golden Pheasant crest feather
*Body:* Under-fur of Grey Fox, spun on
*Ribbing:* Flat gold tinsel
*Wing:* A small bunch of the guard-hairs of a Grey Fox (see comment above).
*Hackle:* A grizzly hackle tied on as a collar (see above)
*Cheeks:* Jungle Cock, short (optional)

Mr. Howard thinks this was the original dressing, although the *Rat* was tied at the same time and may have been the first one. Mr. Thomson experimented with various styles in standard wet fly salmon dressings, low-water and exaggerated (very sparse) low-water types, and others dressed on long-shank hooks as bucktails. Experience proved that the best was a compromise between the low-water and the standard dressing.

During the night a large run of salmon entered the pool and many fish of between seven and fourteen pounds were taken on the *Grey Rat*. Other later variations, discussed as nearly in order of origination as possible are as follows:

## SILVER RAT

This is the same as above except that the body is dressed with flat silver tinsel, with oval gold ribbing. (Remember to use *red* tying thread on this and all other flies in the series.)

## GOLD RAT

This is the same as the *Grey Rat* except that the tag is silver; the tail is Golden Pheasant crest dyed red; and the body is flat gold tinsel ribbed with oval silver tinsel. It was originated in the fall of 1911 by Roy Angus Thomson.

## RAT

This is the same as the *Grey Rat* except that the tag is silver tinsel and the body is dressed with Peacock herl twisted on the red tying thread, with silver ribbing.

These were the first four patterns, and all were originated by Roy Angus Thomson, in spite of what certain fly-dressers in northern New Brunswick might let us think. A *Grey Rat* tied by Roy Angus Thomson in October, 1911, is in the author's collection.

## COPPER RAT

This fly was originated by Herbert L. Howard in November, 1911. In addition to the usual wing and throat hackling it has a copper tag, a short and small tail of two or three Peacock sword fibers and a body of flat copper tinsel ribbed with oval copper tinsel or copper wire. (Jungle Cock cheeks are included optionally on all the patterns.)

## BLACK RAT

This fly was originated either by Mr. Thomson, Colonel Monell, or by Dr. Orrin Summers when he was a neighbor of Mr. Howard at Bound Brook, New Jersey. (See *Summers Gold* bucktail in *Streamer Fly Tying and Fishing*.) It is the same as the *Grey Rat* except that it has a tag of flat silver tinsel and a black Seal's fur body, ribbed with flat silver tinsel.

### RUSTY RAT

*This fly was originated by Dr. Orrin Summers. Many anglers consider it the best of the series.*

*Tag:*  Oval gold tinsel
*Tail:*  Three or four Peacock sword fibers, tied in rather short
*Body:*  Rear half: Bright yellow floss. Forward half: Peacock herl. A length of the yellow floss extends as a veiling from the middle of the body nearly to the end of the body on top of the fly.
*Ribbing:* Oval gold tinsel
*Wing:*  A small bunch of the guard hairs of a Grey Fox
*Hackle*  A grizzly hackle tied on as a collar (see first paragraph)
*Cheeks:* Jungle Cock (optional)

### RED RAT

*Tag:*  Oval or flat silver tinsel
*Tail:*  Two small and short sections of barred Wood Duck
*Body:*  Red Seal's fur, spun on
*Ribbing:* Flat gold tinsel
*Wing:*  A small bunch of the guard hairs of a Grey Fox
*Hackle:* A grizzly hackle tied on as a collar
*Cheeks:* Jungle Cock (optional)

## BROWN RAT

This is the same as the *Red Rat* except that the body is of fiery brown Seal's fur, spun on.

Except for the original of the *Grey Rat*, which was tied by Roy Angus Thomson, the other flies in this series illustrated in this book were dressed by Herbert L. Howard, now the greatest authority on the subject. Several other variations of the *Rat* flies were experimented with, but the nine described here proved to be the best ones. Mr. Thomson went into military service the day after World War I started in August 1914, and was killed in action.

When Grey Fox fur cannot be obtained, several substitutes will do almost as well. In approximate order of preference these are guard hairs from the Silver African Monkey; from Raccoon; mixed black and white Monga Ringtail; or any other mixture of fairly straight black and white hairs, such as white bucktail with black Skunk tail or Black Bear hair. Usually a mixture of about two-thirds of black and one-third of white is the best proportion. The use of kinky and curly hair, such as Impala, calf, etc., is not advised because the hair of the wing for these flies should be straight.

The importance of the *Rat* series is indicated by the experiences of numerous angling groups when polls were taken of the flies which caught salmon. As discussed in this book's notes about fishing in the Province of Quebec, during the summer of 1965, a group of anglers at a camp on the Government waters of the Restigouche took 221 salmon and 159 of these were taken on flies of the *Rat* series. The *Rusty Rat* accounted for 64, the *Silver Rat* for 56, the *Black Rat* for 34, the *Gold Rat* for 3 and the *Brown Rat* for 2. While twenty different patterns were used at the time, we don't know what preference was given to members of the *Rat* series during the action. However, it is quite obvious that the *Rusty Rat*, *Silver Rat* and *Black Rat* are necessities on Quebec rivers such as the Restigouche and the Matapedia, as well as elsewhere.

No one except the salmon knows why salmon will take one fly pattern in preference to another although anglers, based on their experiences, have evolved various theories and procedures about it. Charlie De Feo, who knows as much about it as anybody, is quoted as having remarked that the *Rat* flies resemble the Stone Fly, an insect prevalent at times in the Restigouche area. The *Rusty Rat* has been compared to a hair-wing version of the *Jock Scott*, the *Silver Rat* to the *Silver Grey*, and the *Black Rat* to the *Black Dose*—all very important patterns. Regardless of this, the author never would go salmon fishing without an abundant supply of *Rats*, especially the *Rusty Rat*, and these famous flies have helped him to hook more big salmon than any others.

## RED ABBEY

*Head color:*   Black or red     Hook sizes: 10 to 7/0
*Tag:*              Flat embossed or oval silver tinsel
*Tail:*             A small section of the wing of red Ibis, Swan or Goose, or a very small bunch of red bucktail
*Body:*          Red silk floss, or wool
*Ribbing:*      Flat embossed or oval silver tinsel
*Throat:*       A few turns of a brown hackle applied as a collar, pulled down and tied back slightly
*Wing:*         A small bunch of light brown Squirrel tail hairs, or brown bucktail
*Cheeks:*      Jungle Cock (optional)

An American pattern dating about 1913, this is especially popular in the Restigouche area of Quebec. The account of the " Patent " method of fishing herein noted that Colonel Lewis S. Thompson used a 5/0 "Abbey" when he discovered the method. The fly was a favorite of Richard Hunt and of Walter Teagle (retired Chairman of the Board of Standard Oil of New Jersey), both members of the Anglers' Club of New York. Gold tinsel sometimes is used instead of the silver. Presumably this is an adaptation of an old feather-wing trout pattern, as were so many others of the era.

A similar trout fly, called the *Abbey,* has a tail of Golden Pheasant crest, red silk body, gold tinsel tag and ribbing, and a wing of Grey Squirrel tail hair of grey Mallard flank feather. The throat is brown, or natural red cock. For a black winged fly with the same body, see the British *Black Brahan.*

## ROSS SPECIAL

*Head color:*   Black
*Tag:*              Silver oval tinsel
*Tail:*             A Golden Pheasant crest feather
*Body:*          Red wool, dressed fairly full
*Ribbing:*      Silver oval tinsel
*Throat:*       A yellow hackle, tied on as a collar and pulled down
*Wing:*         A small bunch of Red Squirrel tail hairs
*Cheeks:*      Jungle Cock

This fly was illustrated in the *Fortune* article, "Atlantic Salmon," in June, 1948. It is a popular pattern on Canadian rivers, especially the Margaree. It is rather similar to the *Red Abbey* and the *Abbey* British trout fly. Thus, it seems to be an adaptation.

## SHRIMP

*Head color:* Black
*Tag:* Fine oval gold tinsel
*Tip:* Pale yellow silk floss
*Tail:* A small section of a Golden Pheasant tippet; 6 to 10 strands, tied in upright, showing second black band
*Body:* Pink silk floss, slightly shaped
*Ribbing:* Flat gold tinsel
*Throat:*
*(Hackle)* A few turns of a yellow hackle *before* the wing is applied, and a few turns of an olive-green hackle *after* the wing is applied
*Wing:* A small bunch of Silver Monkey hair, topped with a very small bunch of mixed brown and white bucktail. The wing extends to the tip of the tail.

This is a Canadian pattern, not to be confused with several patterns from the British Isles with the same name. It is an original pattern, dressed by L. A. Lapointe in 1949. He and his brother, D. A. Lapointe, were famous fly-dressers who supplied most of the flies used in New Brunswick and on the Gaspé. The fly was sent to the author by one of his fishing companions, Jean-Paul Dubé, of New Carlisle, Quebec, who owned a tackle shop between 1948 and 1956 which employed L. A. Lapointe. Mr. Lapointe had a reputation for dressing excellent hair-wing flies "which could kill many salmon before coming apart." He had his own tackle shop in Matapedia from 1956 to 1966.

## SILVER DOWN-EASTER

*Head color:* Black
*Tag:* A very few turns of fine oval silver tinsel
*Tail:* A Golden Pheasant crest feather
*Butt:* Two or three turns of black Ostrich, very sparse
*Body:* Medium flat silver tinsel
*Ribbing:* Fine oval silver tinsel
*Throat:* A bright orange hackle, sparse and short, tied on as a collar before the wing is applied
*Wing:* A small bunch of black Squirrel tail hairs or Black Bear hair, rather sparse and extending to the bend of the hook

This is an important and popular pattern on Maine and on Canadian salmon rivers. It is attributed to Bert Miner, of Doaktown, New Brunswick, and is one of several similar patterns described in this book under the *Blackville.*

## SILVER GREY

*Head color:* Black
*Tag:* Silver tinsel
*Tip:* Two or three turns of yellow silk floss
*Tail:* Golden Pheasant crest
*Butt:* Two or three turns of black Ostrich herl
*Body:* Flat silver tinsel
*Ribbing:* Oval or round silver tinsel
*Throat:* A small bunch of Badger hackle or Widgeon, fairly short (this also can be applied as a collar)
*Wing:* A bunch of grey Squirrel tail hairs into which are mixed a few hairs dyed red, yellow, blue or green, or any combination of these
*Cheeks:* Jungle Cock (optional)

This is a simple hair-wing version of the classic British fly which is dressed with a feather wing, as discussed under feather-wing flies in this book, and is quite similar to the popular *Silver Rat*.

## SILVER SATAN

*Head color:* Red
*Tag:* Fine oval silver tinsel
*Tip:* Radiant orange floss
*Tail:* A Golden Pheasant crest feather
*Butt:* About two turns of very bronze Peacock herl
*Body:* Rear two-thirds: Flat silver tinsel. Front third: Black floss
*Ribbing:* Oval silver tinsel, over all
*Wing:* A few Golden Pheasant tippet fibers, over which is a small bunch of Grey Squirrel tail hair
*Cheeks:* Jungle Cock, very small and short
*Hackle:* About two turns of a Plymouth Rock hackle applied as a collar

This fly was originated by Charles De Feo, of New York City, and has been used very successfully on many North American rivers. It bears considerable resemblance to the *Silver Rat* and to a hair-wing version of the *Blackville*.

## TOBIQUE SPECIAL

*Head color:* Black
*Tag:* A few turns of fine oval silver tinsel
*Tail:* About a half-dozen fibers of a Golden Pheasant tippet, long enough to show two black strands
*Body:* Rear half: medium yellow wool. Front half: black wool
*Ribbing:* Fine oval silver tinsel, over entire body
*Wing:* A small bunch of Pine Squirrel tail hair, extending very slightly beyond the bend of the hook

*Hackle:* A few turns of a buttercup-yellow hackle, rather sparse and about half as long as the wing, applied as a collar and tied back slightly after the wing has been put on

This is merely an adaptation of one of the prolific "Yellow butt, black body" hair-wing designs. It is a recent pattern, included here because it is popular by name in the Tobique Valley of Canada's Tobique River.

# XII Dry-Fly and Nymph Patterns

Those having access to old books in angling libraries realize that the art of salmon fishing has diversified remarkably since the days of Kelson. The beautiful color plates in his thick volume, *The Salmon Fly* (1895), illustrate many of the 300 or so patterns he advocated. Modern anglers notice that in general all these were essentially of the same style and type, differing principally only in color. Now, color is of lesser importance and what counts more is variation in type or shape, as well as size. Evidently anglers of the Victorian era were confined to a wealth of color schemes in a very limited range of types, and these were in wet flies alone. The old-timers knew nothing about dry flies and nymphs, which are now essential in our bag of tricks.

As this is written, the techniques of using dry-flies and nymphs still are ignored almost everywhere but in North America. Our friends across the sea should learn to benefit from them because it seems inconsistent to suppose that salmon will accept them so readily on one side of the Atlantic while rejecting them everywhere else.

255

Earlier we discussed the enigma of why salmon take flies. In addition to other theories it could be that, even though the desire to feed is absent in fresh water, the everlasting instinct to hunt remains. This instinct very fortunately is not confined to things under the water.

While we may need, or think we need, a variety of color combinations in wet-flies, the need for them in dry-flies is very much less, perhaps confined to light and dark and maybe a shade in between. In dry flies, while floatability is important, what seems most necessary is a small collection of various shapes in a restricted range of sizes, some of which are very large.

In dry-flies this book offers ten different shapes which can be dressed in as many color combinations as desired. Favorite color variations also are provided. If somebody's pet pattern has been left out it may be because it is considered unnecessary. The popular Wulff patterns are essential, and so are the long caterpillar-like floaters such as the *Bomber* or the *Bottlewasher* and their close cousin, *Whiskers*. The latter three can be fished by several different techniques as we have seen.

Many anglers who have assembled a collection of these think that anything else is superfluous. However, a skater or a skittering fly or two may be handy, and so might a few of the clipped deer hair-bodied flies like the *Irresistible* and the *Rat Face*. Another type listed under the *Silver Grey* is popular in some places. The formerly fashionable La Branche palmers are included more for historic interest than from necessity. Most of us think that later developments are better.

Some will wonder why nymphs are included in a chapter primarily devoted to floaters. Nymphs and dry-flies both are of relatively recent origin and both are exclusively American, so it doesn't seem improper to link them together. While they are important, so few nymph patterns are necessary that it seems needless to give them a chapter all to themselves. We have noted that a very few simple ones will do as well as many, but it doesn't seem out of order to presume that more complicated, more lifelike ones will do better. While George La Branche pioneered or popularized the dry fly, he later was matched by Charles De Feo in the development of nymphs for salmon fishing. Charlie was kind enough to send me some of his favorite patterns, and it is an honor to be able to include them, as well as three from the bench of another prominent expert in the field, Bill Keane.

Readers will note that the patterns provided in this chapter therefore are divided into two parts. First are the dry flies, followed in a second section by the nymphs.

## DRY-FLIES

### BOMBER

*Head color:* Use any appropriately colored thread     Hook sizes: 2 or 4, 4x long, forged Viking.

*Tail:* A fairly large and rather short bunch of the same deer body hair that will be used for the body of the fly. (Other materials are often used, such as calf, Woodchuck, etc.)

*Wing:* A fairly short bunch of the same body hair tied so as to extend forward at an angle of about 45°. (This forward and upward bunch of hair is called a "wing" for want of a better term. The upward slant keeps it free of the eye of the hook.)

*Body:* Natural deer body hair (grey, brown or white are regularly used) spun on, tightly massed, flared out and clipped to a smooth cigar-shape, tapering toward the tail and slightly toward the head. The body should be clipped so that about one-third is below the hook-shank and two-thirds above it to allow plenty of clearance between body and barb. To produce a dense body, rather small bunches of body hair should be used. Many anglers like the body rather roughly clipped

*Ribbing:* A large brown hackle (or one of any other desired color) tied in at the tail and palmered through the clipped body from tail to head.

The *Bomber* dry flies should not be confused with wet-fly patterns of the same name. They were developed in approximately 1967 for use on New Brunswick's Miramichi River, where they have been very effective. They are dressed in various color combinations, another one being all white with red hackle ribbing. It is important that they should be in large sizes. As stated in the text, they are fished dry, dry and dragging (with a fast skittering motion) or wet with a sinking line. They are effective in each technique.

### GOURDEAU'S BOTTLEWASHER

*Head color:* Black     Hook sizes: 1–1/2″ to 2″; low-water

*Tip:* A double tip, dressed thin. Rear part: black wool. Forward part: yellow wool, each 1/8 inch long in proportion to a hook 1–7/8 inches long*

* Hook length measurements do *not* include the eye.

*Body:*       Heavily palmered throughout with wide brown hackles whose
  width is about 3/4 inch at the front (in the above size), tapering slightly toward
  the tail

This is an elongated palmered dry-fly originated in 1958 by François deB. Gourdeau, an official of the Fish & Game Branch of the Department of Tourism of the Province of Quebec. He says, "I fish this dry-fly upstream with four or five casts directly in front of the fish, leaving the fly on the water surface for about two seconds. It usually does not take long before the fish gets mad and goes for it. We have had success with this fly on most Gaspé waters. It always should be dressed on large, long-shank low-water hooks. It is especially successful (during low-water conditions) in August."

The author also suggests using this as a "last resort" fly, and sees no reason why it should not be tied in various colors.

### IRRESISTIBLE

*Head color:*  Use black or brown thread        Hook sizes: 4 to 8; low-water
*Tail:*        A moderate bunch of brown deer tail hair, tied in over tip of barb,
  about as long as the hook
*Body:*        Of grey deer body hair, spun on, tightly massed, flared out and
  trimmed to egg-shape except that the forward part is flat. The body is tapered
  toward the tail and occupies half the distance from point where tail is tied in
  to eye of hook
*Hackle:*      Wide grizzly hackles, heavily applied as a collar from front of
  body to eye of hook

This is one of the favorite dry-fly patterns adapted in large sizes for salmon, but originally tied for trout. It is an excellent floater, even on fast, broken water. Fly dressers make adaptations in various colors, similar to the Wulff patterns. Very little is said in American angling books about this important pattern. Reuben Cross, in his *The Complete Fly Tier* (1950), calls it "a comparatively new and very effective trout fly, used with good success for salmon in sizes 10 to 4." His dressing is the same except that the hackling is blue dun.

### THE "LA BRANCHE" SERIES

In his book, *The Salmon and the Dry Fly*, the noted American angler, George M. L. La Branche, gives the dressings of four bivisibles or heavily palmered dry flies which were popular when the book was written in 1924. While these are not among current favorites (because more effective patterns have since been devised), they are notable as being among the first named dry-flies used for salmon. George La Branche fished for salmon with Colonel Ambrose Monell, famed for his interest in the *Rat* wet hair-wings, as we have noted.

Judging from La Branche's book, it was Colonel Monell who taught him the art of dry-fly fishing for salmon, and La Branche says that Monell was the first angler to take a salmon on a dry fly, this evidently having been on the Upsalquitch, in New Brunswick. In discussing the flies, La Branche says, "Cock's hackles, being of finer quality than hen's hackles, were used exclusively. Dyed feathers were avoided because of an apparent tendency to absorb water, so the colours that could be used were limited to a few shades of brown and grey. While the hooks are small, the flies are large, looking much like pine cones, bottle brushes and fuzzy caterpillars, certainly quite unlike anything the fish have ever seen before. Whatever the flies may look like to the fish, the fact remains that they are accepted, and that it is much more important to place them properly on the water than to consider what form or colour they should possess. The four are merely adaptations of well-known trout flies (the one named for Colonel Monell being his favorite.)"

While the flies are heavily palmered, especially at the heads, they are not hackled so heavily as to more than half conceal the bodies. These are the four dressings:

## COLONEL MONELL

*Tail:* Five or six whisks of grey Plymouth Rock Cock's hackle
*Body:* Peacock herl, with a rib of red, lightly dressed
*Hackle:* Grey Plymouth Rock Cock's hackle, tied Palmer

## SOLDIER PALMER

*Tail:* Five or six whisks of brown or brownish-red hackle
*Body:* Red dubbing, with rib of tinsel, lightly dressed
*Hackle:* Brown or brownish-red, tied Palmer

## MOLE PALMER

*Tail:* Five or six whisks of dark brown hackle
*Body:* Brown dubbing or quill, lightly dressed
*Hackle:* Dark brown, lightly mixed with grey at shoulder, tied Palmer

| SKITTER FLY | WHITE WULFF | BLACK WULFF |
|---|---|---|
| Dressed by | Originated and | Originated and |
| Mr. Burt Carpenter (P) | Dressed by | Dressed by |
| | Mr. Lee Wulff (A) | Mr. Dan Bailey (P) |

| GOURDEAU'S BOTTLEWASHER | WHISKERS |
|---|---|
| Originated and | Originated and |
| Dressed by | Dressed by |
| Mr. Francois deB. Gourdeau (A) | Mr. Louis Butterfield (A) |

| SILVER GRAY | MACINTOSH | PINK LADY |
|---|---|---|
| Dressed by | Dressed by | Dressed by |
| Mr. Herbert Howard (P) | Mr. Keith Fulsher (A) | Mr. Herbert Howard (P) |

| GRAY BIVISIBLE | GINGER SKATER | IRRESISTIBLE |
|---|---|---|
| Dressed by | Dressed by | Dressed by |
| Mr. Robert Jacklin (P) | Mr. Harry Darbee (P) | The Orvis Company (P) |

| WHITE-WINGED RAT-FACED MacDOUGALL | BOMBER | WHITE-WINGED BLACK GNAT |
|---|---|---|
| Dressed by | Dressed by The | Dressed by |
| Mr. Harry Darbee (P) | Rev. Elmer J. Smith (A) | Mr. Harry Darbee (P) |

FIG. XII-1

Varieties in Dry-Flies for Salmon

260

## PINK LADY PALMER

*Tail:*       Five or six whisks of ginger-colored hackle
*Body:*       Light pink silk; rib of gold tinsel, lightly dressed
*Hackle:*   Ginger-colored, with one or two turns of light yellow at head, tied Palmer

Mr. La Branche's reference to these flies resembling bottle brushes reminds us of similar ones of double or triple length which are used effectively as this is being written, such as the *Gourdeau's Bottlewasher.* The La Branche flies presumably were developed by one or more of four men who frequently fished together. In addition to La Branche, these are Colonel Monell, Roy A. Thomson and Dr. Orrin Summers.

## RAT-FACED MacDOUGALL

*Head color:*  Thread used      Hook sizes: 2 to 12 (light wire)
*Tail:*       A dozen or so stiff ginger hackle fibers, fairly long. (A small bunch of deer hair or other straight hair about as long as the hook-shank can be used on flies in the larger sizes.)
*Body:*       Of clipped deer hair, light ginger color. (The body is clipped to the shape of an elongated egg, tapering to the rear.)
*Hackle:*     Ginger hackles applied as a collar in the same manner as the Wulff patterns (see page 265)
*Wings:*      Each a small bunch of white calf hair, splayed upward at a 45° angle (V-shaped) and set upright

This is the pattern for the *White-winged Rat-Faced MacDougall*—a popular dry-fly pattern on all salmon rivers in North America. Except for the wings it is almost identical with the *Irresistible*, and is dressed in several color combinations. The *White-Winged Black Gnat* is dressed similarly, with black hair tail, black (dyed) deer hair clipped body, black hackles, and white calf hair wings. The patterns are dressed on Wilson dry fly hooks, but any strong, light-wire hook can be used. The fly originally was a trout fly, later adapted to dry-fly salmon fishing for conditions under which the dry-fly seems appropriate.

## SILVER GREY

*Head color:*  Red      Hook sizes 4 to 8, low-water
*Tag:*        Embossed flat silver tinsel
*Body:*       Dubbing of underfur of Grey Fox
*Ribbing:*    Embossed flat silver tinsel
*Wing:*       A bunch of white bucktail tied flat along the body, extending slightly beyond bend of hook. The wing hair envelops the upper half of the body and flares out slightly
*Throat:*     From 4 to 6 grizzly hackles wound on as a collar after the wing is applied. The hackling is very thick

# Dry-Fly and Nymph Patterns

This is a bass dry-fly which was adapted to salmon in 1914 by Dr. Orrin Summers and Colonel Ambrose Monell. It is indicative of a type, a somewhat similar one being the *Mackintosh*, which is composed only of tail and forward hackle. The tail of rather bushy Fox Squirrel is tied in at the base of the hackle, or at about the center of the hook shank. Several dark ginger or light red-brown hackles are applied bushily as a collar. Herbert Howard, who fished with Dr. Summers and Colonel Monell, reports that a Miramichi guide remarked that, if the *Silver Grey* were tied with brown and black in it, it would look like a Stone Moth. In 1922 Mr. Howard originated the *Stone Moth*, which is the same type, with an oval gold tinsel tag, Peacock herl body, oval gold ribbed, a wing of brown bucktail, and a collar of two or three each of brown and black hackles, mixed. These flies can be very successful when used with the surface fishing techniques described herein. Sometimes a trailing tail is applied above the barb, forward of which is a body of tinsel or something else. *Mackall's Anticosti Fly* (by John Mackall, of Baltimore, Maryland) is an example of this type. It has a trailing Grey Squirrel tail, a silver body and grey collar hackling applied thickly.

## SKATER

*Head color:* Thread used  Hook sizes: Model Perfect TDE (short) 2–12
*Body:* Heavily hackled from a point above the tip of the barb forward to the eye with the longest, stiffest and widest hackles obtainable (suitable to hook-size), in any desired color, such as ginger, black, white, etc. The hackles at the front face of the fly are vertical to the hook shank (not tied back). Hackles should be tied in at their tip ends, making a widening taper toward the eye. On a size 4 (short shank) hook, for example the hackles should be about an inch wide, providing a fly whose circular front face is about two inches in diameter. In this case, the length of the dressing on the shank should be 3/8 of an inch. Model Perfect hooks with short shank and turned-down eye are suggested because their light wire provides good floatability and their round bend decreases the chance of their pulling out after the fish is hooked.

The pattern takes the name of the color of hackle used. For example, if ginger hackles are used, the fly would be called a *Ginger Skater*. The pattern was originated by the late Edward R. Hewitt, famous angler and angling author, in the 1930's. Originally it was a trout fly, dressed to imitate a butterfly flying low over a body of water, and has been a popular dry fly for salmon for many years. The fly should be given a skating motion by the angler, a motion which excites all game fish and which provides great excitement during the strike. The stiffest hackles obtainable are necessary to insure the proper skating action.

## SKITTER FLY

*Head color:*   Yellow or red      Hook sizes: 2 to 10; low-water
*Tail:*           A bunch of brown bucktail, fairly long
*Body:*          Yellow wool, moderately thick
*Ribbing:*       Black silk, fairly wide
*Wings:*        A large bunch of brown bucktail, widely divided to splay out nearly flat and tilted back slightly
*Hackle:*      Several turns of a brown hackle, in front of the wing

This is a Miramichi pattern of about 1935. It is fished in the surface film, drifting, dragging or skating, as described in the text.

## WHISKERS

*Head color:*   Black      Hook size: 6 or 8; low-water (or #4, 6, 8, streamer hooks, 4x long)
*Tail:*           A fairly large bunch of Grey Squirrel tail hairs, quite long
*Body:*          Angora yarn of any color, such as brown, red, green or black, moderately palmered with stiff, brown hackles. A turn or two of the yarn is made as a tip to hold up the tail
*Wing:*         A fairly large bunch of deer body hair dressed fan-shaped in a semi-circle on top of the hook, upright and facing slightly forward. The deer hair is tied in first, over the forward two-thirds of the body, which then is covered by the yarn and hackles.

This dry-fly was originated by Louis M. Butterfield, of Stratham, New Hampshire, who owned a camp (now a club) on Black Brook, near where the Cains River flows into the Miramichi. He says that (over a great many years of salmon fishing) he has "caught thousands of salmon and grilse on *Whiskers*." A way to describe the fly might be that it looks like a Wulff pattern (with the wing fan-shaped but not separated) with a fairly long *Wooly Worm* body. As in most dry flies, the head is insignificant. Many color combinations and types of hair are used.

## THE "WULFF" SERIES

We have seen in the account of the "La Branche" series of bi-visibles, that one of the greatest innovations in modern salmon fishing is the development of the dry-fly and the various methods of fishing it effectively. Whatever its type of pattern, we know it must float "high" on the water and remain so for a reasonable time despite attempts of currents to sink it.

This didn't seem to make any very devastating impact on Atlantic salmon angling until the great American angler, Lee Wulff, developed his three Wulff patterns and proved to all who would pay attention that we really were missing something. Originally, he developed these for trout, with the cooperation of another famous angler, Dan Bailey, of Livingston, Montana. He soon realized that, by making the flies bigger and bushier, they would float cockily high on big salmon rivers and that there they would take salmon which were reluctant to bother with almost anything else.

My good friend, A. I. Alexander, III, wrote about the genesis of the Wulff patterns in the Spring, 1968 issue of *Trout* as follows:

"Most fishermen, I imagine, associate the *Grey Wulff* with a big, rough, rock-strewn salmon river in Newfoundland or Labrador. With its high degree of floatability, the *Grey Wulff* has become a favorite with Atlantic salmon fishermen who need a dry fly that will ride high on the water and require a minimum of attention to keep it afloat. It was conceived, however, not on a brawling salmon river but on a gentle trout stream: the Ausable, in New York State.

"On Labor Day, 1930, Lee Wulff, dissatisfied with the then current dry-fly patterns, sought to imitate a large greyish mayfly that was prevalent on the water. He was particularly interested in creating an artificial that had a larger and fuller body than the existent patterns and one that was not quite so susceptible to fish slime which, of course, is detrimental to the floating quality of a fly.

"Wulff, whose inventive and original thinking has contributed much to American angling, made a radical departure from the traditional flies in his choice of materials. He used natural brown bucktail for the tail and wings and grey Angora rabbit fur (in the trout pattern) for the body. For hackles he used two blue-grey saddle hackles. One must remember that in 1930 the American fly-fisherman was still very much influenced by the English style of fly and the use of hair in any insect imitation was virtually unknown. It is still rarely used by English fly-dressers. The result of Wulff's effort was a durable fly that would float, take trout, and still float after a few false casts.

"Encouraged with his initial effort, Wulff then went on to create the *White Wulff* and the *Royal Wulff* in the same manner. The Wulff patterns that came later, the *Blonde, Grizzly, Brown,* and *Black Wulff,* were from the vise of another talented fisherman, Dan Bailey, who was Lee Wulff's partner that September day on the Ausable. It is the *Grey Wulff* that is important, however, in that it was the first, and it established a distinct American style of dry fly. The fact that it has been accepted as a standard fly pattern in such a relatively short time attests to its effectiveness."

This book illustrates original patterns by Lee Wulff and by Dan Bailey. Commercial tyers often substitute materials and thus sometimes lose the original rough and bushy character which the flies should have. In salmon fishing the flies are tied on light-wire hooks, usually in sizes from No. 4 to No. 10. Sometimes, hard-to-cast giant sizes on larger hooks are employed as attractors.

In common with some of the world's best fly-dressers, Lee Wulff ties flies with his fingers, without bothering with a vise. He explained this in the 68th issue of the *Bulletin* of the United Fly Tyers Club, of Boston, Massachusetts. Whether or not the fly-dressers who read this use a vise, they may be interested in his methods in order to obtain faithful reproductions:

"In tying a Wulff dry-fly I still prefer to use bucktail, the original material, although calf's tail is somewhat easier to use since it doesn't take the extra time to match up the hair ends and is just about as effective. Tying them in my fingers, my first step is to pick up the hook and start the dinging (attaching thread to hook) with a piece of thread long enough to tie the fly. For these flies the thread should be fairly strong as it takes a firm pressure and a small wall of thread around the base of the wings to hold them in position.

"I hold the eye of the hook between the nails of thumb and first finger of the left hand, doing the winding of the thread with my right. When the shank is wound I can either hold the thread in place by pressure between thumb and finger below the eye of the fly, or take a couple of half-hitches to hold the thread in place.

"Next I cover the wrapped shank with lacquer. I like to feel that the flies I tie will stay together for catching a lot of fish and so want the solid body permanence lacquer gives as well as the security against twisting. I use unwaxed thread as waxing prevents the lacquer from penetrating into the thread. The tail is cut to length and wrapped to the shank. I like a good thick tail to hold up the heavy end of the hook and having the bucktail run the length of the shank (1X long hooks preferred) starts building up the body as well as making the tail more secure.

"Again the thread is clamped between the left thumb and finger, or the head of the fly may be put between my lips to keep the thread from unwinding while I pick up the Angora wool, or roll rabbit's fur around the thread to make the body. Normally, I use wool as it's easier to handle and, seemingly, just as acceptable to the fish. I wind the body from head to tail and back again, shaping it into a natural insect form, and winding over it with thread near the head.

"The fly at this stage is either held between the lips or the thread is given two half-hitches to hold it while I cut the bucktail for the wings. I cut it long and then pull out the longer hairs and reset them until all the natural ends are approximately even and the hair is matched up. Then it's cut to length which is about 1/8 inch longer than the wings should normally be.

"The hair is placed, facing forward, at the right place at the head of the body. It is wrapped tightly with several turns of the thread about 1/8 of an inch or less behind the winding. Then the hairs are lifted and thread is wound in front of the vertical hair until it stands upright and can be split by windings around the shank and a figure of eight or two. The butt ends of the hair, protruding behind the first windings, tend to give a natural humpbacked look when the fly is finished.

"Next, two saddle hackles are set in with two winds of thread. They face forward, on top of the hook, their bare butts fitting in between the rising wings. The fly, in all this tying, is still held between the nails of the left thumb and forefinger. A big drop or two of lacquer is then put on the base of the wings to penetrate well and set everything up when it dries. While it is still wet the two hackles are wound. The first wind is through the top between the wings, then two or three winds behind the wings and a wind back through between the wings. The tip is gripped between finger and thumb to hold it until ready to tie off. The second hackle is wound entirely

ROYAL COACHMAN
(LOW-WATER DRESSING)
Dressed by
Mr. Robert Jacklin (P)

SWEEP
Dressed by
Hardy Brothers (P)

SILVER BLUE
(LOW-WATER DRESSING)
Dressed by
Mr. Robert Cavanagh (A)

LADY AMHERST          BLACK FAIRY
The patterns above were dressed by Mr. Colin Simpson (P)

BROWN TURKEY
Dressed by
Mr. Colin Simpson (P)

GENERAL
PRACTITIONER
Originated and
Dressed by
Col. Esmond Drury (A)

JEANNIE
Dressed by
Miss Megan Boyd (P)

ELVER
Dressed by
Mr. Harry Willcox (P)

MARCH BROWN
Dressed by
Hardy Brothers (P)

MUSKER'S FANCY No. 1
Dressed by
Miss Megan Boyd (P)

BLACK HERON
Dressed by
Miss Megan Boyd (P)

USK GRUB          GOLDEN SHRIMP          RED SHRIMP
The patterns above were dressed by Mr. Jimmy Younger (P)

PLATE VI

Popular British Feather-Wing Patterns

268

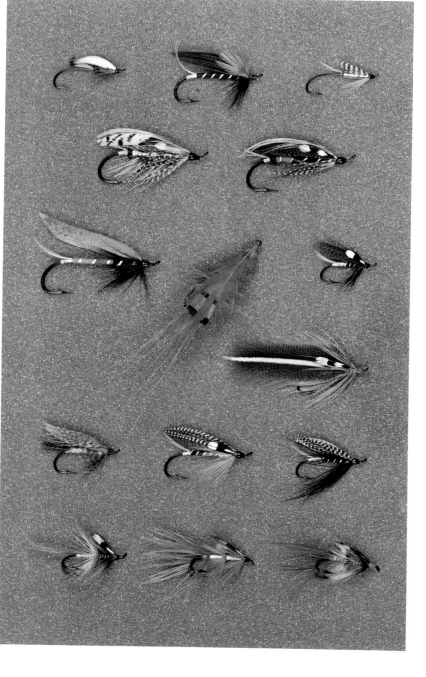

in front of the wings and its tip secured along with that of the first hackle. Now the final wind or two at the head; three half-hitches to secure things, and a drop of lacquer goes at the head and the place where the tail joins the body to make everything secure."

These are the seven original dressings:

### GREY WULFF (WULFF)
*Tail:*    Natural brown bucktail
*Body:*    Blue-grey wool
*Wings:*   Natural brown bucktail
*Hackle:*  Two blue-grey saddle hackles

### WHITE WULFF (WULFF)
*Tail:*    White bucktail
*Body:*    Cream-color wool
*Wings:*   White bucktail
*Hackle:*  Two light badger hackles

### ROYAL WULFF (WULFF)
*Tail:*    White bucktail
*Body:*    Rear and front quarters are butted with Peacock herl; middle half is scarlet wool or silk
*Wings:*   White bucktail
*Hackle:*  Two brown saddle hackles

### BROWN WULFF (BAILEY)
*Tail:*    Brown Impala hair
*Body:*    Cream Angora
*Wings:*   Brown Impala hair
*Hackle:*  Two badger hackles

### BLACK WULFF (BAILEY)
*Tail:*    Black Moose hair
*Body:*    Pink silk, lacquered
*Wings:*   Black Moose hair
*Hackle:*  Two furnace hackles

### GRIZZLY WULFF (BAILEY)
*Tail:*    Brown bucktail
*Body:*    Light yellow silk, lacquered
*Wings:*   Brown bucktail
*Hackle:*  One brown and one grizzly hackle, mixed

### BLONDE WULFF (BAILEY)
*Tail:*    Light tan Elk hair
*Body:*    Light tan Angora
*Wings:*   Light tan Elk hair
*Hackle:*  Two light ginger hackles

As with other successful styles in flies, there have been many adaptations of the Wulff patterns (so named by Dan Bailey). One worthy of note was taken from the colors of the famous *Cosseboom* wet hair-wing:

## COSSEBOOM

| | |
|---|---|
| *Tail:* | Grey Squirrel, dark, with white tips |
| *Body:* | Bright green wool |
| *Wings:* | Grey Squirrel, dark, with white tips |
| *Hackle:* | Two bright yellow saddle hackles |

Readers who dress these flies are reminded of a suggestion made previously: to make hair tips even without manual adjustment, cut off the necessary amount and drop the bunch tip-first into a small and short vial or cup such as the cap on a lady's lipstick. Tap the container on a hard surface, and all hair-tips become even immediately. (*This method works best with straight hair.*) Kapok, in the correct shade, often is used for body dubbing because of its excellent floatability.

# *NYMPHS*

## DE FEO'S SALMON NYMPHS

Charles De Feo, prominent commercial artist of New York City, is famous for his development of (and success with) nymphal imitations for salmon fishing. The following six are among his favorite patterns. Dressings start on the hook-shank above middle of barb.

## BLACK NYMPH

| | |
|---|---|
| *Tag:* | Fine flat gold tinsel |
| *Tip:* | Orange floss |
| *Tail:* | Three or four brown Mallard fibers extending to hook-bend |
| *Butt:* | Peacock herl |
| *Body:* | Black Seal's fur, gold ribbed |
| *Throat:* | A very few brown Mallard fibers extending to hook-point |
| *Wing:* | One small Jungle Cock hackle tip set flat on top extending to butt |

## BROWN NYMPH

| | |
|---|---|
| *Tag:* | Fine flat gold tinsel |
| *Tip:* | Orange floss |

*Tail:* Three or four brown Mallard fibers extending to hook-bend
*Butt:* Peacock herl
*Body:* Fiery brown Seal's fur, gold ribbed
*Throat:* A very few brown Mallard fibers extending to hook-point
*Wing:* One small Jungle Cock hackle tip set flat on top extending to butt

## GOLD NYMPH

*Tag:* Fine flat silver tinsel
*Tip:* Orange floss
*Tail:* Three or four brown Mallard fibers extending to hook-bend
*Butt:* Peacock herl
*Body:* Rear half of oval gold tinsel, front half of Peacock herl
*Throat:* A very few brown Mallard fibers extending to hook-point
*Wing:* One small Jungle Cock hackle tip set flat on top extending to butt

## SILVER NYMPH

Same as above except that the rear half of body is oval silver tinsel.

## GILL'S GIRL NYMPH

*Tag:* Fine flat gold tinsel
*Tip:* Orange floss
*Tail:* Three or four lemon Wood Duck fibers extending to hook-bend
*Body:* Peacock herl ribbed with gold tinsel and palmered beside ribbing with a black body hackle of moderate width
*Head:* Red

## GILL'S LADY NYMPH

*Tag:* Fine flat silver tinsel
*Tip:* Orange floss
*Tail:* Three or four lemon Wood Duck fibers extending to hook-bend
*Body:* Mixed black and fiery brown Seal's fur ribbed with silver tinsel and palmered beside ribbing with a black body hackle of moderate width

In dressing the above nymphs hooks usually are Model Perfect in sizes 4–10. Tags and tips are very small. All heads are black except as noted. The Gill's nymphs have been used in Iceland with great success but, under conditions noted in this book, all six nymphs should be effective everywhere.

## W. J. KEANE'S SALMON NYMPHS

Bill Keane is a salmon angler and professional fly-dresser of Bronxville, New York. He dresses his nymphs on Veniard's low-water hooks in sizes from 4 to 10, with No. 10 his favorite. These are three of his favorite patterns:

FIG. XII-2

## NYMPHS FOR SALMON

TOP ROW: Nymphs by Charles DeFeo: *Gold Nymph*, *Gill's Girl Nymph* and *Black Nymph*. BOTTOM ROW: Nymphs by William J. Keane: *Olive Nymph*, *Leadwing Coachman Nymph* and *March Brown Nymph*.

## MARCH BROWN

*Head color:* Brown
*Tail:* Three cock Pheasant tail fibers, tied in over point of hook to angle apart to right, center and left, extending slightly beyond bend of hook
*Body:* A dubbing of blended tan Fox and amber Seal
*Ribbing:* Dark brown cotton thread
*Legs:* Body plumage of dark brown Partridge, the fibers angling out to right and left like a jet aircraft's wings, extending slightly beyond rear of wing case
*Wing case:* A section of a dark brown Turkey tail feather (shiny side up), tied down and lacquered

## LEAD-WING COACHMAN

*Head color:* Dark brown or black
*Tail:* Three small dark grey hackle tips, tied in as above
*Body:* A dubbing of blended Black Bear under-fur, dark grey dyed Fox and fiery brown Seal
*Ribbing:* Dark brown cotton thread
*Legs:* A section of a dark grey hen's hackle, tied in as above
*Wing case:* A section of a dark grey duck or goose wing feather, tied down and lacquered

272

## OLIVE NYMPH

*Head color:* Brown or black
*Tail:* Three cock Pheasant tail fibers, tied in as above
*Body:* A dubbing of blended cream Fox under-fur and medium green wool fibers
*Ribbing:* Amber cotton thread
*Legs:* A section of a medium brown Partridge body feather, tied in as above
*Wing case:* A section of a light brown mottled Turkey tail feather, tied down and lacquered

In these nymphs the wing case covers the top of the front half of the body. Bill Keane usually fishes his nymphs by the "Greased Line" method and he says, "You will note that, while I mix colors in accord with Atherton's 'impressionist' theory, I mix textures so that one ingredient is soft to bind the dubbing together, another relatively wiry to give the body resilience, to keep it from matting, and to retain translucency. The dubbings for all three nymphs have one highly visible color."

## ROSGEN SALMON NYMPH

*Head color:* Black    Hook sizes: 6, low-water
*Tail:* About four whisks of soft black hackle
*Body:* In five equal sections: Three black chenille body rings separated by two rings of flat, fairly wide silver tinsel
*Throat:* About six whisks of soft black hackle

This simple pattern is a favorite of Bill Rosgen, of Winsted, Connecticut, who fishes often on Canadian rivers. He has used this nymph since 1952 and also makes it in *Green Highlander* green and *March Brown* brown. He uses them during low-water conditions and also in the early season when water is clear. He says there is no need to make the nymph any smaller because salmon will take the number 6 size well and this size holds them effectively.

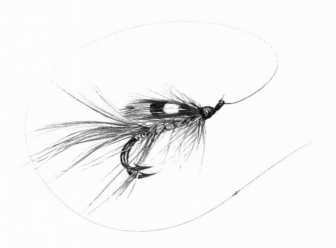

# XIII

# British Feather-Wing Patterns

This chapter contains pertinent information and the most authentic dressing instructions available on about fifty British feather-winged Atlantic salmon flies which are at present nationally or internationally popular. While an attempt has been made to omit famous classics described in other books (such as Kelson and Pryce-Tannatt) the descriptions of a few have seemed necessary either because they still are in widespread use in many areas or because the description of their dressings shows how they can be simplified into reduced or hair-wing versions. Notably among these are the *Green Highlander*, *Black Dose*, *Silver Grey*, the three *Doctors*, (*Black*, *Blue* and *Silver*) and *Dusty Miller*, all extremely popular in one or more of their various versions in Canada and other countries as well as in the British Isles. Many readers may enjoy attempting to dress these beautiful classics, but the principal reason for their inclusion is to demonstrate various ways in which they can be simplified.

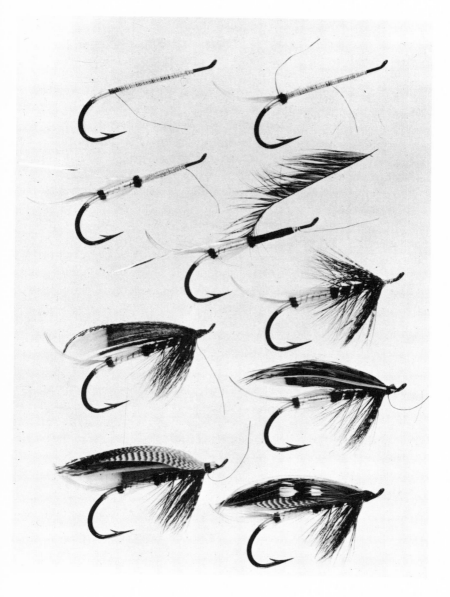

FIG. XIII-1

A "JOCK SCOTT" IN THE MAKING

Most of the flies described here are relatively easy to tie and have been selected for that reason as well as for their popularity. Some also have been chosen because they are different, thus perhaps showing how North American fly-dressers can vary their efforts at the tying bench by adapting successful British ideas to American uses. Salmon often respond to flies which are out of the ordinary, and the flowing hackles of the Heron patterns and the unusual dressings of the various shrimps and grubs which are described and illustrated should provide suggestions for creative variation.

Finally, a few flies are included only because they are outstandingly beautiful. The author is of the opinion that, while most American dressings are very practical, they do not offer sufficient creative challenge. It is hoped that some of the dressings will inspire fly-tying competitions such as are sponsored by the Fly-Dressers' Guild in the United Kingdom. These patterns include *Apollo 11*, *Colonel Bates*, *Prince Philip*, *Gordon* and *Salscraggie*, the latter two being proved angling patterns. The originals have been dressed by several of the world's most proficient fly-dressers: Miss Megan Boyd, Alex and Colin Simpson, and Jimmy Younger (who currently is the British champion). The author apologizes for including a pattern named after himself, but it is one of the beautiful creations of Jimmy Younger, and it seemed too good to keep hidden. A special color plate has been prepared for these Exhibition Patterns because they are examples of the peak of the art in Atlantic salmon fly-dressings, and many Atlantic salmon flies are the loveliest and most difficult dressings in the world.

## AKROYD (DEE TYPE)

*Head color:*  Black
*Tag:*  Gold *oval* tinsel
*Tail:*  A Golden Pheasant crest feather, over which are between 5 and 10 Golden Pheasant tippet fibers, half as long as the crest
*Body:*  In two equal parts: Rear half: yellow Seal's fur palmered with a yellow hackle whose fibers are as long as the gape of the hook. The rear section is ribbed with oval *gold* tinsel. Front half: black silk floss palmered with Black Heron. The Heron fibers are as long as the wing and extend to or beyond the bend of the hook. The front half is ribbed with oval *silver* tinsel.
*Wing:*  Two narrow strips of cinnamon Turkey wing feathers, reaching to the tip of the tail and set medium low over the body
*Cheeks:*  Jungle Cock, medium long and set drooping, that is, set *under* the hook, pointing to the barb

This is the correct dressing, as given to the father of Miss Megan Boyd, the celebrated fly-dresser of Scotland, by the originator, Mr. Charles Akroyd, of "Duncraggie," Brora, Sutherland, Scotland. Miss Boyd sent to the author an *Akroyd* dressed by Mr. Akroyd himself in 1878. This one has a wing of *white* Turkey. Evidently both were used. The ribbing on large sizes from 3/0 to 8/0 is flat tinsel, oval tinsel in the smaller sizes. Mr. Akroyd liked "simple" flies such as this one, and nicknamed it the *Poor Man's Jock Scott*. He considered that the fly would fish well anywhere. It is an excellent Dee pattern, used on all rivers, especially the Brora and Helmsdale Rivers in Scotland. The fly also is used on Canada's Grand Cascapedia River. (Also note the simplified hair-wing version.)

## APOLLO 11 (AN EXHIBITION PATTERN)

*Head color:* Black
*Tag:* Oval silver tinsel
*Tip:* Yellow silk floss
*Tail:* A Golden Pheasant crest feather, over which is a shorter section of Indian Crow
*Butt:* Black Ostrich herl
*Body:* Rear half: Yellow silk floss, ribbed with fine oval silver tinsel. Middle butt: Black Ostrich herl, veiled with Indian Crow above and below. Forward half: Flat silver tinsel, ribbed with fine oval silver tinsel
*Hackle:* A bright yellow hackle palmered over the silver tinsel of the front half of the body
*Throat:* A purple Vulturine Guinea fowl feather, wound on as a collar, and with an added small bunch of the fibers set below the hook
*Wing:* Two strips of yellow Swan, covered by two yellow hackles, covered by two red Golden Pheasant sword tail feathers, outside of which are two black, blue and white Vulturine Guinea fowl hackles with points cut off half the length of the wing, plus sides of yellow Toucan with red points
*Cheeks:* Jungle Cock
*Topping:* A Golden Pheasant crest feather

While the American astronauts of Apollo 12 were on the moon the author received this beautiful dressing, commemorating the flight of Apollo 11, from the renowned fly-dresser, Alex Simpson, of Aberdeen, Scotland. It is included here, not as a fishing fly (because it should be kept for exhibition), but rather as a challenge to fly-dressers who want to attempt to duplicate a fly which is outstandingly beautiful and rather difficult. The author has the honor of quoting from the letter from Mr. Simpson in which the fly was enclosed:

"You have the only *Apollo 11*, which I am pleased to enclose. This fly was designed by me during the moon walk. Bill, my eldest son, and I sat up all night watching the moon walk on television and Bill asked me to design a salmon fly to commemorate the event. The body had to have silver to represent the rocket, and the red Toucan butts on the body represent the rocket's firing. With the rocket hurtling through space there had to be heat, so the wings had to be red and yellow. Different colours were encountered around the moon: intense darkness, bright light and the blue-grey of the moon's surface. This is represented by the blue, black and white Vulturine Guinea fowl hackle with the points cut off. The purple Guinea fowl throat hackle also represents heat, and the Jungle Cock represents the eyes guiding the rocket to the moon. All this sounds romantic, doesn't it? But to me, it was true and it turned out to be a beautiful-looking fly, with colours which appeal to salmon."

Some day the author hopes to duplicate this fly, and to catch a salmon with it. Mr. Simpson deserves the picture! Quite obviously he has out-Kelsoned Mr. Kelson.

## BEAULY SNOW FLY (SPEY TYPE)

*Head color:* Orange Seal's fur, spun on behind the black tip of the head
Hook sizes: 1/0 or larger
*Body:* Pale blue Seal's fur (sparse)
*Ribbing:* Broad, flat silver tinsel, edged with fine oval gold tinsel or gold twist
*Hackle:* A black Heron's hackle wound forward from the third turn of tinsel, quite full at the throat, the longest fibers extending to bend of hook
*Wing:* A fairly large bunch of Peacock herl fibers (in strands) covering that part of the Heron's hackle which is above the hook. The hackle is pulled up and down to expose the body

This is a classic Scotch Spey fly, used mostly in the spring. There is considerable latitude in dressing Spey flies, since each dresser has his own variation.

## BLACK DOCTOR

*Head color:* Black, with inside rim of red
*Tag:* Fine silver wire
*Tip:* Pale yellow silk floss
*Tail:* A Golden Pheasant crest feather, over which is a much shorter tip of Blue Chatterer or Indian Crow
*Butt:* Scarlet Berlin wool
*Body:* Black silk floss (or wool or Seal's fur) not built up
*Ribbing:* Oval silver tinsel

*Hackle:* A cock's hackle dyed dark claret or magenta, palmered from forward third of body

*Throat:* A bunch of speckled Gallina fibers, tied under the hook, extending nearly to the hook point

*Wing:* (Mixed wing) An underwing of strands of a Golden Pheasant tippet with strips of Golden Pheasant tail over it; a sheath of married single Swan strands dyed (from bottom to top) scarlet, blue and yellow, with Florican, Bustard, Peacock wing, mottled and cinnamon Turkey tail, married narrow strips of Teal and barred Wood or Summer Duck fastened in across the sheath; plus narrow strips of bronze Mallard edging the top of the sheath

*Cheeks:* Jungle Cock, about half as long as the wing

*Horns:* Blue Macaw

*Topping:* A Golden Pheasant crest feather

The wings are the same in the *Silver Doctor* and the *Blue Doctor* as in the *Black Doctor*.

The *Silver Doctor* is the same as above except the tip is golden yellow floss; the body is flat silver tinsel; and the throat is a pale blue hackle followed by Widgeon, without the claret hackle.

The *Blue Doctor* is the same as above except the tip is golden yellow floss; the tail is a topping and tippet in strands; the body is pale blue floss; the hackle is pale blue, and the throat is of Jay fibers.

The cheeks and horns often are omitted in all three patterns.

This one of a very few complicated dressings given in this book is included merely as an example of fancy dressings rather typical during the Kelson era of the 1890's. Except for making exhibition dressings, most fly-dressers will prefer the much simpler hair-wing and reduced dressings included herein. Readers interested in complicated dressings are referred to the works of Kelson and of Pryce-Tannatt. Pryce-Tannatt's book, *How to Dress Salmon Flies*, is a recently reprinted classic recommended by the author for reference because the *methods* of dressing complicated flies are as important as the descriptions of the patterns. (See Chapter IX herein.)

## BLACK DOSE

*Head color:* Black

*Tag:* Silver thread or fine oval silver tinsel

*Tip:* Light orange silk floss

*Tail:* A Golden Pheasant crest feather, over which are two married strips (back to back) of Teal and scarlet Swan, about half as long as the tail, and very thin

*Body:* Two or three turns of pale blue Seal's fur or silk floss (sometimes omitted); the rest black Seal's fur (left smooth) or black silk floss

*Ribbing:*     Oval silver tinsel
*Hackle:*      A black hackle palmered forward from first turn of tinsel
*Throat:*      Two or three turns of a light claret or fiery brown hackle, applied
as a collar and pulled down (This sometimes is omitted and two or three turns
of the black body hackle are used instead.)
*Wing:*        A pair of Golden Pheasant tippets, back to back, veiled with
married strands of scarlet and green Swan, light mottled Turkey tail and Golden
Pheasant tail, with a few strands of Peacock herl over this (The author notes
that on some dressings the Peacock is omitted and that an outer veiling of
brown Mallard over barred black and white Teal is used instead, set over the
upper part of the wing.)
*Topping:*     If the topping of Peacock herl is not used, a Golden Pheasant
crest feather is used
*Cheeks:*      If the Golden Pheasant crest topping is used, cheeks of Jungle
Cock are included. If the Peacock herl topping is used, there are no cheeks
*Horns:*       Blue and yellow Macaw (optional)

This classic dressing of the still-popular British fly is included
because its hair-wing and reduced simplifications also are given in
this book. There is a Norwegian dressing of the same name which is
an entirely different fly pattern.

## BLACK FAIRY

*Head color:*  Black
*Tag:*         Fine round gold tinsel
*Tip:*         Golden yellow silk floss
*Tail:*        A Golden Pheasant crest feather
*Butt:*        Black Ostrich herl
*Body:*        Black Seal's fur or silk floss
*Ribbing:*     Oval gold tinsel
*Throat:*      A black hackle, wound on as a collar and pulled down
*Wing:*        Strips of brown Mallard

Another version eliminates the butt in the above dressing and
uses the tip as a butt. This dressing, popular on Canadian rivers, is
almost identical to the popular *Jeannie*, whose hair-wing versions
include the *Black Bomber* and the *Black Star*. A third, more complicated, more attractive and probably more authentic dressing which
is popular in Scotland was sent to the author by Alex Simpson and
his son Colin, prominent dressers of classical British salmon flies in
Aberdeen. This is as follows:

*Tag:*         Fine oval silver tinsel
*Tail:*        A Golden Pheasant crest feather, over which is a shorter section of
Indian Crow
*Butt:*        Black wool

*Body:*      Rear third: dark red wool     Forward two-thirds: black wool
*Ribbing:*   Oval silver tinsel
*Hackle:*    A Black Heron feather (tip tied in first) palmered forward over the
             the black wool
*Throat:*    Barred black and white Teal, fairly long
*Wing:*      Strips of brown Mallard
*Cheeks:*    Jungle Cock
*Topping:*   A Golden Pheasant crest feather

## BLACK HERON
*Head color:*  Black
*Tag:*         Silver tinsel
*Tail:*        A Golden Pheasant crest feather (or red Ibis)
*Body:*        Two turns of yellow silk floss, with the rest of the body black
silk floss
*Ribbing:*     Oval or round silver tinsel
*Throat:*      About two turns of a black Heron feather, with an added small
bunch tied under the hook, all very long, extending well beyond the bend of
the hook
*Wing:*        Two strips of barred black and white Teal

This fly was a favorite of the late English angling authority,
Mr. Anthony Crossley. Mr. Frederick Hill, in his excellent book,
*Salmon Fishing—The Greased Line on Dee, Don and Earn* (1948),
says, "It is a very plain and simple fly and effective in low water. I
like it in dark, dirty weather, especially just before a rise in the river,
but it also takes in brilliant sunlight."

## BLUE CHARM
*Head color:*  Black
*Tag:*         Two or three turns of fine silver wire
*Tip:*         Golden yellow silk floss (left out on low-water pattern)
*Tail:*        A Golden Pheasant crest feather
*Butt:*        Black Ostrich herl (left out on low-water pattern)
*Body:*        Black silk floss, quite slim
*Ribbing:*     Oval silver tinsel or fine silver wire
*Throat:*      A deep blue hackle, wound on as a collar and pulled down before
the wing is applied (the hackle should be very short and sparse on the low-
water pattern).
*Wing:*        Strips of mottled brown Turkey tail or brown Mallard, veiled with
an overwing of narrow strips of Teal along the upper edge (the Turkey wing
is set upright).
*Topping:*     A Golden Pheasant crest feather

This is a relatively simple British classic pattern which is "good
everywhere" and which is a highly favored fly in anglers' fly boxes

generally. The low-water version is dressed very sparsely and simply on long-shanked, light-wire hooks usually in sizes from 4 to 10, the body occupying no more than half of the length of the hook-shank. Presumably, if an international poll were taken of anglers' favorites in low-water patterns, the *Blue Charm, Logie* and *Black Jack* would rank at the top, and probably in that order. This dressing is the most popular one, although there are slight variations among the classical authors.

The *Blue Charm* (HW) is as above except that it has no tip, butt or topping. The throat is applied as a beard and the wing is Grey Squirrel.

## BRORA

*Head color:* Black
*Tag:* Oval silver tinsel
*Tip:* Lilac-pink silk floss
*Tail:* A Golden Pheasant crest feather, over which are a few fibers of blue Kingfisher, half as long as the crest
*Body:* Rear half: Oval silver tinsel, veiled at the front with gold Toucan, top and bottom    Front half: Black silk floss, ribbed with oval silver tinsel
*Hackle:* About two turns of a black Heron feather, extending to the bend of the hook
*Wing:* Two cinnamon Turkey strips, outside of which are married strips of blue and white Swan, outside of which are strips of Pintail two-thirds as long as the inside strips. The Swan is not quite as wide as the Turkey, and the Pintail is not quite as wide as the Swan

This pattern was sent to the author by Miss Megan Boyd, the noted fly-dresser of Brora, who thinks it was originated by Mr. Charles Akroyd, of Brora, Sutherland, Scotland. It is a beautiful fly which resembles the much simpler predominantly black patterns so successful on North American rivers, such as the Miramichi. Mr. Akroyd was the originator of the *Akroyd* pattern, which it resembles slightly.

## BROWN FAIRY

*Head color:* Black
*Tag:* Gold tinsel
*Tail:* A Golden Pheasant crest feather
*Body:* Fiery brown Seal's fur, brown wool yarn, or brown silk floss
*Ribbing:* Oval gold tinsel
*Hackle:* A brown hackle palmered over front half of body

*Throat:*     A small bunch of brown hackle fibers, tied full under the wing (if the palmering is insufficient or has been omitted)
*Wing:*      Brown (bronze) Mallard, in strips
*Topping:*   A Golden Pheasant crest feather (sometimes omitted)

This (with the *Yellow Fairy*) is a variation of the *Black Fairy*. In the above dressing a butt of black Ostrich herl is often included. In another variation of the same fly the tinsel is silver and the hackle and throat are black. This relates it more closely to the *Black Fairy*, which is also done in a more complicated dressing. It is a favorite fly on many rivers, especially the Miramichi. An almost identical fly is the *Brown Bomber*, also used on Canadian rivers. It has a Red Squirrel wing instead of the Mallard.

## BROWN TURKEY

*Head color:* Black
*Tag:*       Very narrow flat silver tinsel
*Tail:*      A Golden Pheasant crest feather
*Body:*      Rear third: yellow-orange mohair     Middle third: scarlet
mohair     Front third: black mohair, not built up
*Ribbing:*   Flat silver tinsel
*Hackle:*    Several turns of a black hackle, tied back slightly but not pulled down; of moderate length and fullness
*Wing:*      Sections of brown Turkey, medium width

In his authoritative *Fly Dressers' Guide*, John Veniard gives a slightly different dressing. It is without a tag. The rear half of the body is yellow Seal's fur; front half, claret Seal's fur, ribbed with oval silver tinsel. The hackle is brown and the wing is composed of sections of Golden Pheasant tippet veiled with strips of light cinnamon Turkey. This, evidently, is the English dressing. The one given above is favored in Scotland.

Two other similarly named flies of a later date are the *Gold Turkey* and the *Silver Turkey*, which seem to be North American adaptations and are described elsewhere in this book.

## COLONEL BATES (An Exhibition Pattern)

*Head color:* Black, with red center band
*Tag:*       Fine oval silver tinsel
*Tip:*       Pale yellow silk floss
*Tail:*      A Golden Pheasant crest feather, over which are two small strips of red Goose and Kingfisher, both half as long as the tippet
*Butt:*      Scarlet wool
*Body:*      Flat silver tinsel

*Ribbing:*    Oval silver tinsel
*Throat:*    About two turns of a Guinea Fowl hackle, forward of which are about two turns of a red game-cock's hackle, both applied as a collar, pulled down and tied back slightly
*Wing:*    Four golden yellow saddle hackles, with a white saddle hackle on each side half as long as the yellow. Over this on each side is a fairly wide strip of a yellow Swan wing feather as long as the wing, with thin strips of red Swan wing feather married to it, top and bottom. Over this is a wide strip of barred Mandarin Duck to level with the butt (both feathers on each side)
*Topping:*    Two Golden Pheasant crest feathers
*Shoulders:*    Jungle Cock, of moderate length
*Cheeks:*    Kingfisher, over the Jungle Cock, and shorter

This fly was originated in 1969 by Jimmy Younger, champion fly-dresser of the British Fly-Dressers' Guild, and was adapted from the streamer fly of the same name. It is one of a few Exhibition Patterns given in this book and is intended primarily to demonstrate fly-dressing ability in tying rather complicated and attractive patterns for exhibition.

## CARRON (Spey Type)

*Head color:*    Black    Hook sizes: 3–1/0; (usually) low-water
*Body:*    Orange Berlin wool, dressed thin
*Ribbing:*    Flat silver tinsel: scarlet silk floss and fine oval silver tinsel or silver wire
*Hackle:*    A black Heron hackle, doubled, tied in at the point at the fourth turn of tinsel and wound forward between the flat silver tinsel and the scarlet wool, with the fine oval silver tinsel wound in an opposite direction between the fibers, one turn of the tinsel covering each turn of the hackle.
*Throat:*    A bunch of barred grey Teal feather fibers tied under the hook as a beard (to allow the wings to hug the body), extending to the point of the hook
*Wing:*    On each side, narrow brown Mallard strips (showing brown points and light roots) set low and tied on points down, extending to the bend of the hook

This is one of the old standard Spey patterns, which include the *Lady Caroline* and later ones such as the *Grey Heron* and the *Black Heron*, all distinguished by their thin, drab bodies and long, flowing hackles for best action in fast water. Spey flies are discussed on pages 184 to 187. Evidently there is no such thing as standard dressings for these flies because every dresser had his own variation. However, the dressings in this book are consistent with those given in British classics, such as Kelson and Pryce-Tannatt.

## DUNKELD

| | |
|---|---|
| *Head color:* | Black |
| *Tag:* | Fine oval gold tinsel |
| *Tip:* | Orange silk floss |
| *Tail:* | A Golden Pheasant crest feather (A pair of Jungle Cock points, back to back, can be set over the topping, but often are omitted.) |
| *Butt:* | Black Ostrich herl |
| *Body:* | Flat gold tinsel |
| *Ribbing:* | Oval gold tinsel |
| *Hackle:* | An orange hackle, wound forward from the second turn of tinsel |
| *Throat:* | A small bunch of Jay fibers |
| *Wing:* | Two strips of Peacock wing, partly veiled by strips of Mallard |
| *Cheeks:* | Blue Chatterer |
| *Topping:* | A Golden Pheasant crest feather |
| *Horns:* | Blue and red (or yellow) Macaw |

This is the simplified dressing from Kelson. Pryce-Tannatt gives one in which the wings are much more complicated. Kelson says, "This old standard pattern has undergone considerable change and now universally is dressed as above. Formerly the body was made with gold embossed tinsel, which I prefer. I believe it was invented by W. J. Davidson."

Jimmy Younger, the celebrated Scotch fly-dresser, sent the author a simple *Dunkeld* (*hw*) with a Tag of oval gold tinsel; Tail: Golden Pheasant crest; Body: Flat gold tinsel; Ribbing: Oval gold tinsel; Throat: Orange cock fibers; Wing: Squirrel tail dyed orange; Cheeks: Jungle Cock. Given one or two body embellishments from the fancy dressing, we would almost exactly duplicate the American *Orange Blossom*, which presumably was arrived at independently.

## DUSTY MILLER

| | |
|---|---|
| *Head color:* | Black |
| *Tag:* | Silver thread |
| *Tip:* | Golden yellow silk floss |
| *Tail:* | A Golden Pheasant crest feather, over which is Indian Crow, half as long |
| *Butt:* | Black Ostrich herl |
| *Body:* | Rear two-thirds: Embossed silver tinsel     Front third: Orange silk floss |
| *Ribbing:* | Fine oval silver tinsel |
| *Hackle:* | A Golden yellow hackle palmered over the floss only (and sometimes omitted) |
| *Throat:* | A small bunch of speckled Gallina |

*Wing:*        A pair of black white-tipped Turkey tail strips (back to back); over these but not entirely hiding them is a mixed sheath of married strands of Teal, yellow, scarlet and orange Swan, Bustard, Florican and Golden Pheasant tail; over but not entirely hiding these are married narrow strips of Pintail and barred Summer Duck, with narrow strips of brown Mallard over these, at the top of the wing
*Topping:*     A Golden Pheasant crest feather
*Cheeks:*      Jungle Cock
*Horns:*       Blue and yellow Macaw

This is the classic British dressing as done by Pryce-Tannatt. It is included in this book with its hair-wing and reduced variations to show how the classic patterns have been simplified in modern dressings. Olaf Olsen, the famous fly-dresser of Laerdal, Norway, dresses a fly of the same name which is entirely different. In fact, many Norwegian dressings having the names of British classics are quite different from the British ones.

## ELVER (or BLUE ELVER or RANSOME'S ELVER)

*Head color:*  Red        Hook sizes: 4–6, low-water
*Body:*        Black silk floss, dressed thin
*Ribbing:*     Oval or flat silver tinsel
*Wing:*        Two Blue Vulturine Guinea Fowl feathers with white stripe, nearly twice as long as the hook and tied low, back to back, to cover the shank of the hook. (Vulturine feathers come from the African Guinea Fowl. They should be 2-1/2 inches long for hook sizes 6 or 4.)
*Hackle:*      Three or four turns of a plain Blue Vulturine feather (without the white stripe) ahead of the wing and tied back to blend with the wing. The fibers should be very long, extending beyond the bend of the hook

This modern and unusual British fly of the streamer type was popularized by Arthur Ransome in a radio broadcast in England. He observed that elvers (young eels) breed in the Atlantic off Bermuda and travel in the Gulf Stream to American and British rivers in astounding numbers. Therefore, they must be a staple food for salmon. The young elvers, at one stage, are only about 2-1/2 inches long, very fat, and translucently dark. Mr. Ransome indicates that this fly, dressed to resemble a young elver, is successful for salmon, and it should be equally successful in North American rivers, into which they migrate. Richard Waddington, in his book, *Salmon Fishing*, devotes a chapter to the elver and maintains that large flies of this type are excellent for "Greased Line" fishing. For these reasons the pattern is included with the thought that other anglers may wish to try it. It has been noted that streamer fly and bucktail fishing for Atlantic salmon is becoming more and more productive as experience makes it better understood.

## EVENING STAR

*Head color:*    Black
*Tag:*    Silver tinsel
*Tip:*    Yellow floss
*Tail:*    A Golden Pheasant crest feather
*Butt:*    Black Ostrich herl
*Body:*    Black silk floss, not built up
*Ribbing:*    Oval silver tinsel, with a black cock hackle palmered between the ribbing of the front half
*Throat:*    A small bunch of dark blue hackle fibers
*Wing:*    Four Jungle Cock feathers, the inside pair extending to the end of the tail, the outside pair somewhat shorter to expose the eyes of the inside pair
*Topping:*    A Golden Pheasant crest feather

This is an old standard British pattern which was sent to the author by the famous English fly-dresser, Mr. Harry Willcox, of Alnwick, England.

## FIERY BROWN

*Head color:*    Black
*Tag:*    Fine oval gold tinsel
*Tip:*    Claret floss
*Tail:*    A Golden Pheasant crest feather
*Body:*    Fiery-brown mohair, moderately slim
*Ribbing:*    Fine oval gold tinsel
*Hackle:*    A light fiery-brown hackle is palmered forward from the second turn of the tinsel to the throat and one or two extra turns are made at the throat. The longest fibers of the throat extend to the tip of the barb
*Wing:*    An underwing of sections of Golden Pheasant tippet, veiled by bronze Mallard sections, slightly longer than the tippet sections
*Horns:*    Blue Macaw (optional)

This is the accepted simplified pattern, as described by Duncan Frazer, a very old British angling author. The fly is a nineteenth century Irish classic, described by Kelson (1895) who differs in the description slightly, as follows (other elements are the same): Tip: light orange silk; Body: fiery-brown Seal's fur; Head: finished with black herl. The *Fiery Brown* has several variations, depending on the materials which each ghillie or fly-dresser happened to have on hand. All, however, feature the fiery-brown coloration. Some of the dressings are very complicated, including the one given in

Pryce-Tannatt, which is too involved for most fly-dressers to attempt or to bother with.

## THE GENERAL PRACTITIONER

Since salmon attain their pink-red flesh color by feeding on shrimp (called "prawns" in the British Isles), it follows that flies dressed to imitate them should be effective. By far the best imitation is Colonel Esmond Drury's *General Practitioner*, which he originated in 1953 and which has been eminently successful ever since. The fly is not an easy one to dress but, between the following step-by-step instructions, the drawings, and the illustration in the color plates, it should not present great difficulty. In the British Isles, treble hooks usually are used. In North America we would use doubles, or perhaps singles, preferably size No. 2 long-shank, fine wire, with red-orange tying thread. After each winding of hackle, the hackle on the top of the shank is clipped off to allow the Golden Pheasant neck feathers to lie as flat as possible. When the fly is completed, stroke the feathers backward so they will lie flat and close to the body to give the effect of the scales of a shrimp. The diagram positions the 15 steps, as follows:

1. Wind tying thread to bend and tie in ten thick-rooted bucktail hairs dyed hot-orange. (These represent the shrimp's whiskers and they should project two inches beyond the bend of the hook.)
2. Tie in at the same spot, *concave* side upward, a small orange-red Golden Pheasant neck feather.
3. Tie in, *concave* side upward, another small orange-red Golden Pheasant neck feather. These feathers, 2 and 3, should lie one on top of the other. They represent the head of the shrimp.
4. Tie in a long hot-orange cock's hackle and a strip of fine oval gold tinsel.
5. Dub tying thread liberally with pinkish-orange mohair or Seal's fur.
6. Wind dubbed silk to "A" and secure.
7. Wind about three turns of ribbing tinsel to "A" and secure.
8. Wind the hackle between the ribbing to "A" and secure.
9. At "A" tie in, *convex* side up, a slightly larger Golden Pheasant neck feather long enough to cover feathers 2 and 3. Tie this down to lie flat.
10. Prepare the eyes of the shrimp by cutting a "V" from a Golden Pheasant tippet (see sketch). Tie this in to lie flat on top of feather 9.
11. Dub a further length of tying thread and wind it to "B". Wind three turns of tinsel and hackle to "B". Tie these in and cut off.
12. Tie in, *convex* side up, a Golden Pheasant neck feather. This should be tied down to lie along the body so that it will veil, but not cover, feathers 9 and 10.

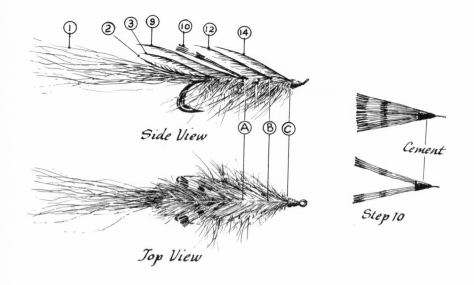

Side View

Top View

Cement

Step 10

13. Dub a further length of the tying thread; wind this to "C" and secure it.
14. Tie in, *convex* side up, a Golden Pheasant neck feather. Tie this down so it will lie flat along the body.
15. Finish the fly with a whip-finish and apply red varnish to the head.

This dressing was sent to the author by Colonel Drury, and the fly in the color plate facing page 268 was dressed by him for this book. He says, "I do not use wax on the tying silk, but apply little dubs of Bostick clear adhesive where necessary, including at the roots of the Golden Pheasant feathers to keep them in place. If I wish to tie a smaller fly, such as size 6, I omit feather number 12. I fish the large fly slowly on a sinking line and the small fly on a floating line; sometimes fishing it fast by stripping in line." The *General Practitioner* may be a new type of fly to North American anglers, but those who try it should find it successful particularly when salmon are reluctant to strike.

## GOLDEN SHRIMP (CURRY'S GOLDEN SHRIMP)

*Head color:* Red or black
*Tag:* Three or four turns of oval or flat silver tinsel
*Tail:* Several turns of a yellow Golden Pheasant body feather, tied backward to an angle of about 30° from horizontal, extending a bit longer than the body

289

*Body:*        In two equal halves, both of embossed silver tinsel ribbed with oval silver tinsel. Some dressings call for veiling both halves with orange Toucan or a substitute. The two halves are separated by a middle hackle of two or three turns of an orange hackle, slanted backward as above

*Throat:*      As a front hackle: Two or three turns of an orange hackle a bit longer than the middle hackle, and slanted backward as before

*Wing:*        Two Jungle Cock feathers, back to back, set in a "V" shape and meeting at the tops, edging the throat hackling and reaching to end of body

## GOLD TURKEY

*Head color:*  Black
*Tail:*        A few honey dun hackle fibers
*Butt:*        Fluorescent orange floss
*Body:*        Flat gold tinsel
*Ribbing:*     Gold wire
*Throat:*      Honey dun hackle fibers optionally applied as a collar or bunched under the hook
*Wing:*        A small bunch of Canadian Pine Squirrel tail hairs, over which are sections of gold barred wild Turkey feather, both of same length

The classic Turkey-winged fly is the *Brown Turkey*, popular in the British Isles. A companion fly to this is the *Silver Turkey*, evidently of North American origin.

## GREEN HIGHLANDER

*Head color:*  Black
*Tag:*         Silver twist or tinsel
*Tip:*         Canary-yellow silk floss
*Tail:*        A Golden Pheasant crest feather, over which are a very few fibers of Teal or barred Summer Duck half the length of the topping
*Butt:*        Black Ostrich herl
*Body:*        Rear three-quarters: Canary yellow silk floss. Remainder: Green Seal's fur or floss
*Ribbing:*     Oval silver tinsel
*Hackle:*      A green hackle palmered over green part of body
*Throat:*      Two or three turns of a canary-yellow hackle, wound on as a collar and pulled down
*Wing:*        Two Golden Pheasant tippets, back to back; veiled by married strips of yellow and green Swan and grey mottled Turkey; veiled by black and white barred Teal, with narrow strips of bronze Mallard over, at top
*Topping:*     A Golden Pheasant crest feather
*Cheeks:*      Jungle Cock (sometimes with Indian Crow over)
*Horns:*       Blue and yellow Macaw (optional)

This is one of the most famous of the British classic patterns, still very popular throughout the world. The reduced and hair-wing versions are also given herein. The fly was designed by a Mr. Grant, of Wester Elchies on Speyside in the late 1800's. When green is mentioned in the dressing it should be the special *Green Highlander* green, for which a dye can be purchased. It is a very bright grass-green shade. The pattern is mentioned in many of the British classics, including Francis.

## GREY HERON (SPEY TYPE)

*Head color:*  Black    Hook sizes: 3–1/0, (usually), low-water
*Body:*       Rear one-third: lemon Berlin wool    Forward two thirds: black Berlin wool
*Ribbing:*    Flat silver tinsel; oval silver tinsel and fine oval gold tinsel
*Hackle:*    A grey Heron hackle, doubled, tied in at the point and wound forward from the rear of the body between the flat silver tinsel and the oval silver tinsel, with the oval gold tinsel wound in an opposite direction between the fibers, one turn of the tinsel covering each turn of the hackle
*Throat:*    A bunch of speckled grey Gallina (Guinea Fowl) feather fibers tied under the hook as a beard (to allow the wings to hug the body), extending to the point of the hook
*Wing:*    On each side, narrow brown Mallard strips (showing brown points and light roots) set low and tied on points down, extending to the bend of the hook

This Spey fly is the favorite of the celebrated English professional fly-dresser, Geoffrey Bucknall, who tied the pattern for this book. He says it is "almost a Spey version of the *Jeannie*" and discusses the dressing on page 185. Flies of this type are tied on low-water hooks due to their lightness and extra length. They are very productive on fast rivers in the British Isles and should be more popular in North America as they become better known.

## IAN WOOD

*Head color:*  Black    Hook sizes: 4 to 6, singles or doubles
*Tail:*       A Golden Pheasant crest feather
*Body:*       Flat gold tinsel
*Ribbing:*    Oval gold tinsel
*Throat:*    A ginger hackle wound on as a collar, pulled down and tied back slightly, *or* a small bunch of ginger hackle fibers applied as a beard
*Wing:*    Sections of black and white Turkey wing feathers

This fly was originated in 1950 by Ian Wood, formerly editor of *Trout and Salmon*, and enabled him to break many fishing records. Although dressed as a salmon fly it has proved excellent in small sizes for sea trout and Brown Trout. Mr. Wood uses two of these flies on his loch casts and says he gets most of his salmon by carefully working the bob fly. He very often takes salmon on a hackle-less version of the fly and always makes a point of splitting the wing fibers of a new fly with a pin because he believes that the Turkey feather, so treated, works better in the water——has more "play" in other words. (This, of course, is a recommendation for a hair-wing version.)

## JEANNIE

| | |
|---|---|
| *Head color:* | Black |
| *Tag:* | Silver tinsel |
| *Tail:* | A Golden Pheasant crest feather |
| *Body:* | Rear third: lemon yellow silk floss        Front two-thirds: black silk floss |
| *Ribbing:* | Oval silver tinsel |
| *Throat:* | A small bunch of (natural) black hackle fibers (sometimes wound on as a collar) |
| *Wing:* | Two strips of a brown Mallard feather, set upright |
| *Cheeks:* | Jungle Cock |

The *Jeannie* is internationally popular both as a standard pattern and as a low-water dressing. There are several hair-wing versions of it, where straight black hair (such as Black Bear hair) is used as a wing instead of the Mallard. In the British Isles, this version is called the *Black Bomber*, which is similar to *Black Maria*. It is the same as North America's *Black Star*, except that the yellow floss is used as a tag and the body is all black silk. With the addition of a few Peacock sword fibers mixed into the black hair wing, it would be a simplified version of the popular hair-wing *Black Dose*.

## JUNGLECOCK

| | |
|---|---|
| *Head color:* | Black |
| *Tag:* | Three or four turns of fine oval silver tinsel or round silver wire |
| *Tip:* | A few turns of bright yellow silk floss, about twice as long as the tag, and quite thin |
| *Tail:* | A Golden Pheasant crest feather, over which is a shorter red Indian Crow feather |
| *Butt:* | Two turns of black Ostrich herl |
| *Body:* | Rear two-thirds: Embossed silver tinsel        Forward third: Bright orange silk floss |
| *Ribbing:* | Oval silver tinsel, over entire body |
| *Hackle:* | The orange floss is palmered with several turns of an orange hackle of the same shade |
| *Throat:* | A small bunch of Guinea Fowl fibers, tied under the hook, slightly longer than the orange hackle and extending nearly to the barb of the hook |

*Wing:*       Three pairs of Jungle Cock feathers, each pair back to back. The inside pair extends to the end of the tail and the other two pairs are graduated shorter

*Cheeks:*     Blue Kingfisher, extending the length of the orange floss

*Topping:*    A Golden Pheasant crest feather

This pattern should not be confused with one of the British "lake flies" of the same name. In common with many other patterns, this one has the popular *Dusty Miller* body, but with an all-Jungle-cock wing. As one of the "bright" patterns, it is preferred for high or discolored water, and it has been used occasionally on North American rivers since 1955.

## LADY AMHERST

*Head color:* Black

*Tag:*        Fine oval silver tinsel, or silver wire

*Tip:*        Golden-yellow silk floss

*Tail:*       A Golden Pheasant crest feather (over this sometimes a few wisps of Teal are added).

*Butt:*       Black Ostrich herl

*Body:*       Flat silver tinsel

*Ribbing:*    Oval silver tinsel

*Hackle:*     A badger hackle palmered forward from the second turn of tinsel

*Throat:*     About two turns of a barred black and white Teal body feather, tied on as a collar and pulled down, the longest fibers extending to the barb of the hook (the Teal fibers sometimes are applied as a beard, but this is less attractive)

*Wing:*       Strips of Amherst Pheasant center tail (barred black and white Amherst Pheasant neck feathers often are substituted, especially on large flies)

*Shoulders:*  Jungle Cock, of moderate length

*Cheeks:*     Blue Chatterer, smaller and shorter than the Jungle Cock, but veiling it (Blue Kingfisher can be substituted.)

*Topping:*    A Golden Pheasant crest feather

This is one of the classic salmon fly patterns often used during conditions of high or discolored water.

## LADY CAROLINE (SPEY TYPE)

*Head color:* Black       Hook sizes: 3–1/0 (usually), low-water

*Tail:*       A very small bunch of red-brown Golden Pheasant breast feather fibers

*Body:*       Olive-green and light brown Berlin wools wound together in proportion of two of the brown to one of the olive-green

*Ribbing:*    Flat gold tinsel, oval silver tinsel and fine oval gold tinsel

*Hackle:*    A grey Heron hackle tied in at the point and wound forward from the rear of the body between the flat gold and the oval silver tinsel, with the fine oval gold tinsel wound in an opposite direction between the fibers, one turn of the tinsel covering each turn of the hackle

*Throat:*    Two turns of a red-brown Golden Pheasant breast feather wound on as a collar and tied back slightly

*Wing:*    On each side, brown Mallard strips (showing brown points and light roots), set low and extending to the bend of the hook, tied on points down

Spey flies, originally designed for use in the fast currents of the Spey River, are tied on light wire (low-water) hooks which are one size longer in the shank than ordinary salmon hooks. Flies of this type have thin, drab woolen bodies palmered with very long, flowing, doubled Heron hackles (or other extremely long-fibered rump feathers) and nearly horizontal slim Mallard wings. The *Lady Caroline* was famous before the days of Kelson (1895) and still is popular on fast rivers in Europe as well as (more recently) in North America. Flies of this type are described in more detail on page 184.

## LADY SEAFIELD (or COUNTESS OF SEAFIELD)

*Head color:*    Black       Hook size: #1 light iron, usually

*Tag:*    Fine oval silver tinsel

*Tail:*    A Golden Pheasant crest feather *or* a few fibers from a red Golden Pheasant breast feather

*Butt:*    Black Ostrich herl (on larger sizes only)

*Body:*    Rear two-thirds: Embossed silver tinsel    Front one-third: Yellow Seal's fur, palmered with a yellow hackle

*Ribbing:*    Oval silver tinsel

*Throat:*    A light blue hackle, applied as a collar

*Wing:*    Two narrow strips of cinnamon Turkey, set medium-low over the body and extending to the tail

This fly was originated jointly by Mr. William Popner and Miss Megan Boyd in the presence and with the approval of Lady Seafield, of Cullen House, Scotland, when she visited Miss Boyd's workshop. It is a popular fly on the River Spey, used by many anglers on the northern rivers of Scotland, as well as in Sweden, when a light and bright fly seems to be needed. The *Lady Seafield* (*hw*) is as above except that the palmering of the body is eliminated, and the wing is brown Squirrel tail.

## LOGIE

There are several somewhat similar dressings for this famous pattern. One of the earliest (1895) is from Kelson, as follows:

*Head color:* Black
*Tag:* Silver tinsel
*Tail:* A Golden Pheasant crest feather
*Body:* Dark claret silk floss
*Ribbing:* Oval silver tinsel
*Throat:* A bunch of light blue hackle fibers, tied full under wing
*Wing:* Two strips of Swan, dyed yellow, set upright and slightly covered by broad strips of brown Mallard
*Cheeks:* Jungle Cock

Pryce-Tannatt's dressing is essentially the same except for the body. The first two-fifths of the body is pale primrose (light yellow) floss; remainder is ruby-red floss. His dressing does not call for Jungle Cock cheeks. Veniard agrees with Pryce-Tannatt. Leonard's dressing is the same as Kelson's except that he adds a tip of orange floss; calls the body "brown-red," and dresses the wing with brown (bronze) Mallard, without the yellow Swan strips. He does not include the Jungle Cock cheeks.

Of the three, I like Kelson's dressing best, and it probably is the most authentic. It would make a good hair-wing pattern if a small bunch of yellow under dark brown hair should replace the feathered wing. Kelson says that his dressing is "an excellent summer pattern in dull weather on the Dee. It is dressed on small double hooks."

## MARCH BROWN

*Head color:* Black
*Tag:* Round gold tinsel
*Tail:* A Golden Pheasant crest feather
*Body:* Fur from a hare's face, spun on and well picked out
*Ribbing:* Oval gold tinsel
*Throat:* A small bunch of Partridge feather fibers (from the back for small sizes; from the rump for larger sizes)
*Wing:* Strips from a hen Pheasant tail

Veniard's dressing is the same as above except that silver tinsel is used instead of gold. This salmon fly pattern is adapted from the trout fly pattern, which is dressed as a dry fly, as a standard wet fly and as low-water pattern. There is a dry-fly hair-wing version which uses barred brown Squirrel tail as a wing. In this one the throat is brown and grizzly cock, mixed (or "cree" hackle, which has brown, black and white bars). This could be tied *Wulff* fashion, and it also is tied as a wet fly. In all its variations it is a popular salmon fly pattern on many rivers.

## F. G. MORGAN

*Head color:* Black
*Tag:* Gold tinsel
*Tail:* A Golden Pheasant crest feather, over which are a few black and white tippet fibers, about half as long as the crest feather
*Butt:* Black Ostrich herl
*Body:* Flat gold tinsel, with a very small section of scarlet floss in the middle, occupying about one-fifth of the body
*Ribbing:* Oval gold tinsel
*Throat:* A small bunch of red claret hackle fibers
*Wing:* A mixed wing of red, blue and yellow Swan, outside of which is a section of a Teal feather of the same length
*Cheeks:* Jungle Cock, about half as long as the wing
*Topping:* A Golden Pheasant crest feather

This is a British pattern.

## MUSKER'S FANCY (No. 1)

*Head color:* Black
*Tag:* Silver tinsel
*Tail:* A Golden Pheasant crest feather
*Body:* Fairly thin. Rear third: Black silk floss  Middle third: Red silk floss  Front third: Oval silver tinsel
*Ribbing:* Oval or round silver tinsel
*Throat:* A few turns of a light blue hackle, tied on as a collar and pulled down, extending nearly to the point of the barb
*Wing:* Teal and Mallard, mixed
*Cheeks:* Jungle Cock

The *Musker's Fancy* was originated in 1943 by Frederick Hill, the English author of *Salmon Fishing—The Greased Line on Dee, Don and Earn*, and was named by him in honor of his employer, Captain H. T. Musker. It was made to represent a combination of the *Blue Charm*, *Logie* and *Silver Blue*. In the British Isles it is favored especially for the "greased line" method of fishing.

There are two other variations of this fly, all by Mr. Hill. The *Musker's Fancy, No. 2* is the same as above except that black hackle is used instead of blue, and there is no Jungle Cock. *Musker's Fancy, No. 3* is the same as above except that brown hackle is used instead of blue (with Jungle Cock).

In North America this fly is dressed as a hair-wing using red-phase Squirrel (dark in color). The No. 1 version then is called *Cole's Modified Musker*.

## PRINCE PHILIP (An Exhibition Pattern)

*Head color:* Black
*Tag:* Fine oval gold tinsel
*Tip:* Light blue silk floss
*Tail:* A Golden Pheasant crest feather, over which are two small sections of light blue and of red Swan about half as long as the topping
*Butt:* White Ostrich herl
*Body:* Royal purple silk floss, or wool
*Ribbing:* Flat gold tinsel, followed by heavy gold twist
*Hackle:* A claret cock's hackle palmered ahead of ribbing over front half of body
*Throat:* A few turns of a magenta hackle, forward of which are a few turns of a light blue hackle, both pulled down and tied back
*Wing:* Two strips of white-tipped brown mottled Turkey, back to back, over which on each side are married strips of blue and black Swan, set low, over which are broad strips of Amherst Pheasant tail feather, set high, over which are strips of brown Turkey or Mallard set mid-wing
*Topping:* A Golden Pheasant crest feather
*Shoulders:* Jungle Cock, of moderate length
*Cheeks:* Kingfisher, over the Jungle Cock, and shorter

This fly was originated in January, 1969, by Jimmy Younger, great-great-grandson of John Younger, eighteenth-century fly-dresser and angling author who lived at Kelso-On-Tweed. It earned him the title of champion fly-dresser of the British Isles in the 1969 competition of the Fly-Dressers' Guild. The original was tied on board the ship *Clansman* on the Thames in London to be presented to the Duke of Edinburgh on his opening the Highland Fling Exhibition of Scottish Crafts. The pattern in this book was dressed for the author by Mr. Younger. In his notes he says, "The claret body hackle should be tied in halfway down body and wound to the right of the flat gold, the gold twist being wound to the left. The married strips of blue/black Swan are tied in on the lower half of the white-tipped Turkey wing and the Amherst Pheasant on the top half. On the larger hooks of 2/0 and over, use two Golden Pheasant toppings. The Jungle Cock should be one-third down wing."

## RED SANDY

*Head color:* Black, ringed with red at rear (or with scarlet wool)
*Tag:* Oval silver tinsel
*Tail:* A Golden Pheasant crest feather, over which is a slightly shorter one of Indian Crow
*Butt:* Scarlet wool

*Body:*        In two sections of oval silver tinsel, butted in the middle with
scarlet wool and veiled above and below with Indian Crow. The forward
section is palmered with a scarlet hackle (quite heavily).
*Wing:*        Two extended Jungle Cock feathers, back to back, enveloped on
each side by two double Indian Crow feathers overlapping each other
*Throat:*        Additional turns of a scarlet hackle wound on as a collar after
the wing is applied
*Topping:*        Two Golden Pheasant crest feathers
*Horns:*        Red Macaw

This nineteenth-century classic pattern is a fly-dresser's delight
because of its unusual beauty. Kelson says it is "a good fly on the
Halladale, and highly prized in Iceland." Pryce-Tannatt's dressing
differs so much from Kelson's that it seems to be a different pattern
entirely, and he could have confused it with something else. Since
Kelson's dressing is the earlier one, simpler, and more unusual, it
is given here. Veniard publishes Pryce-Tannatt's dressing, which
includes a wing almost identical to the *Jock Scott*. This fly is dressed
as a standard pattern but also is recommended as an Exhibition
Pattern.

### RED SHRIMP (CURRY'S RED SHRIMP)

*Head color:*   Red
*Tag:*          Three or four turns of oval or flat silver tinsel
*Tail:*          Several turns of a red Golden Pheasant body feather, tied backward to an angle of about 30° from horizontal, as long as the hook
*Body:*          In two equal halves: the tail half of bright red silk floss ribbed
with fine oval silver tinsel, the front half of black silk floss ribbed with thicker
oval silver tinsel. Both halves are veiled with Indian Crow or substitute. The
two halves are separated by two or three turns of a badger hackle over the
veiling
*Throat:*        As a front hackle: Two or three turns of a badger hackle which is
a bit longer in fiber than the middle hackle. Both hackles are slanted backward
at the same angle as the tail
*Wing:*          Two Jungle Cock feathers, back to back, set in a V shape and meeting at the tops, edging the throat hackling and reaching to end of body

### THE "SHRIMP" PATTERNS

*Head color:*   Black        Hook sizes: 2, 4, 6, 8
*Tag:*          A few turns of fine oval gold tinsel
*Butt:*          Several turns (as a collar) of a red-brown Golden Pheasant breast
feather whose fibers should be as long as the hook (from eye to bend). These
windings are fairly bushy and are tied back very slightly (about 30° from the
vertical). The forward two collars are tied back on the same slant

*Body:*  *Rear half:* Medium yellow silk floss ribbed with fine oval gold tinsel. *Middle butt:* Veiled both on top and bottom with a burnt-orange Toucan feather extending to the tail. Immediately forward of this is wound (as a collar) about three turns of a dark-orange cock's hackle or a Golden Pheasant breast feather whose fibers are two-thirds as long as the butt and tied back as above. *Front half:* Black silk floss ribbed with fine oval gold tinsel

*Hackle:*  About three turns of a Golden Pheasant breast feather, applied as a collar as above. The fibers are as long as those of the middle butt

*Wing:*  Two Jungle Cock eye feathers nearly as long as the collar fibers and slanted similarly to a wing

The *Shrimp* flies are very popular, attractive and unusual British patterns which are dressed in several variations, often on double hooks. The first salmon fly to be called a *Shrimp* was originated by Hardy Brothers, of Alnwick, England, and evidently was based on the *Usk Grub* type of fly, which is quite similar. The above is the original dressing, provided by the famous fly-dresser, Jimmy Younger, of Brora, Scotland. The success of the fly has led to the development of many patterns of the same or similar name.

Another version, by the same fly-dresser, uses a hot-orange hackle between the two body halves, with a black hackle at the throat. The Jungle Cock eyes are tied in high and short (below the first black bands, with both feathers meeting at the top). The tag and the ribbing over the yellow part of the body are oval gold tinsel, with silver over the black part.

A less heavily dressed version, provided by Alex and Colin Simpson, expert fly-dressers of Aberdeen, differs from the first dressing (above) as follows: Tag: Silver; Butt: (same); Body: *Rear half:* (same) ribbed silver; *Middle butt:* Veiled above and below with narrow sections of red Toucan, Ibis or Swan extending slightly longer than rear half of body, then a few turns of a white hackle, slanted backward like rear butt; *Front half:* (same) ribbed silver; Throat: The red veiling is duplicated above and below the throat, following which the throat is wound with two or three turns of a badger hackle; Wing: (same) extending slightly beyond rear butt.

Separate dressings are given in this book for the *Curry's Red Shrimp*, the *Curry's Golden Shrimp* and the *Usk Grub*, all of which are somewhat similar.

| BLACK BOMBER | HAIRY MARY | STOAT'S TAIL |
|:---:|:---:|:---:|
| Dressed by | Dressed by | Dressed by |
| Miss Megan Boyd (P) | Mr. Jimmy Younger (P) | Mr. Harry Willcox (P) |

| WATSON'S FANCY | BUCKTAIL & GOLD | JERRAM'S FANCY |
|:---:|:---:|:---:|
| Dressed by | Dressed by | Dressed by |
| Mr. Jimmy Younger (P) | Mr. Harry Willcox (P) | Mr. Harry Willcox (P) |

GARRY
(or "YELLOW DOG",
HAIR-WING VERSION)

BLUE DOCTOR
(HAIR-WING VERSION)

The Patterns above were dressed by Mr. Alex Simpson (A)

DUNKELD
(THE HAIR-WING VERSION ON AN ARTICULATED HOOK)
Dressed by Mr. Jimmy Younger (P)

FIERY BROWN
(HAIR-WING VERSION)

JOCK SCOTT
(HAIR-WING VERSION)

The Patterns above were dressed by Mr. Geoffrey Bucknall (P)

BLACK BRAHAN

RED DRAGON

The Patterns above were dressed by Mr. Geoffrey Bucknall (P)

AKROYD
(HAIR-WING VERSION)
Dressed by
Mr. Colin Simpson (P)

SILVER DOCTOR
(HAIR-WING VERSION)
Dressed by
Mr. Herbert Howard (P)

PLATE VII

Typical British Hair-Wing Patterns

300

In addition to the above dressings, the shrimp (or prawn) is imitated by the *General Practitioner*, which is more life-like than any of the others. Anglers in North America should take special interest in these patterns. Another which is quite different, but which should be mentioned here, is the *Crayfish*, listed under American featherwing patterns.

## SILVER BLUE (SILVER AND BLUE)

*Head color:* Black     Hook sizes: 4 to 10, (usually), low-water
*Tag:* Silver tinsel (optional)
*Tail:* A Golden Pheasant crest feather
*Body:* Flat silver tinsel
*Ribbing:* Fine oval silver tinsel
*Wing:* Two strips of barred black and white Teal breast feather (sometimes brown Mallard is used)
*Throat:* A very small bunch of fibers from a pale blue dyed hackle (Cambridge blue)

The *Silver Blue* is an old British pattern most popular as a low-water fly, the dressing then being very sparse and occupying only the forward half of the long-shanked light-wire hook. As such, it is one of the principal patterns in North America and in the British Isles. It also is tied as a hair-wing pattern, using a very small bunch of Grey Squirrel tail hairs for the wing.

## SILVER GREY

*The simplified pattern:*

*Head color:* Black
*Tag:* Silver tinsel
*Tip:* Two or three turns of yellow silk floss
*Tail:* A Golden Pheasant crest feather
*Butt:* Two or three turns of black Ostrich herl
*Body:* Flat silver tinsel
*Ribbing:* Oval or round silver tinsel
*Throat:* A badger hackle, two or three turns of which are wound on as a collar and tied back slightly. Widgeon sometimes is substituted
*Wing:* A lightly barred grey wing, such as sections of Widgeon, Teal, Mallard or Pintail side feathers. Egyptian Goose is used in large flies, if the other feathers are not long enough. The wing should be horizontal; close to the hook
*Cheeks:* Jungle Cock (optional)

*The classic British pattern:*

The body is the same except that a badger hackle is palmered forward from second turn of tinsel, with a small and fairly long bunch of Teal fibers at the throat. The wing is horizontal. There is an inner wing of Golden Pheasant tippets and tail fibers; green, blue and yellow married Swan wing feather sections, and Guinea fowl, Amherst Pheasant or Teal. The outer wing is brown Mallard with grey Mallard or Teal. There are Jungle Cock cheeks and a topping of a Golden Pheasant crest feather.

The classic version is included in most of the works of British authors, all of whom differ somewhat. For instance, Pryce-Tannatt recommends an inner wing of married white, yellow and green Swan, Bustard, Florican and Golden Pheasant tail, an outer wing of married strips of Pintail and barred Summer Duck, with brown Mallard strips over this. He also recommends horns of blue and yellow Macaw, plus some other embellishments. For those who don't want to go to all this trouble, a very attractive reduced variation can be made by putting a married Swan section, in colors as above, between the grey wing sections in the above simplified version. Kelson says the fly is "good on all rivers," but he lists slight differences in the pattern. A popular hair-wing version is described elsewhere in this book.

### SILVER TURKEY
*Head color:*  Black
*Tail:*  A few dark dun hackle fibers
*Butt:*  Fluorescent red floss
*Body:*  Flat silver tinsel
*Ribbing:*  Silver wire
*Throat:*  Dark dun hackle fibers, optionally applied as a collar or bunched under the hook
*Wing:*  A small bunch of black Fitch tail hairs, over which are sections of wild Turkey body feather, both of same length

The classic turkey-winged fly is the *Brown Turkey*, popular in England and Scotland. A fly similar to this is the *Gold Turkey*, which seems to be of North American origin.

### SIR CHARLES
*Head color:*  Black
*Tag:*  Round silver tinsel
*Tail:*  A Golden Pheasant crest feather, over which is a section of Indian Crow, half as long
*Body:*  Fairly thin, of golden silk floss
*Ribbing:*  Fine oval silver tinsel

*Throat:* A few turns of a pale blue hackle, wound on as a collar and pulled downward, almost as long as the body
*Wing:* Several Peacock herl tips, over which are two strips of black and white barred Teal, of equal length. (Some dressings call for two strands of Peacock sword instead of the larger amount of herl tips.)

This is the classic standard dressing. The noted British author and angler, Frederick Hill, gives a variation he likes better. He fishes the above dressing only in bright sunlight and uses the following variation "in all weathers, from May onwards." It is the same in wing and proportions as the above. The tag is gold tinsel; Tail: a Golden Pheasant crest feather (only); Body: Olive-green silk; Ribbing: embossed gold tinsel; Throat: pale navy-blue hackle.

## SWEEP

*Head color:* Black    Hook sizes: 6 to 8
*Tag:* Oval gold (or silver) tinsel
*Tail:* A Golden Pheasant crest feather
*Butt:* Black Ostrich herl
*Body:* Black silk floss
*Ribbing:* Oval gold (or silver) tinsel
*Throat:* A black cock's hackle, wound on as a collar and pulled down; quite long, full and mobile
*Wing:* Any black feather such as Crow or dyed Goose
*Cheeks:* Blue Kingfisher or Jungle Cock
*Horns:* Blue Macaw

This is a favorite pattern in Scotland. Correctly dressed, the throat is of a Spey-cock's (a certain breed of domestic fowl) hackle obtained from the lateral tail feathers of the bird. These are scarce, especially in the United States. Black Heron's hackles are often substituted.

## THUNDER AND LIGHTNING

*Head color:* Black
*Tag:* Fine oval gold tinsel, or wire
*Tip:* Yellow silk floss
*Tail:* A Golden Pheasant crest feather, over which is a shorter section of Indian Crow
*Butt:* Black Ostrich herl
*Body:* Black silk floss, not built up
*Ribbing:* Oval gold tinsel
*Hackle:* A deep-orange hackle, wound forward from the second turn of the tinsel
*Throat:* A small bunch of Jay fibers

| *Wing:* | Strips of brown Mallard, set upright |
| *Cheeks:* | Jungle Cock |
| *Topping:* | A Golden Pheasant crest feather |
| *Horns:* | Blue and yellow Macaw |

This dressing is from Kelson, with whom Pryce-Tannatt agrees. Kelson says, "This fly is exceedingly popular and has a well-earned reputation for its destructive qualities when rivers begin to rise after rain. General B---- puts an underwing of tippet, and brown mottled Turkey strips." Also note the British hair-wing version.

## TORRISH

| *Head color:* | Black |
| *Tag:* | Silver thread or tinsel |
| *Tip:* | Golden yellow silk floss |
| *Tail:* | A Golden Pheasant crest feather, over which are a few strands of Golden Pheasant tippet *or* red Ibis, half as long as the crest feather |
| *Butt:* | Black Ostrich herl |
| *Body:* | Rear two-fifths (or half): Oval silver tinsel, butted forward with black Ostrich herl veiled above and below with Indian Crow |
| | Forward three-fifths (or half): Oval silver tinsel palmered with a lemon-yellow hackle and ribbed with fine oval silver tinsel |
| *Throat:* | A deep red-orange hackle, the color of Indian Crow |
| *Wing:* | A pair of black white-tipped Turkey tail strips (back to back) outside of which but not entirely concealing them is a mixed sheath of married strands of Teal, yellow, scarlet and orange Swan, Bustard, Florican and Golden Pheasant tail, outside of which are married narrow strips of Pintail and barred Summer Duck, outside of which are narrow strips of brown Mallard |
| *Cheeks:* | Jungle Cock and/or Indian Crow |
| *Topping:* | A Golden Pheasant crest feather |
| *Horns:* | Blue and yellow Macaw |

This dressing essentially is the one recommended by Dr. Pryce-Tannatt. Miss Megan Boyd, the celebrated Scotch fly-dresser, gives a somewhat different and simpler formula for the wing. In addition to the Turkey she uses Bustard, Peacock wing, Golden Pheasant tail, married strands of red and blue Swan and Gallina, plus the Mallard. She also sent the author a different and very popular "cousin" of this fly:

## PALE TORRISH (OR SALSCRAGGIE)

In this fly the head, tag, tip, tail, butt and topping are as above. The rear section of the body is oval silver tinsel butted forward with a turn or two of yellow hackle and Ostrich herl. The forward part is yellow Seal's fur ribbed with oval silver tinsel.

The underwing is cinnamon Turkey, outside of which are married strands of red, yellow and blue Swan, plus Amherst Pheasant, grey mottled Turkey tail and Pintail. The throat is a deep yellow hackle, and the cheeks are Jungle Cock.

These two flies are named after places in Scotland's Strath of Kildonan, through which flows the famous Helmsdale River. Though the flies were made chiefly for use there, their popularity is worldwide. Hardy Brothers includes the *Torrish* in their most popular twelve classic patterns.

## USK GRUB

*Head color:* Red or Black
*Tag:* Three or four turns of fine round silver tinsel
*Tail:* A small bunch of fibers from a red Golden Pheasant body feather, nearly as long as the hook
*Body:* In two equal halves; the tail half of orange wool, silk or Seal's fur ribbed with fine oval silver tinsel; the front half of the same material in black ribbed with fine oval silver tinsel. The two halves are separated by about two turns of a white hackle immediately forward of which are about two turns of hot-orange hackle, both slanted backward slightly.
*Throat:* As a front hackle: Two or three turns of a Coch-y-bonddu hackle longer in fiber than the middle hackles and slanted backward at an angle of about 30°
*Wing:* Two Jungle Cock feathers, back to back, set in a V shape and meeting at the tops, set high and reaching to the ends of the middle hackling

## YELLOW FAIRY

*Head color:* Black
*Tag:* Silver tinsel
*Tail:* A Golden Pheasant crest feather
*Body:* Yellow Seal's fur or yellow silk floss
*Hackle:* A yellow hackle palmered over front half of body
*Ribbing:* Oval silver tinsel
*Throat:* A small bunch of yellow hackle fibers, tied full under the wing (if the palmering is insufficient or has been omitted)
*Wing:* Brown (bronze) Mallard, in strips
*Topping:* A Golden Pheasant crest feather (sometimes omitted)

This seems to be a variation of the *Black Fairy*, which is dressed both in a simple version similar to the above, and in a more complicated dressing which can be adapted to this one, if desired.

# XIV Britain Hair-Wing Patterns

Since hair-wing salmon flies are relatively late arrivals in British angling (few dating before 1960) we include here only about thirty patterns. These are in addition to the hair-wing simplifications suggested for many of the British feather-wing flies given in the preceding chapter. About ten additional hair-wing adaptations of classic British feather-wings are included here also.

Undoubtedly the growing use of hair-wings in the British Isles was stimulated by their success in North America. Several of the patterns resemble the familiar *Butts* used principally on New Brunswick's rivers. Very probably we substituted the hair-wings for the feathers on some of the British designs and then gave the adaptations back to Britain.

Among the classic adaptations, we have seen that the *Green Highlander, Black Dose, Dusty Miller, Thunder and Lightning* and the three *Doctors* are excellent North American hair-wing patterns, and their popularity in this simplified form should spread around the

Atlantic. Fly-dressers who want to adapt the patterns to their use should note the references to them in Chapter XIII as well as here. The dressing of the *Jock Scott* is not given in the chapter on British feather-wings because it is a very difficult one to tie, but it is an important fly on North American rivers, so the hair-wing version is included.

Probably the most prominent British hair-wing pattern is the *Hairy Mary*, and there are several very different dressings going by that name. The author has included Jimmy Younger's version of it, which seems to be the basic one. Others worthy of special note are *Dunkeld, Garry, Black Bomber* and *Stoat's Tail*. These various patterns are from the benches of several of the United Kingdom's best experts. These artists include Megan Boyd, Geoffrey Bucknall, Hardy Brothers, the Simpsons, Harry Willcox and Jimmy Younger. Since readers may wish to purchase authentic patterns made by these professionals, their addresses will be found on page 345.

We should note that fly-dressers are advised to copy standard patterns exactly, perhaps omitting some of the embellishments such as butts and cheeks if they choose to. However, the hair-wings which simulate the feathers on classic patterns are composed as each fly-dresser thinks best in order to obtain satisfactory color imitations. The best imitations (which have stood the tests of time) are given in this book, and it is suggested that they should be adhered to unless there is reason to the contrary.

Beginners in fly-dressing, usually with insufficient experience in angling, are prone to "invent" new patterns. These usually turn out to be relatively ineffective, not good enough either to fish with or to give away. While it may be fun to originate flies it usually seems preferable to take advantage of the skill and experience of others before trying to compose new ones, of which there are too many already!

Favorite British hair-wing patterns include:

## AKROYD

*Head color:* Black
*Body:*   Rear half: orange Seal's fur
  Front half: black silk floss
*Ribbing:*   Oval silver tinsel

*Hackle:*     A yellow hackle palmered over the orange; a black Heron hackle palmered over the black
*Throat:*     A small bunch of Teal hackle fibers, tied under the hook
*Wing:*     A very small bunch of white bucktail, over which is a very small bunch of Red Squirrel tail hair

This is a simplified version of the feather-wing pattern (which see).

## ARNDILLY FANCY

*Head color:*     Red Ostrich herl (but usually a ring of red Cellire next to the wing, with the rest of the head black)     Hook sizes: 7 to 10, low-water, double
*Tag:*     A few turns of oval silver tinsel
*Tail:*     A Golden Pheasant crest feather
*Body:*     Yellow silk floss
*Ribbing:*     Oval silver tinsel
*Throat:*     A small bunch of bright blue hackle fibers, tied in under the hook
*Wing:*     A small bunch of black Squirrel tail hairs
*Cheeks:*     Jungle Cock (very small)

This fly was originated by Miss Megan Boyd, one of Scotland's leading professional fly-dressers.

## BLACK BOMBER

*Head color:*     Black
*Tag:*     Silver tinsel
*Tail:*     A Golden Pheasant crest feather
*Body:*     Rear third: lemon yellow silk floss
     Front two-thirds: black silk floss
*Ribbing:*     Oval silver tinsel
*Throat:*     A small bunch of (natural) black hackle fibers (sometimes wound on as a collar)
*Wing:*     A bunch of straight black hair, such as Black Bear hair

This is the British version of the *Black Bomber* and a hair-wing version of the *Jeannie* (which see). The Canadian version is the same except that the yellow floss is used as a tip, with the body all black floss. This version also calls for Jungle Cock cheeks and a topping of a Golden Pheasant crest feather. Another North American fly called the *Black Star* is exactly the same, without the topping. Jungle Cock eyes often are added. This general dressing, with or without the embellishments, is one of the most popular flies on Canada's Miramichi River. There, following early traditions, it is called by a descriptive name such as *Black Bear, Yellow Butt.* On the Miramichi and other rivers the butt or tag or rear third of the body is in a choice of colors, such as yellow, orange, green and red. These often are fluorescent colors, which seem to the author (and to many others) to make the fly much more productive. The wing should be sparse and applied close to the body.

## BLACK BRAHAN

*Head color:* Black    Hook sizes: 6 to 10 (Preferably 8 or 10 doubles, low-water irons)
*Tag:* Three turns of oval silver tinsel
*Body:* Red Lurex* or red silk floss
*Ribbing:* Oval silver tinsel
*Throat:* A small bunch of black (sometimes of hot-orange) hackle fibers tied in under the wing
*Wing:* Black Squirrel

This fly was designed by John MacKenzie, a ghillie on the River Conon, and is named for the Brahan beat on that river. It is a Welsh border salmon fly, popular on the Wye and the Usk. Another version, in bucktail form, was sent to the author by Geoffrey Bucknall, of London. It has a red head; a tail of a small bunch of black Squirrel tail, about as long as the body; same body, ribbing and throat; and a wing of a small bunch of black Squirrel tail extending to the end of the tail, which is quite long.

## BLACK DOSE

*Head color:* Black
*Tag:* Silver tinsel
*Tip:* Palest yellow floss
*Tail:* A Golden Pheasant crest feather, over which is Indian Crow (or a few red hackle fibers), half as long (the latter often omitted)
*Body:* Black silk floss, or wool
*Ribbing:* Oval silver tinsel
*Hackle:* A black hackle palmered forward from first turn of the tinsel
*Wing:* Three or four Peacock sword fibers, over which is a small bunch of black Impala tail hairs, or black bucktail, all of even length
*Throat:* A few turns of a black hackle, wound on as a collar and tied back slightly
*Cheeks:* Jungle Cock

This is a hair-wing version of the classic British pattern. Another version, with the same tag, tip, tail and body, calls for additional

---

* *"Lurex"* is the trade name for a plastic material which has the appearance of tinsel and is obtainable in many colors. It is not as strong as tinsel, and therefore should always be ribbed.

turns of the body hackle wound as a throat before the wing is applied. The wing is extremely small bunches of mixed black and dark blue bucktail, over which are extremely small bunches of mixed red and yellow bucktail. Adding Peacock herl or sword fibers is optional, as is Jungle Cock for cheeks. In North America the *Black Dose* is one of the top favorites in the Matapedia-Restigouche area of Quebec. A very dark fly such as this is considered to be particularly effective on dark, cloudy days.

## BLACK DRAGON
*Head color:*   Black
*Tail:*         A very small bunch of black bucktail, as long as the body
*Body:*         Black chenille
*Ribbing:*      Narrow embossed silver tinsel
*Wing:*         A very small bunch of black bucktail, extending to the end of the tail (both tail and wing are very sparse).
*Hackle:*       About two turns of a stiff black hackle, wound on as a collar, extending outward at right angle to the hook in all directions

This is another of the few British bucktail-type salmon flies, usually used on low water. A companion fly called the *Red Dragon* is the same except that the head and all other elements are red. The ribbing is narrow embossed gold tinsel. These two flies were dressed by Geoffrey Bucknall, of London, and are listed in his catalog.

## BLACK MARIA
*Head color:*   Black      Hook sizes: 6 to 10
*Tag:*          Fine oval silver tinsel
*Tail:*         A Golden Pheasant crest feather
*Body:*         Rear half: yellow silk floss
  Front half: black silk floss
*Ribbing:*      Oval silver tinsel
*Hackle:*       A black hackle palmered from tail to head
*Throat:*       A small bunch of Guinea Fowl hackle fibers
*Wing:*         A small bunch of black bucktail

This fly was popularized by Mrs. N. K. Robertson, of Slavey, Ireland.

## BLACK MARIE
*Head color:*   Black      Hook sizes: 6 to 10
*Tag:*          Gold tinsel
*Tail:*         A Golden Pheasant crest feather
*Body:*         Black silk floss

*Ribbing:*     Fine oval silver tinsel
*Throat:*     A small bunch of mixed scarlet and yellow hackle fibers, tied in under the hook
*Wing:*     A small bunch of Stoat's tail hairs (any fairly straight black hair)

This is a British pattern, attributed to a Brigadier Gibson.

## BLUE DOCTOR

*Head color:*  Red
*Tag:*     Oval silver tinsel
*Tail:*     A Golden Pheasant crest feather
*Butt:*     Bright red silk floss
*Body:*     Light blue silk floss, dressed thin
*Ribbing:*     Oval silver tinsel
*Throat:*     A light blue hackle applied as a collar and tied back slightly; fairly long
*Wing:*     A small bunch of Grey Squirrel tail hair

This is an attractive hair-wing version of the classic British feather-wing pattern which also is given in this book.

## BRAHAN SHRIMP

*Head color:*  Red Cellire     Hook sizes: 6 to 10 (preferably 8 or 10 double, low-water irons)
*Tag:*     Copper tinsel
*Tail:*     A Pheasant rump feather, dyed black
*Body:*     Red Lurex
*Ribbing:*     Copper tinsel
*Throat:*     A small bunch of hot-orange hackle fibers, tied under the hook
*Wing:*     Two very small Jungle Cock feathers, back to back

This fly (and the *Black Brahan*) was designed by John MacKenzie, a ghillie on the River Conon, and was named after the Brahan beat on that river. Alex Simpson, of Aberdeen, who sent the author this dressing, reports, "Most of the salmon up north (in 1969) were caught on the *Brahan Shrimp* and the *Black Brahan*, and also lots of sea-trout."

## BUCKTAIL AND GOLD

*Head color:*  Black
*Tag:*     Several turns of fine round or oval gold tinsel
*Tail:*     A Golden Pheasant crest feather
*Body:*     Flat gold tinsel
*Ribbing:*     Oval gold tinsel
*Throat:*     Several turns of a medium blue hackle feather, wound on as a collar and pulled down before the wing is applied. The longest fibers extend nearly to the point of the hook

*Wing:*      A small bunch of brown bucktail, with a bit of blue bucktail on each side, extending to the end of the tail

This fly was originated in 1962 by Harry Willcox, of Alnwick, England, and is used extensively in Scotland. The originator prefers to dress it on double-hooks.

## DUNKELD

*Head color:*    Black
*Tag:*          Fine oval gold tinsel
*Tail:*         A Golden Pheasant crest feather, over which is a shorter one of Indian Crow (or a few red hackle fibers)
*Butt:*        Black Ostrich herl
*Body:*       Embossed gold tinsel
*Hackle:*     About three turns of a hot-orange cock's hackle, not pulled down
*Wing:*       A moderate bunch of Grey Squirrel tail hair dyed orange
*Cheeks:*     Jungle Cock

This dressing is by Jimmy Younger, winner of the annual competition of the Fly-Dresser's Guild of 1969. He sent the dressing on an articulated (linked) hook. On this type of hook the bodies of both linkages are the same, and a collar of hot-orange hackle is applied to the forward end of the rear linkage of the hook. Another version of the hair-wing *Dunkeld* is added to this fly's dressing in the British feather-wing section (Chapter XIII).

## DUSTY MILLER

*Head color:*    Black
*Tag:*          Silver thread or oval silver tinsel
*Tip:*          Golden yellow silk floss
*Tail:*         A Golden Pheasant crest feather, over which is a shorter section of Indian Crow
*Butt:*        Black Ostrich herl
*Body:*       Rear two-thirds: Embossed silver tinsel      Front third: Orange silk floss
*Ribbing:*     Fine oval silver tinsel
*Hackle:*     A golden olive hackle over the orange floss only (this palmered hackle sometimes is omitted)
*Throat:*      A turn or two of a speckled Gallina feather wound on as a collar before the wing is applied
*Wing:*       A section of a grey Mallard breast feather, over which is a very small bunch of dyed brown Polar Bear hair, over which are two or three Peacock sword fibers mixed with a few Polar Bear hairs dyed scarlet, blue and yellow. Sometimes the wing is of dyed brown bucktail or Polar Bear only.
*Cheeks:*     Jungle Cock

This is a hair-wing version of the classic British feather-wing pattern which is included in that section. The brown Polar Bear hair should be the same color as brown Mallard. While most anglers prefer Polar Bear hair because of its sheen and translucence, bucktail may be substituted.

## GARRY (OR YELLOW DOG)

*Head color:* Black
*Tag:* Fine oval silver tinsel
*Tail:* A Golden Pheasant crest feather, over which are a few strands of a Golden Pheasant tippet (or a very thin section of a red Ibis feather, or red Duck, Goose or Swan) about half as long as the tippet
*Butt:* Black Ostrich herl (optional)
*Body:* Black silk floss, with a black hackle palmered forward two-thirds of the body and tapering back to its beginning
*Ribbing:* Oval silver tinsel
*Throat:* A blue Gallina feather, tied on as a collar before the wing is applied (this is imitated by Guinea hackle, dyed blue)
*Wing:* A small bunch of (dyed) yellow Goat hair or bucktail, with a few strands of red hair underneath
*Cheeks:* Jungle Cock often is used, but the pattern doesn't call for it.

In John Veniard's excellent book, *Fly Dressers' Guide*, he says that the *Garry* was originated by the late John Wright, son of James Wright, the noted fly-tyer of Sprouston, near Kelso-On-Tweed, before 1950. It was named for the local minister's dog, a Golden Retriever, who happened to walk into the shop when some black-bodied flies were being tied. A few hairs were cut from its tail and the result was the original of this pattern. The minister caught many fine salmon with it and it became a firm favorite of Tweed fishermen, eventually becoming popular everywhere. A tip of golden yellow silk floss is a later embellishment to the original pattern.

## GREEN HIGHLANDER

*Head color:* Black
*Tag:* Silver tinsel
*Tip:* Palest yellow silk floss
*Tail:* A Golden Pheasant crest feather, over which is Indian Crow (or substitute). or a few Teal fibers. half as long as the crest
*Butt:* Black Ostrich herl
*Body:* Rear third: Light gold floss
Front two-thirds: *Green Highlander* green floss
*Ribbing:* Oval silver tinsel over both sections

*Hackle:* A green hackle of same shade as the forward part of the body, palmered over front two-thirds of body only

*Wing:* A very small bunch of Golden Pheasant tippet fibers, over which is a small bunch of medium to light colored deer tail hairs, *or* sparse green and yellow bucktail, mixed

*Throat:* A few turns of a bright canary-yellow hackle, wound on as a collar and tied back slightly

*Cheeks:* Jungle Cock

This is a hair-wing version of the classic British feather-wing pattern included in that section. It is dressed with whatever combinations the dresser considers will best imitate the feather wing, of which two favorites are given above. This hair-wing version is an international favorite, used extensively in North America and especially in the Matapedia-Restigouche area of Quebec. A bright fly such as this usually is very effective on bright, sunny days.

When dressing very small sizes, such as Nos. 8, 10 and 12, the green palmered hackle in the body can be omitted because it could make the fly look too bulky.

## HAIRY MARY

*Head color:* Black

*Tag:* Gold tinsel

*Tail:* A Golden Pheasant crest feather

*Body:* Black silk floss (black wool sometimes is used)

*Ribbing:* Oval gold tinsel

*Throat:* A bright blue hackle (*Blue Charm* color) tied on as a collar before the wing is applied (Some dressings call for tying the throat under the hook instead of as a collar. Some dressings call for medium or dark blue hackle.)

*Wing:* A small bunch of reddish-brown Fitch tail (Some dressings call for natural brown bucktail. In smaller sizes, brown barred Squirrel tail or hair from the red phase of the Squirrel often is used.)

This fly was originated in the early 1960's by John Reidpath, who had a small fishing tackle shop on Ingles Street, in Inverness. It is one of the first, and probably the best known, of the British hair-wings. Since some of the early dressings call for a wing of "Canadian" deer body hair, it would seem that the idea for the early British hair-wings was inherited from North America, where they were being used before 1930. By using silver ribbing, the fly would be similar to a *Blue Charm*. With black hackle and wing, it would resemble a *Stoat's Tail*.

The above seems to be the original dressing, with later variations given in parentheses. Gold tinsel seems to be preferred, although silver often is used. John Veniard, in his *A Further Guide to Fly*

*Dressing*, says, "Modern variations add various dyed colored fibres to the wing, and colored tinsel bodies are popular in Scotland." He also says that there is a *Hairy Mary* pattern used in the Nith and Tweed districts which is quite different from the above. Since this dressing is a simple one, it seems preferable to stay with the original. If you don't you won't have a *Hairy Mary*! In its original form, it is a very popular pattern. It has been used very successfully in the rivers of Scotland and the Wye these last few years.

## JERRAM'S FANCY

*Head color:* Black
*Tag:* Silver tinsel
*Tail:* A section of dark blue floss (shade 184), as long as the bend of the hook, and cut off
*Body:* Rear half: Scarlet red floss
Front half: Black floss
*Ribbing:* Oval silver tinsel
*Throat:* A small bunch of dark blue hackle fibers
*Wing:* Black hair

This was a favorite of Mr. Tom Jerram, a druggist of Turriff, Aberdeenshire, who was known as "a gentleman in business and a true sportsman on the river." He developed the pattern in 1965 for fishing on the Deveron River. The original dressing had a Black Crow wing, but Mr. Jerram later found that the black hair wing was "more deadly." He liked the fly dressed on double hooks on sizes 8 to 12.

A hair-wing pattern called the *Watson's Fancy* is almost identical to the *Jerram's Fancy* except that tag and ribbing are gold and the tail is a Golden Pheasant crest feather. The throat is of black cock's fibers and Jungle Cock eyes are added.

## JOCKIE

*Head color:* Black    Hook sizes: 6 to 10, Doubles or singles
*Tag:* Oval silver tinsel
*Tail:* A Golden Pheasant crest feather
*Butt:* Black Ostrich herl
*Body:* Rear half: Deep yellow silk floss
Front half: Black silk floss
*Ribbing:* Oval silver tinsel
*Throat:* A small bunch of black hackle fibers
*Wing:* A small bunch of Roe Deer hair
*Cheeks:* Jungle Cock

This is a Brigadier Stevens pattern.

## JOCK SCOTT

*Head color:* Black
*Tag:* Silver tinsel
*Tail:* Golden Pheasant crest, over which is a wisp of Indian Crow, about half as long
*Butt:* Black Ostrich herl
*Body:* Rear half: Yellow floss, ribbed with flat silver tinsel
At joint: Ostrich herl (as a butt) "veiled" with Golden Pheasant crest or Toucan
Front half: Black floss palmered with a black hackle and ribbed with flat silver tinsel
*Ribbing:* As above
*Throat:* A small bunch of spotted Guinea Fowl hackle
*Wing:* A tiny section of a Teal breast feather with a few hairs of brown Polar Bear or bucktail on either side. Over this are two or three green Peacock sword fibers topped with a few hairs of (dyed) scarlet, yellow and blue Polar Bear hair or bucktail, mixed
*Cheeks:* Jungle Cock, with tips of Blue Chatterer over this, but not concealing the Jungle Cock eyes

This is a hair-wing version of the classic British pattern. Blue Jay or tips of a blue hackle can be substituted for the Blue Chatterer, which is difficult to obtain. A much simpler hair-wing version of the *Canadian Jock Scott* (which was probably fashioned after the *American Jock Scott*) calls for a silver tag, a tail of Golden Pheasant crest, rear half of body yellow wool: front half black wool, both halves of body ribbed with oval silver tinsel, a grizzly hackle throat and a Grey Squirrel wing. This pattern bears only slight resemblance to the British original, but it is popular on New Brunswick's Miramichi River. A mixture of the above wing colors instead of the plainer Grey Squirrel might provide a better effect.

## OLD CHARLIE

*Head color:* Red
*Tag:* Flat gold tinsel
*Tail:* A Golden Pheasant crest feather
*Body:* Claret silk floss
*Ribbing:* Wide oval gold tinsel
*Throat:* A small bunch of fibers from a hot-orange cock's hackle
*Wing:* A small bunch of natural brown bucktail, with black tips, if possible
*Cheeks:* Jungle Cock

Veniard says that this is a first-class, all-round hair-wing salmon fly which was designed by Douglas Pilkington, of Stow-on-the-Wold. It is equally good as a low-water fly, used on the Spey and many other rivers.

## POT SCRUBBER

*Head color:*   Black
*Tag:*   A few turns of oval silver tinsel
*Tail:*   A small Golden Pheasant crest feather
*Body:*   Flat copper tinsel
*Ribbing:*   Oval silver tinsel
*Throat:*   A brown hackle, tied on as a collar and pulled down, or applied as a beard
*Wing:*   A very small bunch of Grey Squirrel tail hairs showing brown, black and white parts

This hair-wing pattern was designed in 1961 by John MacKenzie, a ghillie on the River Conon, in Ross-shire, Scotland. It was so named because the original body was made from a copper pot scrubber.

## RED DOG

*Head color:*   Black       Hook size: 6–10, Doubles or singles
*Tag:*   Oval silver tinsel
*Tip:*   Deep yellow silk floss
*Tail:*   A Golden Pheasant crest feather
*Body:*   Flat silver tinsel
*Ribbing:*   Oval silver tinsel (applied after the hackling, to hold it in place)
*Hackle:*   A yellow hackle tied in at tip and wound forward over entire body
*Throat:*   Two turns of a natural red hackle, wound on as a collar
*Wing:*   A small bunch of reddish Roe Deer hair

This is a Brigadier Stevens pattern.

## SILVER DOCTOR

*Head color:*   Red
*Tag:*   Silver tinsel
*Tail:*   Golden Pheasant crest, over which is a Peacock herl fiber about half as long as the crest, or a wisp of red fiber
*Butt:*   Red wool (optional)
*Body:*   Flat silver tinsel
*Ribbing:*   Oval silver tinsel or silver wire
*Throat:*   A small bunch of spotted Guinea Fowl hackle fibers
*Wing:*   A very small bunch of plain brown Squirrel tail hairs, with a few wisps of mixed red, yellow and blue bucktail on each side

*Shoulders:*   Two or three turns of a light blue hackle, wound on as a collar and
  tied back slightly
*Cheeks:*      Jungle Cock (optional)

This is a hair-wing version of the classic British feather-wing
pattern described under *Black Doctor*. There are numerous variations
which can imitate the colorful *Silver Doctor* as a hair-wing, but
this one seems to provide an excellent effect. A further simplification
is to include a small bunch of the blue hackle shoulder as a beard,
in which case the Guinea Fowl throat is optional.

## STOAT'S TAIL (STOAT TAIL)

*Head color:*  Black
*Tag:*         Several turns of fine oval silver tinsel
*Tail:*        A Golden Pheasant crest feather
*Body:*        Black silk floss, not built-up
*Ribbing:*     Fine oval silver tinsel
*Throat:*      A sparse bunch of Stoat's tail hairs or black cock's hackle, tied
  underneath only, of moderate length
*Wing:*        A small bunch of the black points of a Stoat's tail, extending to the
  end of the Golden Pheasant crest feather (black Squirrel or other black hair
  usually is substituted).

("Stoat" is Ermine when in its black color.) This is a British
pattern which has numerous variations, reminding us of the variety
of the black bodied butted hair-wings so popular on the Miramichi
River. Variations include: 1) Eliminate the tag and/or the tail.
2) Use dark claret silk floss for the body, since it becomes almost
black when wet. 3) Wind on a fluorescent thread or fluorescent
"Stren" monofilament beside the ribbing, or include it as a tip.

There is a *Silver Stoat's Tail* dressed with a body and ribbing
of silver tinsel. There is a *Gold Stoat's Tail*, which is a gold-ribbed
pattern having blue hackle at the throat in place of black. Except
for the color of the wing, this fly is very similar to the popular
*Hairy Mary*.

## THUNDER AND LIGHTNING

*Head color:*  Black
*Tag:*         Oval gold tinsel
*Tip:*         Claret silk floss
*Tail:*        A Golden Pheasant crest feather
*Butt:*        Black Ostrich herl
*Body:*        Black silk floss, not built-up

*Ribbing:*     Oval gold tinsel
*Hackle:*      A deep-orange hackle, palmered over front third of body
*Throat:*      A small bunch of blue Gallina (Guinea Hen) fibers
*Wing:*        Orange under brown under yellow bucktail in layers, quite sparse
*Cheeks:*      Jungle Cock

This hair-wing version of the British classic is by the celebrated British fly-dresser, Peter Dean. Another popular way of dressing the wing is to use a section of a dark brown Turkey feather, over which is dyed brown Polar Bear hair, over which is Polar Bear hair dyed yellow.

Jimmy Younger, the modern Scottish authority, sent the author a very simple dressing without tip, butt, topping and horns (as in the classic feather-wing pattern). The throat is a very small bunch of orange cock fibers, forward of which is a very small bunch of blue Gallina fibers. The wing is Squirrel tail, dyed brown and Jungle Cock eyes are included.

## THUNDER STOAT

*Head color:* Black      Hook sizes: 10 to 6 single, or low-water double
*Tag:*         Three turns of fine oval silver tinsel
*Butt:*        Black Ostrich herl (optional)
*Body:*        Black silk floss
*Ribbing:*     Oval silver tinsel
*Throat:*      A small bunch of blue or black cock's hackle fibers, tied in under the hook
*Wing:*        A small bunch of black Squirrel tail hairs, which should not extend beyond the bend of the hook
*Cheeks:*      Jungle Cock

This is a variation of the popular *Stoat's Tail.* There is another variation of the *Thunder Stoat* which has a gold tag and ribbing; a short and spare throat of orange hackle, and a wing of Red Squirrel (instead of black).

## THE TOSH (Also called THE DEVIL or SPEY TOSH)

*Head color:* Black      Hook size: #6, treble (in U. K.)
*Body:*        Black silk floss, sparsely dressed
*Wing:*        Black and yellow bucktail, very sparse and long

This is a new British pattern which was first tied by the head ghillie at Delfour (a famous Spey beat) from hairs of a black and yellow Labrador dog. It is one of the few British flies dressed in the form of the American bucktail. It was tied on the river bank for fun, but it proved to be a good fly which often does extremely well in low water. (Note remarks herein on the use of streamers and bucktails for low-water fishing.) The very simple dressing is body and wing (only).

The fly evidently is tied in several variations, so the name is more for a shape than for a pattern. Regarding this, Colonel Drury says, "A new addition to the killer range is *The Devil* or *Spey Tosh*. This is a simple fly, tied with either yellow or blue badger or squirrel hair or black bucktail with a polythene body. It is tied very thin indeed, a dozen fibers, no more. It is not an attractive fly to look at, but is very attractive to salmon. The only thing these modern spring flies have in common with their Kelson ancestors is size. They are used up to three inches in length, but there the detail resemblance ends."

## VEEVER'S FANCY
*Head color:*    Black      Hook sizes: 6 to 10    Double or single
*Tail:*          A small section of Golden Pheasant tippet, tied upright
*Body:*          Flat silver tinsel
*Ribbing:*       Oval silver tinsel
*Throat:*        A small bunch of yellow hackle fibers
*Wing:*          A small bunch of Grey Squirrel tail hairs
*Cheeks:*        Jungle Cock

## WATSON'S FANCY
*Head color:*    Black      Hook sizes: 4 to 10
*Tag:*           Fine oval silver tinsel, or silver wire
*Tail:*          A small Golden Pheasant crest feather
*Body:*          Rear half: Red silk floss
  Front half: Black silk floss or dubbing
*Ribbing:*       Fine oval silver tinsel, or silver wire
*Throat:*        A small bunch of fibers from a black cock's hackle, tied in under
  the hook
*Wing:*          A small bunch of black Squirrel tail hair
*Cheeks:*        Jungle Cock, very small

This is a British trout fly pattern, now used without change as a popular salmon pattern. The original trout pattern has a wing of sections of a Crow's wings. The hair-wing version uses any fairly straight black hair.

## XV

# Salmon Flies of Other Countries

Many of the flies used in Iceland and all the way down the Continent from Finland to Spain are familiar British classics such as the *Green Highlander, Durham Ranger, Silver Grey* and *Thunder and Lightning.* The latter gets its name because it is known as "the great storm fly," supposedly doing its best after a thunderstorm when streams are high and discolored.

American anglers who fish for salmon in Europe have proved the effectiveness of our hair-wing patterns there, and people from overseas who have fished our waters have found hair-wings at least as effective as their fancier flies and have extolled their value after returning home. Thus, while old habits are slow to break, hair-wing flies (particularly the best of the *Rat* patterns) are growing in popularity to such an extent that future generations may regard the intricate classics primarily as museum pieces; in fact, some of us do now.

However, there are many interesting patterns indigenous to the Continental salmon rivers and, while it doesn't seem necessary to include a great many of them, a dozen or so should be of special interest to American anglers as well as to those in other countries. Since the flies used in Iceland and on the Continent include both American and British patterns, as well as specialized dressings of certain countries, the general favorites are listed in Chapter VIII.

In the Scandinavian countries we find flies bearing the same names as many of the famous British classics. If one is related to the other, the relationship usually is in name only, because the dressings for the most part are entirely different. These are complicated dressings reminiscent of the Kelson era, and Kelson's influence still spreads as far south as Spain.

In the Scandinavian region it is not strange that flies preferred in one country are also popular in others, so one generally can fish from the same fly boxes whether he does it in Finland, in Norway or in Sweden. Thus, we include half a dozen Norwegian flies with the remark that they are also good elsewhere.

Spain has several very beautiful and rather complicated dressings which, while undoubtedly effective on Spanish rivers, are included here primarily because of their excellence as an art form. They are the work of the great professional, Senor B. Martinez, who quite obviously is the peer of any fly-dresser in the world. It is a pleasure to include them as a challenge to all who enjoy dressing beautiful flies, but they are far too good to become messed up, even in the jaws of salmon. They should be framed and admired as the originals of fine paintings are, and the ones Senor Martinez sent to me surely will be!

Here are the dressings of a sampling of these patterns. Most of them are reproduced in Color Plate VIII:

## BLUE SAPPHIRE (ICELAND)

*Head color:*  Black  Hook sizes: 2 to 10
*Tag:*  Two or three turns of round or oval gold tinsel
*Tip:*  Yellow floss
*Tail:*  A Golden Pheasant crest feather on one side of which are a very few red hackle tips; on the other side a very few deep blue hackle tips and barred Guinea Fowl, all half as long as the crest feather and extremely sparse
*Body:*  Black floss, built up slightly

*Ribbing:*      Fine round or oval gold tinsel

*Hackle:*      A black and a wider deep blue hackle both palmered forward from second turn of tinsel, with the black tied off before extra turns of the blue are made at the throat. The throat hackling is pulled down and tied back slightly to accommodate the wing.

*Wing:*      An underwing of strips of dark brown Turkey tail or Mallard; an outerwing of married strips of medium-blue Swan or Goose, mottled Turkey and brown Mallard (the blue at bottom of wing)

*Topping:*      A Golden Pheasant crest feather

This is one of the very few fly patterns used in Iceland which is not one of the British classics. The fly was sent to the author by Johann Sigurdsson, of the Iceland Tourist Information Bureau, and the above dressing was taken from it, so it may not be exactly correct. Bing Crosby, who sings a lot, even while he is fishing for salmon, wrote the author that "most of the standard salmon flies seemed to be productive (in Iceland) but by far the most consistent was the *Blue Sapphire*."

## CROSSFIELD (ICELAND)

*Head color:*      Black

*Tag:*      A few turns of round or oval silver tinsel

*Tail:*      A Golden Pheasant crest feather

*Body:*      Embossed silver tinsel

*Throat:*      A few turns of a medium blue hackle applied as a collar, pulled down and tied back slightly

*Wing:*      An underwing of strips of brown Turkey or Mallard; an outerwing of strips of barred black and white Teal which veils the underwing

This is another of the Iceland patterns sent to the author by Johann Sigurdsson. The above dressing is from inspection of the fly. While the name was spelled *Crossfield* the fly may be a pattern of the eminent British angler and fly dresser, Ernest M. Crosfield. Mr. Crosfield was an exponent of simple patterns, and this is consistent with his opinions.

## EO RIVER (SPAIN)

*Head color:*      Black      Hook sizes: 2 to 5/0

*Tag:*      Fine round or oval gold tinsel, quite wide

*Tail:*      A Golden Pheasant crest feather extending well beyond bend of hook over which are two small Jungle Cock feathers, back to back and vertical, about half as long as the crest

*Butt:*      Bright red wool, small

*Body:*      Rear three-quarters: Embossed gold tinsel

     Front quarter: Yellow chenille

*Ribbing:*      Oval gold tinsel, over whole of body
*Throat:*      A pink hackle, forward of which is a Guinea Fowl hackle, both applied as a collar and pulled down and tied back
*Wing:*      A very small bunch of brown bucktail hairs, over which are about six green Peacock sword fibers, over which is a very small bunch of pink or yellow-red bucktail, all of same length and extending to bend of hook
*Shoulders:*      A narrow strip of barred black and white Teal on each side along middle of wing and as long as it
*Cheeks:*      Jungle Cock, fairly long

This is a pattern from the bench of the famous fly-dresser, B. Martinez, of Pravia, (Asturias), Spain. Judging from his work, Sr. Martinez is one of the world's most skilful craftsmen. He recommends this fly for fishing in light currents at any time of year.

### ESVA RIVER (Spain)

*Head color:*      Black
*Tag:*      About four turns of fine gold wire
*Tip:*      Yellow floss, fairly wide
*Tail:*      One or two Golden Pheasant crest feathers, over which are one or two much shorter Golden Oriole feather tips, with one or two also under the hook extending to its bend
*Butt:*      A turn or two of black Ostrich herl, small
*Body:*      Rear half: Yellow wool palmered with a yellow hackle
Front half: Orange chenille. There is a small black Ostrich herl butt separating the two body sections.
*Ribbing:*      Oval gold tinsel, over all
*Throat:*      A turn or two of a yellow hackle, forward of which is a turn or two of a magenta hackle, both pulled down and tied back
*Wing:*      Married strips of red, yellow and blue Swan and two bright green Peacock herls, outside of which are wide married strips of barred dark Teal, brown Bustard and brown Mallard
*Horns:*      Blue Macaw
*Sides:*      Jungle Cock
*Cheeks:*      Blue Kingfisher
*Topping:*      One or two Golden Pheasant crest feathers

This fly was named for the Esva River, in Spain, where it is one of the favorites. It is a pattern of the celebrated fly-dresser, B. Martinez.

### MARTINEZ SPECIAL (Spain)

*Head color:*      Black
*Tag:*      Several turns of fine gold wire
*Tip:*      Yellow floss
*Tail:*      A Golden Pheasant crest feather, quite long, over which are two very small Jungle Cock tips, back to back

*Butt:* Bright red wool, quite small
*Body:* Rear three-quarters: Flat gold tinsel
Front quarter: Pale greenish-yellow chenille
*Ribbing:* Oval gold tinsel, over all
*Throat:* Two or three turns of a claret hackle, forward of which is a black and white Guinea hackle, both pulled down and tied back
*Wing:* A pair of Golden Pheasant tippets, outside of which are married strips of yellow, red and green Swan, outside of which are wide married strips of dark barred Teal and brown Mallard
*Horns:* Blue Macaw
*Sides:* Jungle Cock
*Cheeks:* Blue Kingfisher
*Topping:* One or two Golden Pheasant crest feathers

This is another origination of B. Martinez, the renowned professional fly-dresser of Pravia, Spain. Beautiful and complicated flies such as this are popular on Spanish rivers and are dressed in large sizes, up to 5/0.

## NAMSEN (NORWAY)

*Head color:* Black
*Tag:* Two or three turns of round silver tinsel
*Tip:* Yellow floss
*Tail:* A Golden Pheasant crest feather, over which is a shorter section of a fiber or two of red Swan or Goose
*Body:* Seal's fur, in four equal parts, from back to front, of yellow, red-brown, blue-green and black
*Ribbing:* Oval silver tinsel
*Hackle:* A black hackle palmered forward from first turn of ribbing, continued full at throat
*Wing:* An inner wing of married strips of yellow, red and dark blue Goose and speckled Turkey tail, over which on each side is brown Mallard, with barred Teal at top of wing over this

Probably the *Namsen*, named for the famous Norwegian salmon river, was first mentioned in Jones' *Guide to Norway and Salmon Fishers' Pocket Companion*, published in London in 1848. He describes a fly called *The Major* and adds that this fly is known in Norway as the *Namsen*. He gives the dressing as follows: Head: Black Ostrich; Tag: Silver thread; Tip: Red silk; Tail: GP crest; Body: Sections of pale blue, orange, wine-red and dark blue pig's wool, palmered wine-red; Throat: Guinea Hen and Bustard; Wing: Two GP feathers, two wine-red hackle feathers; two Snipe feathers, mixed Duck and Argus Pheasant, over which are "two golden threads" (probably GP crest), with yellow hackle around this.

In preparing this book the author obtained several examples of the *Namsen*. All are different, as sometimes is true on various parts of a long river. The above pattern was sent by Yngvar Kaldal, of Oslo, who considers it the most popular one.

## NARANXEIRA (Spain)

*Head color:* Black      Hook sizes: 2 to 5/0
*Tag:*        Fine silver wire or tinsel, small
*Tip:*        Golden yellow floss, quite long
*Tail:*       A Golden Pheasant crest feather extending well beyond bend of hook, over which are a few barred Teal fibers half as long as the crest feather
*Butt:*       Black wool, small
*Body:*       Rear half: Orange silk floss
Front half: Black silk, floss
*Ribbing:*    Oval silver tinsel, over all
*Throat:*     A pink hackle wound on as a collar before the wing is applied, forward of which is a grey hackle wound on as a collar *after* the wing is applied
*Wing:*       A small bunch of Grey Squirrel tail hairs or of mixed dark brown and white bucktail

This is a hair-wing pattern from the bench of the celebrated Spanish fly-dresser, B. Martinez.

## NARCEA RIVER (Spain)

*Head color:* Red, with black center stripe
*Tag:*        About four turns of fine silver wire
*Tip:*        Yellow floss, slim and wide
*Tail:*       A Golden Pheasant crest feather, over which is a shorter tip of red Indian Crow
*Butt:*       Green Peacock herl, quite small
*Body:*       Rear half: Alternating turns of fine yellow and wide bright green chenille (the green strokes back, almost concealing the yellow). Forward of this is a small middle butt of bronze Peacock herl veiled underneath by a Golden Pheasant crest feather pointing downward and extending to point of hook.
Front half: Crimson mohair or floss palmered with a bright green hackle
*Ribbing:*    Oval silver tinsel, over front half of body only
*Throat:*     Several turns of a black and white Guinea hackle, pulled down and tied back
*Wing:*       Two large Jungle Cock feathers, back to back and veiled with Golden Pheasant tippets, outside of which are married strips of yellow, green and red Swan, outside of which are wide married strips of dark barred Teal and mottled light brown Summer Duck (Wood Duck)
*Horns:*      Blue Macaw
*Sides:*      Jungle Cock
*Cheeks:*     Blue Kingfisher
*Topping:*    A Golden Pheasant crest feather

This is one of several originations of B. Martinez, Spain's leading commercial fly-dresser. Although complicated flies such as this are used for angling on Spanish rivers, the author considers them more as Exhibition Dressings and includes them partly because they offer a challenge to fly-dressers who want to copy unusually beautiful patterns.

## OLA (NORWAY)

*Head color:*  Black
*Tag:*  Round silver tinsel
*Tip:*  Dark orange floss
*Tail:*  A Golden Pheasant crest feather
*Butt:*  Black Ostrich herl
*Body:*  Of wool dubbing in two equal parts, Rear half: Silver-grey Forward half: Black
*Ribbing:*  Wide flat and small oval silver tinsel
*Hackle:*  A black cock's hackle palmered over front half of the body only
*Throat:*  A small bunch of Guinea Fowl fibers
*Wing:*  Two sections of white-tipped Turkey tail, with a wide strip of blue Swan or Goose on each side, and strips of brown Mallard over this, edging the top
*Sides:*  Barred Teal, quite long
*Cheeks:*  Jungle Cock, quite long
*Topping:*  A Golden Pheasant crest feather

Veniard lists the tip as of pink floss and calls for the same colors of Seal's fur for the body.

## OTTESEN (NORWAY)

*Head color:*  Black
*Tag:*  Round silver tinsel
*Tip:*  Scarlet floss (Pink sometimes is used.)
*Tail:*  A Golden Pheasant crest feather
*Butt:*  Black Ostrich herl
*Body:*  Flat silver tinsel (Some dressings call for white floss.)
*Ribbing:*  Scarlet floss
*Hackle:*  A scarlet cock's hackle palmered next to the ribbing (Some dressings call for hot-orange.)
*Throat:*  Barred Teal or Widgeon
*Wing:*  Two Golden Pheasant tippets, back to back, over which but not concealing the top and bottom edges are married sections of yellow, red and blue Swan or Goose, with brown Mallard and barred Teal edging the top of the married feathers but not concealing the tips
*Topping:*  A Golden Pheasant crest feather
*Cheeks:*  Jungle Cock, of moderate length

As is often the case, dressings vary in different sections. In this case one should follow the dressing given, using the alternate materials as a variation.

## PEER GYNT (NORWAY)

*Head color:*    Black
*Tag:*    Round silver tinsel
*Tip:*    Yellow floss
*Tail:*    A Golden Pheasant crest feather, over which are a few shorter crimson hackle fibers
*Butt:*    Black Ostrich herl
*Body:*    Flat silver tinsel
*Ribbing:*    Oval silver tinsel
*Hackle:*    A crimson hackle palmered forward from second turn of tinsel
*Throat:*    Spotted Guinea Fowl
*Wing:*    Two strips of brown mottled Turkey, with brown Mallard over it
*Topping:*    A Golden Pheasant crest feather
*Cheeks:*    Jungle Cock, about half as long as the wing
*Horns:*    Blue-yellow Macaw

This fly was originated in 1963 by John Sand, considered to have been the most famous dresser of trout flies in Norway. The above description is from a true reproduction tied by his son, Erling Sand. Sizes most used in Norway are 1 and 1/0 for salmon and size 6 for sea-trout.

## SHERIFF (NORWAY)

*Head color:*    Black
*Tag:*    Fine oval gold tinsel
*Tail:*    A Golden Pheasant crest feather, over which are three or four shorter speckled Guinea Fowl hackle fibers
*Butt:*    Black Ostrich herl
*Body:*    Rear half: Flat gold tinsel
   Front half: Black Ostrich herl
*Ribbing:*    Oval gold tinsel
*Hackle:*    A yellow cock's hackle, wound over the herl only
*Throat:*    A small bunch of speckled Guinea Fowl fibers
*Wing:*    Two strips of dark Turkey tail, with broad strips of brown Mallard on each side
*Topping:*    A Golden Pheasant crest feather
*Cheeks:*    Jungle Cock, half as long as the wing
*Horns:*    Yellow Macaw

This fly was originated by John Sand, the famous Norwegian fly dresser, and the sample from which the above dressing was taken was provided by his son, Erling Sand. Comments about it are the same as for another of Mr. Sand's patterns, the *Peer Gynt*. Both flies should do well on North American rivers.

## SHRIMP (NORWAY)

*Head color:*   Black
*Tail:*   The tip of a hot-orange hackle, upright
*Body:*   Blood-red wool, fairly thick, and tapered
*Ribbing:*   Flat gold tinsel
*Hackle:*   A hot-orange hackle leading the tinsel, with two or three large
hot-orange hackles tied in heavily as a collar at the head of the fly and tied
back slightly (There is no wing.)

*(W. Meinel)*

FIG. XV-1

THE PROUD BEGINNER

Evidently this fly is a copy of the Swedish *Chilimps*. The Chilimps was first tied by Mr. Olle Törnblom on April 28, 1942, and its dressing was suggested by Mr. Rolf Wilhelmson. The story goes that it was tied with hackle from a shaving brush colored with nail polish, and with thread from a skirt; this later evolved into the above pattern. The fly is intended to imitate a shrimp. Mr. Wilhelmson got its name from a Negro boy in London who was selling shrimp but who mispronounced the word as "chilimps".

The fly is tied in many versions in Scandinavia, one being the *Shrimp Silver* or *Silver Shrimp*, which is identical except that the rear half of the body is silver tinsel without hackling. The author's pattern is dressed on a No. 4 hook.

### SILVER MARTINEZ (Spain)

*Head color:* Black, with red center stripe
*Tag:* Fine silver wire, quite wide
*Tail:* A Golden Pheasant crest feather, over which is a shorter tip of blue Kingfisher
*Butt:* Bright red wool, quite small
*Body:* Flat silver tinsel
*Ribbing:* Oval silver tinsel
*Throat:* Two or three turns of a bright green hackle, forward of which are two or three turns of a black and white barred Guinea hackle, both pulled down and tied back
*Wing:* A pair of large Jungle Cock feathers veiled with wide Golden Pheasant tippets, outside of which at top of wing (one on each side) are bright green hackles or strips of bright green Swan, with wide strips of Summer Duck (mottled brown Wood Duck) outside of this and veiling the whole wing
*Horns:* Blue Macaw
*Sides:* Jungle Cock
*Cheeks:* Blue Kingfisher
*Topping:* A Golden Pheasant crest feather

This is another of the originations of B. Martinez. It is a popular fly on Spanish rivers, where complicated dressings are used widely, including many of the British classics.

# Epilogue

For many generations men have watched the hordes of smolt leave their rivers for the sea, there to remain a year or more before returning as mature fish. Men wondered where they went, and it would have been better if they had never learned.

As briefly related in Chapter II, men found out where they went—some of the places, at least. The men were Danes in their colony of Greenland and, while drift-netting for other fish away from their usual fishing grounds in the Davis Strait, their nets suddenly caught salmon. In 1965 their boats netted 36 metric tons, or about 10,000 fish. In 1968 more boats caught 540 metric tons, or about 180,000 adult salmon, 18 times as many as four years earlier. Tagged fish among them indicated that about 60 per cent came from Canada, 32 percent from the British Isles, and the rest from Sweden and the United States (which means the State of Maine). This was by drift-netting, and it does not include a larger number (579 metric tons, or

ESVA RIVER
(SPAIN)
Dressed by
Mr. B. Martinez (P)

BLACK DOCTOR
(ICELAND VERSION)

CROSFIELD
(ICELAND)

NARANXEIRA
(SPAIN)
Dressed by
Mr. B. Martinez (P)

BLUE SAPPHIRE
(ICELAND)

SHRIMP
(NORWAY)
Dressed by
O. Mustad & Son (P)

SHERIFF
(NORWAY)
Dressed by
Mr. Erling Sand (P)

SILVER MARTINEZ
(SPAIN)
Originated and
Dressed by
Mr. B. Martinez (P)

PEER GYNT
(NORWAY)
Dressed by
Mr. Erling Sand (P)

NAMSEN (No. 1)
(NORWAY)
Dressed by
O. Mustad & Son (P)

EO RIVER
(SPAIN)
Dressed by
Mr. B. Martinez

NAMSEN (No. 2)
(NORWAY)
Dressed by
Mr. Erling Sand (P)

NAMSEN (No. 3)
(NORWAY)
Dressed by
Mr. Olaf Olsen (P)

MARTINEZ SPECIAL
(SPAIN)
Originated and
Dressed by
Mr. B. Martinez (P)

PLATE VIII

Favorite Flies of Contintental Europe

about 170,000 fish) caught by inshore nets along the coast of southern Greenland during that one year alone.*

It does not include long-lining off the Lofoten Islands near Norway. Here, in 1968, about 400 boats, each fishing long-lines each strung with between 1,000 and 2,000 hooks, fished during April, May and June and by mid-June had taken 1,000 tons, or about 300,000 more salmon.

It does not include a great deal more.

This modern massacre of the Atlantic salmon has been felt acutely by anglers in the British Isles, in Canada, and in Maine, too, because many who traveled hundreds of miles and invested hundreds of dollars for a week or two of fishing returned only to report that the fishing was lousy.

The fishing on salmon rivers everywhere became so poor that it has attracted very serious attention. An international Conference on Conservation of Atlantic Salmon was sponsored by the Atlantic Salmon Research Trust (ASRT, London) in cooperation with The Atlantic Salmon Association (Montreal). The Conference included fourteen concerned nations: The United Kingdom, Canada, U.S.A., **Norway, Iceland, France, Spain, U.S.S.R., Poland, Italy, Roumania,** Denmark, West Germany and Sweden. Among various remedies, it was suggested that commercial fishing for Atlantic salmon on the high seas should be stopped for a period of ten years to give the salmon stocks time to recover. The first eleven countries listed agreed to this; those that did not agree were Denmark, West Germany and Sweden. Evidently West Germany and Sweden would have agreed if Denmark had done so, and it seemed generally agreed that Denmark is the chief culprit, largely (but not entirely) because of the depredations of its boats in the Davis Strait.

Now, the Danes have no Atlantic salmon fishery of their own. No important breeding rivers exist either in Greenland or in Denmark itself. In preparing this book the author wrote to authorities in Denmark requesting information. They replied, "We regret

---

* In 1969 the estimated total number of salmon taken off Greenland in coastal and international waters was 667,000, weighing an estimated 2,200 metric tons. It was estimated that about 900 metric tons were caught by set gill nets and about 1,300 metric tons by drift nets. ("Trout and Salmon" Magazine, April, 1970)

to inform you that salmon fishing here has practically been ruined owing to water pollution and regulation of our streams. We are of the opinion that the fishing today is so poor that it would be completely misleading to mention (it) in a book."

Thus, the greedy Danes seem to feel that they are going to get all they can, and the devil take conservation and the future of Atlantic salmon for coming generations. When the matter was discussed with the Danish ambassador all that seemed to have resulted was a lot of deprecatory double-talk.

It apparently has been internationally agreed that fish born in the ocean are part of Nature's bounty, free for the taking by anybody in international waters. But this is not so with Atlantic salmon because they are a fresh-water fish born in fresh-water rivers owned by specific nations which invest vast funds to protect and preserve their fisheries. Every salmon is the product of one nation or another even though it roams the open range of the sea for a time before returning home again. Sometimes the fish contain tags to prove this, but that is beside the point. Of course the Danes, who have no salmon themselves because they have defiled their own rivers, know this, but they seem to choose to lower themselves to the level of "thieves and pirates" in order to take what is not theirs.

To add insult to injury, the Danes catch fish belonging to the United Kingdom and then try to sell them to its people. This is something like a hunter going into someone's barnyard and shooting a cow, then attempting to sell it to the farmer who owns it.

Now, if we want to know what else is happening to the salmon, let's go to Canada and sail in to the Bay of Chaleur, into which flows the Restigouche river system composed of the Restigouche, Causapscal, Assemetquagan, Patapedia, Kedgwick and Upsalquitch, once known as the best salmon river system in the world. Salmon heading into this river system must run the gauntlet of 114 stands (of nets) on the Quebec side alone and, if they want to take a little side-trip to the Bay of Gaspé (on their way), they have a choice of 46 other nets wherein they can trap themselves. On the map these nets look like a picket fence laid on the ground, with every picket in the general shape of a hook. Of course a very smart salmon can travel off-shore, but there he has other hazards to contend with before (if he is very,

very lucky) he enters the river to negotiate other nets both legal and those operated by poachers. (The latter don't always use nets; sometimes they take the fish with spears.)

All this suggests what is happening to our salmon fishing. If you fish the Miramichi and catch ten grilse to every salmon (which is about par for the course there) perhaps the reason is that some of the grilse get through the gill-nets, while most of the salmon don't.

Of course there are laws to protect the salmon! One is that commercial fishermen must raise their nets for 36 hours a week to let some of the salmon get through. Far-sighted individuals (many of them dedicated government officials) want this period to be increased by at least another day; they want the netting season shortened; and they advocate much more than the currently too-lenient disciplining of law-breakers (of which there are many).

This is difficult to accomplish, because law-making is in the hands of politicians, and politicians do not forget that poachers and commercial fishermen and their friends all have votes.

Because of ignorance, apathy or the thirst for votes the politicians are depriving their economy of vast sums of money available from visiting anglers, and while future generations may damn them for it, future generations don't yet control votes.

When visiting any of the Canadian provinces for salmon fishing the average American angler currently spends about five hundred dollars in Canada. Of course, some spend a lot more and some quite a bit less, but it's not an unfair average. If the angler catches only one salmon he is usually pleased with the trip. If he returns fishless after one or two unsuccessful visits he is inclined to give up the idea, and to influence his friends to do the same. The current value of a salmon caught by commercial means is about ten dollars. Salmon caught by anglers may average fifty times more than that in value to the economy of the region. If the politicians realized on which side their bread is buttered they would see to it that an ample supply of salmon survive to spawn or to help make angling trips worthwhile. This, in part, may mean buying a lot of the netting rights, a bonanza investment the politicians discuss a lot more than they act upon.

The picture is not all painted in black, however. Maine, wherein are all the Atlantic salmon rivers currently containing stocks in the

Fig. XVI-1

FAR TOO MANY FAIL TO RETURN HOME

United States, is rehabilitating its salmon rivers at a pace that should provide increasingly good fishing for years to come. There still is good salmon fishing in many parts of Canada, although the angler who knows how to fool fish into striking will do much better than the casual neophyte. In the United States it has now through necessity become imperative to combat the increasing pollution of our air, our lands and our waters, almost regardless of cost. Through necessity in Canada, regional and provincial governments should find it economically imperative to take immediate and drastic steps to improve their Atlantic salmon fishery, also almost regardless of cost. It is about time we all got busy with both efforts.

Unfortunately politicians don't often bother to read angling books, but perhaps a few publications will ask permission to reprint this epilogue and thus assure that the message gets through to them. What can the rest of us do? We can join organizations dedicated to the preservation of Atlantic salmon. We can make our feelings known. We can practice the essential rules of conservation. As the good Father Smith so often says, "It's not how many salmon you've *killed* that counts; it's how many you have *fooled* into striking."

I have before me a brief concerning the Atlantic salmon presented by the Restigouche Riparian Association. One of its recommendations is that "the rod-catch limit be reduced from six to four salmon daily and from twenty-one to fifteen weekly." Fifteen still is far too many under present conditions for any conservation-minded angler to bring home. Why not take one for the table, perhaps one for the freezer, and none to give away, carefully liberating the rest with a friendly pat on their tails so they can continue their excursion upstream to do what they have traveled so far to do? By now we must agree that these few survivors of the world's most dangerous expedition deserve to be allowed to finish their trip!

Atlantic salmon anglers should find it rewarding to
join one or more of three very worthy organizations:

**THE INTERNATIONAL ATLANTIC SALMON FOUNDATION**
425 Park Avenue, New York, N. Y. 10022

**THE ATLANTIC SALMON ASSOCIATION**
705 Shell Tower, 1255 University Street
Montreal 110, Quebec, Canada

**THE MIRAMICHI SALMON ASSOCIATION**
Boiestown, New Brunswick, Canada

(The first does not charge dues, but accepts (tax deductible)
donations. Dues currently are $15 for the second,
and $10 for the third.)

# Bibliography

Books about Atlantic salmon fishing techniques and about the flies used to catch salmon are fewer in proportion than those treating with other important angling subjects. Although many of these books have become cherished classics, very few are sufficiently modern to provide authoritative information on the flies and tactics in popular use today.

Thus, their value for the most part is historical, each one helping to unfold the many fascinating steps in the evolution of the sport and also helping readers to compare the opinions of one author with those of others so each of us can decide for himself what seems to make sense.

Since no one book can cover all elements of such a varied group of subjects, this brief bibliography provides references which should add to the salmon angler's fund of knowledge:

*Atherton, John*—THE FLY AND THE FISH, Macmillan, New York, N.Y., 1951. This is a book on fly-fishing which contains a chapter on Atlantic salmon fishing and one on the Atlantic salmon flies preferred by the author, who was a famous angling artist as well as an outstanding angler.

*Bates, Joseph D., Jr.*—STREAMER FLY TYING AND FISHING, Stackpole Books, Harrisburg, Pennsylvania, 1966. While this contemporary book describes fishing methods with streamers and bucktails in fresh and salt water generally, and includes eight color plates of flies and the dressing instructions for about 300 patterns, its interest to Atlantic salmon fishermen lies in the recently popular uses of streamers and bucktails for this type of fishing. Anglers who fish for black salmon will find that this book contains many suitable patterns for this purpose.

*Brooks, Joe*—A WORLD OF FISHING, D. Van Nostrand Co., Inc., Princeton, New Jersey, 1964. This contemporary book, by one of the greatest fly-rod anglers of all time, provides fascinating accounts of fishing trips around the world for sport-fish of all types. Its chapters on Denmark, Norway, the British Isles, Iceland and Newfoundland are of special interest to Atlantic salmon anglers who wish information about fishing in those countries.

*Hewitt, Edward R.*—A TROUT AND SALMON FISHERMAN (FOR 75 YEARS), Charles Scribner's Sons, New York, N.Y., 1948. One of the world's greatest anglers discusses trout and salmon fishing. Mr. Hewitt also is the author of SECRETS OF THE SALMON, published in 1922.

*Hill, Frederick*—SALMON FISHING (THE GREASED LINE ON DEE, DON AND EARN), Chapman & Hall, London, 1948. This is a small (100 pages) book which discusses the "greased line" method and gives dressing instructions for a few patterns favored by the author.

*Hutton, John E.*—TROUT AND SALMON FISHING, Little, Brown & Co., Boston, 1949. An experienced angler gives his opinion of tackle and tactics for both trout and salmon; the salmon section deals principally with fishing in New Brunswick and Quebec.

*Kelson, George M.*—THE SALMON FLY, published by the author, c/o Messrs. Wyman & Sons, London, 1895. This large book provides fly-tying methods, fishing information, and dressing instructions for about 300 salmon flies of the era, with eight color plates of some of them. This classic (and its companion book, TIPS) is long out of print but available in angling libraries and occasionally from dealers in rare angling books.

*La Branche, George M. L.*—THE SALMON AND THE DRY FLY, Houghton, Mifflin Co., Boston, 1924. This book, by a famous expert, describes the genesis of dry-fly fishing for salmon, an art which has changed considerably since the book was written. It is out of print but available in angling libraries and sometimes from dealers in rare angling books.

*Marbury, Mary Orvis*—FAVORITE FLIES AND THEIR HISTORIES, Houghton, Mifflin & Co., Boston and New York, 1892. This famous classic contains 32 excellent lithographed color plates of old trout and salmon flies and the histories of all important patterns of the period, thus making it a valuable reference for those desiring to research the histories of some of the modern flies. This book has been reprinted and is available from The Orvis Company, Inc., Manchester, Vermont, 05254.

*Netboy, Anthony*—THE ATLANTIC SALMON–A VANISHING SPECIES?, Houghton, Mifflin Co., Boston, 1968. This authoritative and well-researched book provides very complete modern information on the life of the Atlantic salmon and the conditions of its existence around the Atlantic.

*Phair, Charles*—ATLANTIC SALMON FISHING, Derrydale Press, New York, N.Y., 1937. This limited-edition classic is extremely rare and valuable, but anglers lucky enough to read it will find excellent (though a bit dated) information on North American angling for Atlantic salmon.

*Pryce-Tannatt, T. E.*—HOW TO DRESS SALMON FLIES, Adam & Charles Black, London, 1914. Now in a modern reprint, this is the most easily understood book on how to dress the classic feather-wing patterns. It contains eight excellent color plates of flies and dressing instructions for 100 patterns.

*Russell, Jack*—JILL AND I AND THE SALMON, Little, Brown & Co., Boston, 1950. Jack Russell, who owned a camp on the Miramichi River, gives an interesting account of Atlantic salmon fishing there at mid-century.

*Taverner, Eric*—FLY-TYING FOR SALMON, Seeley, Service & Co., London, 1942. This famous author of several angling books clearly discusses fly-dressing methods and gives detailed dressings for many patterns of Atlantic salmon flies, some of which are illustrated in three beautiful color plates. The book also includes valuable information on the evolution of the salmon fly and references to many classic books wherein old flies are discussed.

*Veniard, John*—A FURTHER GUIDE TO FLY DRESSING, Adam & Charles Black, London, 1964. This contemporary book is a later edition of John Veniard's several excellent books on worldwide trout and salmon patterns. It contains fly-tying methods and many dressing instructions, including tube flies, fluorescent materials and nine color plates. John Veniard also is the author of several valuable booklets on fly-dressing. For the list, write to E. Veniard, Ltd., 138 Northwood Road, Thornton Heath CR4 8YG, Surrey, England.

*Wulff, Lee*—THE ATLANTIC SALMON, A. S. Barnes & Co., New York, N.Y., 1958. This is an excellent book on the tackle and tactics for North American salmon fishing, written by the greatest expert in the art. In addition to many excellent photographs the book contains four pages of color plates of Atlantic salmon flies and nymphs.

# Professional Fly Dressers

The following professionals have contributed patterns used in this book. Their addresses indicate the regional fly patterns with which they should be primarily familiar:

BAILEY, DAN
  209 West Park Street, Livingston, Montana 59047
BIGAOUETTE, (Mrs.) CARMELLE
  Matapedia, Province of Quebec, Canada
BOYD, (Miss) MEGAN
  Kintradwell, Brora, Sutherland, Scotland
BUCKNALL, GEOFFREY
  72 Loampit Vale, London, SE 13, England
CAVANAGH, ROBERT H., JR.
  147 Pleasant Street, Woburn, Massachusetts 01801
CARPENTER, BURT D.
  14 North Evarts Avenue, Elmsford, New York 10523
DARBEE, HARRY A.
  Livingston Manor, New York 12758
DOAK, WALLACE W.
  P.O. Box 95, Doaktown, New Brunswick, Canada
DRURY, ESMOND, LTD.
  Langton-by-Spilsby, Lincolnshire, England
FOSTER, PHILIP L.
  Drawer 672, Farmington, Maine 04938
HARDY BROTHERS, LTD.
  61, Pall Mall, London, SW1, England
HATHAWAY, NORMAN
  45 Chamberlain Street, Brewer, Maine 04412

HOWARD, HERBERT L.
  1000 Grove Street, Mamaroneck, New York 10543
JACKLIN, ROBERT V.
  413 Dermody Street, Roselle, New Jersey 07203
KEANE, WILLIAM J.
  Box 371, Bronxville, New York 10708
KUKONEN, PAUL
  61 Green Street, Worcester, Massachussetts 01608
MARTINEZ, B.
  Santa Catalina No. 6, Pravia (Asturias), Spain
MUSTAD, O. & SON
  P.O. Box 79, Lilleaker, Oslo, 2, Norway
OLSEN, OLAF
  5890 Laerdal, Sogn, Norway
ORVIS, THE, COMPANY, INC.
  Manchester, Vermont 05254
ROSGEN, WILLIAM
  Box 333, Winsted, Connecticut 06098
SAND, ERLING
  2440 Engerdal, Norway
SHOPPE, CHARLES
  Route 182, Franklin, Maine 04634
SIMPSON, COLIN (AND ALEX)
  34, Seamount Court, Gallowgate, Aberdeen, AB1 1DQ, Scotland
WILLCOX, HARRY
  34, Lisburn Street, Alnwick, Northumberland, England
YOUNGER, JIMMY
  Sutherland Fly, Ltd., Helmsdale, Scotland

# Index

Page numbers preceded by P. refer to color plates; pages containing particulars of fly dress are noted within parentheses.
Other symbols used:

(FW)—feather-wing version
(HW)—hair-wing version
(R)—"reduced" version
(S)—"simplified" version

349